# Free-Commerce

 **University of Hertfordshire**

Learning and Information Services

Hatfield Campus Learning Resources Centre

College Lane Hatfield Herts AL10 9AB

Renewals: Tel 01707 284673 Mon-Fri 12 noon-8pm only

This book is in heavy demand and is due back strictly by the last date stamped below. A fine will be charged for the late return of items.

## ONE WEEK LOAN

ISBN 0-13-033767-6

90000

9 780130 337672

# Free-Commerce
# The Ultimate Guide to E-business on a Budget

Eileen Mullin

Jared T. Rubin

Foreword by Ross Scott Rubin

**Prentice Hall PTR**
**Upper Saddle River, NJ 07458**
**www.phptr.com**

**Library of Congress Cataloging-in-Publication Date**

Mullin, Eileen.
    Free-commerce : the ultimate guide to e-business on a budget / Eileen Mullin and
Jared T. Rubin ; foreword by Ross Scott Rubin.
        p.   cm.
    Includes index.
    ISBN 0-13-033767-6
    1. Electronic commerce. 2. Electronic commerce—Finance. I. Rubin, Jared. II. Title.

HF5548.32 .M85 2001
658.8′4—dc21

2001016423

Editorial/Production Supervision: *Donna Cullen-Dolce*
Acquisitions Editor: *Jill Harry*
Editorial Assistant: *Justin Somma*
Manufacturing Manager: *Alexis Heydt*
Art Director: *Gail Cocker-Bogusz*
Interior Series Design: *Meg Van Arsdale*
Cover Design: *Nina Scuderi*
Cover Design Direction: *Jerry Votta*

PH
PTR

© 2001 Prentice Hall PTR
Prentice-Hall, Inc.
Upper Saddle River, NJ 07458

The publisher offers discounts on this book when ordered in bulk quantities.
For more information, contact

Corporate Sales Department,
Prentice Hall PTR
One Lake Street
Upper Saddle River, NJ 07458
Phone: 800-382-3419;
FAX: 201-236-7141
E-mail (Internet): corpsales@prenhall.com

Printed in the United States of America

10  9  8  7  6  5  4  3  2  1

ISBN 0-13-033767-6

Prentice-Hall International (UK) Limited, *London*
Prentice-Hall of Australia Pty. Limited, *Sydney*
Prentice-Hall Canada Inc., *Toronto*
Prentice-Hall Hispanoamericana, S.A., *Mexico*
Prentice-Hall of India Private Limited, *New Delhi*
Prentice-Hall of Japan, Inc., *Tokyo*
Pearson Education Asia Pte. Ltd., *Singapore*
Editora Prentice-Hall do Brasil, Ltda., *Rio de Janeiro*

To our parents—Eileen, Jim, Irene, and Nat—for all the good things they taught us.

# Contents

# Acknowledgments

We are most grateful to our family, friends, and colleagues, who have encouraged us and helped this book along. We owe special thanks to Eric Robinson for his invaluable fact-checking and proofreading assistance, especially while weathering computer software incompatibilities. Karen Whitehouse provided early support when the manuscript was just a gleam in Ross's eye. Carole McClendon at Waterside Productions deserves tremendous kudos for spurring us to action and navigating the bumps along the road. Wyndham Morgan Resorts in St. Lucia provided the perfect setting for us to begin outlining the book.

We're obliged to Gene DeRose of Jupiter Media Metrix, who allowed us to move forward with this project. We're grateful to Leslie Fagenson and the whole Global HR Information Systems & Solutions team at Merrill Lynch. Joanne Kissane, James Cha Yoo, Dan Kwok, Anne Savino, Tom Eyestone, Inara Angelis, and Michele Durst deserve special thanks for helping to keep the human resources Web sites humming.

Our sincerest thanks go to Jill Harry and Donna Cullen-Dolce for their eagle-eyed attention during the editing, copyediting, and permissions stages. Grateful thanks are also due Samantha Shurety for her technical review, and also to Justin Somma. We're especially grateful to the production and design teams at Prentice Hall for the good-looking final results.

Eileen Mullin

My first book was an exciting journey, and I have many people to thank who helped me along the road. My mother and father provided love and support. Bari's inspiration and understanding were essential in the book's final days. Shani lent her heart and ears to my computer-crashing woes. All my friends made the moments away from my monitor more enjoyable. Finally, let me give special thanks to my brother Ross, who never fails to amaze me: Your insight and foresight helped throughout this book and continue to help me throughout my life.

Jared T. Rubin

# Foreword: Why Free?

W hatever you may think of Bill Gates, chairman of Microsoft and arguably one of the world's wealthiest individuals, you must give him credit for seeing—and capitalizing on—the rise of the personal computer. Therefore, it was more than mere press release fodder when the bespectacled billionaire proclaimed the Internet the most significant advancement since the personal computer.

He was wrong, though, or at least uncharacteristically understated. The Net has been far more significant than the PC. Although the PC has been instrumental in driving adoption of the Net, particularly in the United States, the Internet and World Wide Web were born independently of it. While most people access the Internet from Windows today, the PC's Net suitability and Microsoft's Internet strategy were late to blossom. The Net holds promise for having its greatest impact yet outside the U.S. through non-PC devices, such as advanced mobile phones, which are more common in Japan and Europe.

The real reason why the Net is far more important than the PC ever was, though, is that the PC failed to fundamentally change the economy. The PC may have improved productivity in virtually all industries. It may have created sea changes in many industries, such as publishing and film production. It may have even virtually created intrinsic industries, such as software development. However, the PC failed to tear down walls among industries. It did not raise the questions of whether music artists should distribute their music without their labels' involvement. It did not cause CNN and the *New York Times* to compete in the same medium. It did not give rise to retailers like Amazon.com that have Wal-Mart in their sights. It did not cause NBC to question whether it was a media or commerce company.

Calling the Internet a force in the evolution of the PC is like saying that television's major impact was changing radio.

# LOOKING, HOOKING, AND BOOKING . . . . . . .

There is another way the Internet has changed our thinking about the economy. The Net's unique combination of direct marketing potential and wildfire distribution combined with new financial valuation models and a glut of startups, all desperate to rise above the fray, has led to a new way of thinking about customers. This is a world that has seen the tremendous success that companies like America Online have had once they have acquired customers. All AOL has really done, though, is replicate what financial and telecommunications companies have known for years. Once you have a billing relationship with customers, it is relatively simple to extract additional revenue from them through premium services, cross-sold services, merchandise, bundles, and other marketing techniques.

The difference in the Net space, though, in spite of the market correction of early 2000, is that investors have been willing to forego the billing relationship for extended periods on the logic that it is only after getting someone's attention that you can sell them goods and services. Microsoft bought Hotmail, which provided free Web-based e-mail, for over $400 million because it had acquired millions of users who might be more easily converted into customers. Regardless of whether their revenue model includes advertising (as many sites profiled in this book do) every company with a Web presence must understand the principles of media.

That was only in the first wave, though. The Internet has certainly blurred boundaries across media and channels, but motivating consumers is still a difficult task, particularly since the low bandwidth available to the Web makes it difficult to elicit the kinds of emotional responses possible in television. The rise of online retail, the transformation of online media, and the investment in crossover online services have pushed the Net from the domain of the consumer out to meeting the needs of businesses, particularly small businesses.

# AN EVOLUTION OF SERVICES . . . . . . . . . . . . .

The first wave of excitement around the Net came around selling access to consumers. Early Internet service providers such as Netcom seemed poised to dominate the landscape. Then came flat-rate pricing, which wiped away the juicy margins in the access business. Furthermore, as we'll discover, distracted Internet service providers were so focused on survival that they slowly saw most of their value-added services, such as e-mail and home pages, usurped by more nimble Web sites.

Selling goods to consumers marked the second phase. Amazon.com started with a franchise in book sales and has slowly branched out to music, video, toys, and even consumer electronics. Amazon's blitzkrieg quickly forced consolidation in sectors ranging from CD sales to beauty supplies, where the retailer has a major investment in Drugstore.com. Undeterred in its strategy of horizontal domination, Amazon has embraced consumer-to-consumer auctions and even launched zShops, which leads smaller vessels of commerce into its raging river.

What is often overlooked about Amazon, though, is that its storefront masks a services play. Books were merely an early vehicle through which to develop tools that provide one of the best online shopping experiences today, including excellent customer service, recommendations driven by collaborative personalization, and a huge selection. And what is selection if not a way to avoid running around, i.e., a convenience service?

Despite Amazon's success, though, the bloom is off online retail's rose. The threat of shopping bots that compare prices across Web sites; the eventuality of established branded retailers moving online; the reality of lowballers such as Buy.com, who are willing to trade profits for advertising revenue; and the twist of reverse auctioneers such as Mercata, which allow consumers to aggregate demand, have made selling goods online something less than the frictionless mecca it once seemed.

Similarly, in the media side of the Web, major portals such as Yahoo!, which has established itself as one of the few successful online media companies (and only through strong offline ties, at that), have made a fundamental shift in the past few years. Most of the attention on its transition over the past few years has focused on the migration from a search site pointing consumers to resources to a directory focusing on internal resources. The more significant change, however, has been Yahoo!'s development of a series of communications and transactional services, all under a unified login—Yahoo!'s answer to Amazon's one-click ordering. Yahoo! itself has started offering its own wallet, from which its members can shop at sites from such retail stalwarts as Macy's and Nordstrom's.

# AN OVERLAP OF MARKETS . . . . . . . . . . . . . . .

The relatively distinct market for consumer goods has little overlap in terms of corporate competition. Outside of uniforms, most corporations have little use for clothing. Outside of functions, they have little need for food. And outside of desks, they have little use for furniture. A floor of 200 people, each of whom may have his or her own VCR at home, may share a single VCR in a corporation. Likewise, the average consumer has little use for copy machines, and the largest consumer PC companies in the world derive only a small fraction of their total revenue from the consumer market. Moreover, these markets account only for finished goods, leaving out major sectors of the economy focused on components and parts.

On the other hand, while some services, such as health care, education, and entertainment, remain largely consumer-focused, what consumers spend on some of their most expensive services is dwarfed by what corporations spend on those services in real estate, telecommunications, insurance, financial services, and travel.

We are at a crossroads in the Net's evolution. It's not that the Internet economy has given up on the consumer. It's that business models—ever craving the steady renewable revenue that services can bring—are evolving to a point where it's easier to make the case to the business customer than to the consumer. The disadvantage is that while changes in the consumer Internet economy led to a crumbling of walls among industry and through the supply chain, the business Internet economy will have relatively low impact in comparison.

# ENTER THE ENTREPRENEUR . . . . . . . . . . . . .

As an entrepreneur, you represent a very attractive target to the provider of free services. You're willing to take action and responsibility, and may even influence the spending of others, such as employees and customers. Furthermore, while the key to motivating customers is often to evoke an emotional reaction, capitalism's unadorned invisible fingers—seeking opportunity, saving costs, and improving efficiency—guide entrepreneurs.

Sites such as eToys had to invest millions of dollars to buy their servers, develop their Web sites, get online, host their sites, promote their brands, and communicate with their customers. They also had to spend millions to shore up their own organizational needs.

Today, technology has advanced and organizations have launched to greatly ease the pain of starting a robust commercial site. Web content management systems, team development environments, and commerce servers have allowed new online stores to get up and running faster. Application service providers and commerce service providers let you rent programs and outsource development so you don't have to hire as much staff to build your own engines of e-commerce.

Nevertheless, we won't kid you. To launch a world-class commerce site still costs millions of dollars because the bar has been raised. Now, for example, staying on customers' radar involves personalized opt-in direct mail campaigns, auctions, and sophisticated data management. However, while the Internet may not quite have allowed all of the smallest guys to unseat the biggest guys, it has allowed the smallest guys to take on the somewhat bigger guys. SOHO (small office/home office) is really where free-commerce has bloomed, allowing entrepreneurs to concentrate on their skills and look to other resources to mind the shop.

# SELLING YOUR SOUL: BEST OF BREED
# VS. INTEGRATION . . . . . . . . . . . . . . . . . .

Even though some services profiled in *Free-Commerce* have a strong offline component, Web-based services have, in general, started to push the limits of Web development. Desktop.com, for example, has made extensive use of JavaScript to create an online experience that behaves more like a traditional Windows desktop than a Web page. Other advanced developments lurk behind the interface. As has often happened when weighing costs and benefits, decisions need to be made between choosing the best of breed and an integrated experience.

For example, in the PC market, the best-of-breed components won. Apple's Macintosh may not have had the best video cards, the biggest hard disk, or the widest selection of software, but its integrated experience allowed a user experience that many argue the PC still has not matched. Nevertheless, the PC far outsold the Mac. Advocates of Microsoft Office argue that each of its applications were best of breed, but in the productivity applications space, the packaging together of word processor, spreadsheet, presentation program, and database unseated the former leaders of those categories—WordPerfect, Lotus 1-2-3, Harvard Presents, and dBase.

With that in mind, let's return to Yahoo!, which along with other portals, has built some of the Web's most comprehensive service offerings. Among its prodigious collection are Yahoo! Messenger, Yahoo! Finance, Yahoo! Mail, and Yahoo! Auctions. Registering for one of these services registers you for all of them, but they have other ties. For example, Yahoo! Calendar can be accessed easily from within Yahoo! Mail, which can be monitored from My Yahoo!, the site's personalized "front door." Undoubtedly, moving from Yahoo! service to service is more convenient than having to log in to several different services on different sites.

But while Yahoo!'s services are generally good, they are not necessarily the best. Other free mail programs, for example, offer the option to have text read over the phone or free mail forwarding. Yahoo! Messenger has far fewer members than the equivalent service by America Online, while Yahoo! Auctions has a far smaller audience than eBay. Datek and Realtimequotes.com offer free real-time market information; Yahoo! Finance's quotes are delayed by 20 minutes.

The competitive nature of the Web means that no one should own an advantage for too long. The integrated sites are certainly worth registering for and provide an easy way to experiment with services you might not ordinarily try. They also tend to be more established compared to many startups. In general, it's not very difficult to switch among services online, but sites use features such as personalization to raise those barriers.

# THE PRICE OF FREEDOM . . . . . . . . . . . . . . . .

Almost all the free services have a price, and that's personal information. Often times, it can be as innocuous as your name and e-mail address, but it often includes more sensitive items like your address, phone number, and income. Surprisingly, few ask much about the specifics of your business, apart from company size and industry.

Critics contend that privacy online is like a nuclear plant. Everyone enjoys the cheap power until someone's space gets contaminated. Increasingly, Web sites offer privacy policies that describe what they will and won't do with data you provide, but there have been instances of companies breaching their policies intentionally or with the unsolicited help of hackers. Worse than having your free service provider abuse your trust is having one of its partners solicit you after buying or trading for their member list.

Efforts to enforce strict privacy standards have ranged from industry organizations such as TrustE to largely stillborn technical standards with obscure acronyms like P3P. Technology companies such as Zero Knowledge Systems and eNonymous have also been sprung up to "anonymize" the online experience. In fact, they don't even know who their own users are.

If your privacy is tantamount to you, your safest bet is to avoid these services. A less extreme measure is to limit your relationships to those you trust or to companies that have more to lose than you by violating their own policies. In general, that means larger companies like America Online and Microsoft, but smaller companies also have their reputation on the line. The main difference between the Net and other channels, though, is the speed with which information travels. Don't do or divulge anything online that you wouldn't want the rest of the world to know about, although determined snoops can probably get the information through other means.

If other companies, like banks and telcos, were held to the same strict standards privacy advocates are proposing for the Net, we could kiss junk mail and telemarketing goodbye. Privacy concerns also tend to be overstated by the media and are a price of progress. The telephone represented a major threat to privacy. And yet, as we complain about telemarketers who are far more annoying than direct e-mail marketers, we rush to adopt cellular telephones to ensure we have even less privacy.

# ABOUT FREE-COMMERCE · · · · · · · · · · · · · · · ·

There may be other prices to pay for free services. Some companies explicitly request the right to send you e-mail as part of the registration. Many of the free PCs discussed in Chapter 1 are tied to contracts. These have parallels in the physical world, where cellular carriers like AT&T Wireless have offered free cellphones in the past in exchange for annual or even multi-year contracts.

Nevertheless, the shift of the Net to services and the attractiveness of the small business as a target customer have allowed you to get things done on the Net. You can get online, find the right software, build your Web site, attract and retain customers, and stay organized throughout it all—all without spending a penny.

There are over 150 free services profiled in *Free-Commerce,* each with information on what they offer, what they'll ask for, and even some inexpensive premium services they offer for you big spenders. The book seeks to provide access to the best and most useful services to you in running your business; we didn't include many free consumer services because they just couldn't be tied back to productivity gains.

Whether you already run a small business with a few employees or have thought about launching a home office, embracing free-commerce will let you focus on what you need to, including the bottom line.

Ross Scott Rubin
Vice President & Chief Research Fellow,
Jupiter Research

# 1

# Getting Online

..........................

**W**hether your motivation is communicating with your clients, selling your services, or detailing demand, you'll need to find a way to connect to the Net. There's no shortage of companies that are vying to sell you your ticket to the online marketplace—but there are several ways to avoid paying the toll.

To get online you basically need two things—a device that can support a Web browser, usually a PC, from which to navigate, and an Internet service provider (ISP), which you call for connection to the Internet. In the Net's early days, ISPs were thought to hold the keys to the kingdom, but now the role of Net access, and indeed the boxes they connect, have willingly been sacrificed in the name of customer acquisition.

## MAKING A SUCCESS OF ACCESS . . . . . . . . . . .

In spite of their allure, most free PC offers are not worth it. A typical ISP costs about $20 per month and lets you access the Internet at up to 56 kilobits per second (Kbps), but faster connections are on the way, and we've yet to see a free PC that has a guaranteed upgrade to a broadband connection like those offered by ADSL and cable modems.

Why is this important? First, in addition to being many times faster than dial-up modems, both ADSL and cable modems offer persistent connections. You don't have to dial up, so there are no busy signals or disconnections. The Net is always waiting for you, like electricity. If you've experienced Internet access at a large corporation or college, you have some idea of how accessing the Internet with these technologies feels. If you'd only experienced the Net this way, the dial-up experience would seem broken. It's taking large phone and cable companies years to roll out these

1

technologies, but they should be available throughout much of their service areas by the end of 2001, two years before most of the three-year service plans typical of free-PC offers expire, assuming you signed at the beginning of 2001.

Second, if you think you're saving $2,000 for the cost of a new PC, you haven't been shopping for a PC for a while. At the time of this writing, $2,000 bought you a nearly top-of-the-line 866 MHz Pentium III, with 128 MB of RAM, a 40 GB hard disk, DVD player, 3D acceleration, and a 17" monitor from Dell—in short, a PC that could eat most free PCs as a light snack. The subsidized PCs that many companies are offering would sell for closer to $600. One particular weak spot is the hard disk, which at 6 GB and under is barely big enough to load Microsoft Office and a couple of games. Remember that virtually all of the value of these PCs to the companies that supply them depend on your going online, so the PC has been built with that in mind.

Finally, the "standard" ISP rate of $20 per month is increasingly starting to crumble in places. Several national players offer Internet access for $15 per month or lower. And after several false starts, it seems that free, ad-supported ISPs are starting to gain momentum in the United States. The next section discusses free ISP options for existing PC owners.

# HARD LESSONS IN HARDWARE . . . . . . . . . . .

The free PC craze began to sweep the industry in 1999. However, the promise was a little ahead of the reality. Indeed, "free PCs" were so scarce that Gateway, which had survived its share of computing fads, ran a television commercial that likens them to other myths, like the Loch Ness monster and Bigfoot. The free PC is typically exchanged for one or more of the following:

- permisson to target ads at you
- a commitment to join the company's ISP or its partner ISP
- signing up for a credit card, bank account, or buyers' club

The only one that was truly "free" in terms of monetary exchange was Scenario 1. Free-PC was launched in 1998 with the idea of giving away computers (with free Internet access) in exchange for filling part of the hard disk and screen with advertising (see Figure 1.1).

Shortly after Free-PC's announcement, a group of companies began offering "free" PCs with the stipulation that consumers sign contracts for Internet access for several years. Taking this almost lease-based approach, other inexpensive PC makers quickly followed suit by partnering with or becoming ISPs, and finally some of the

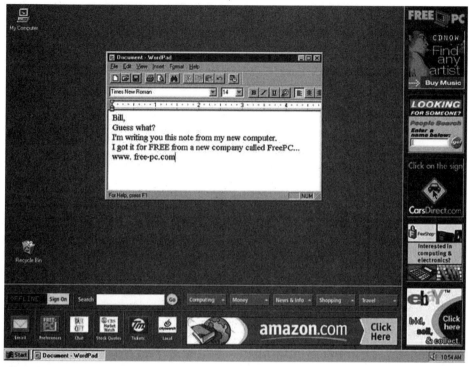

**Figure 1.1**
Free-PC offered consumers a sub-$1,000 Compaq PC plus Internet access in exchange for constantly downloading and viewing advertising that displayed in a strip on the right side of the screen.

more established companies did the same. Table 1.1 summarizes some options available to you if you're willing to lock in your Internet service for some time to come.

All the companies have more powerful PCs available, and some let you buy the PC and Internet access in advance. Be wary that other companies that have tried giving away computers in exchange for Internet access have fallen by the wayside. Microworkz, which had hawked low-cost PCs in addition to a low-cost device connected to your television, called the iToaster, eventually became toast itself. And Enchilada, which offered a high-end version called "The Grand Enchilada," went south—and not just south of the border. Furthermore, even the survivors listed in Table 1.1 are sometimes sporadic in accepting online orders. Table 1.1, at this writing, lends credence to Gateway's television commercials.

Having your PC provider go broke, though, may not be as bad as it sounds. After failing to attract enough advertising dollars, Free-PC was ultimately bought in early 2000 by E-Machines. The lucky few who received its computers were allowed to keep them and were given instructions for removing the advertising.

**Table 1.1**   Comparing Free PCs with Long-term Internet Access Contracts

| Company | PC offered* | Monthly fee* | Contract length | Notes |
|---|---|---|---|---|
| DirectWeb http://www.directweb.com/ | 450 MHz AMD-K6-2, 64 MB RAM 4 GB hard drive | $24.95 | 3 years | PC is IBM Aptiva. Shipping and processing fees are extra. |
| Gobi http://www.gobi.com/ | 366 MHz Celeron 32 MB RAM 4.3 GB hard drive | $25.99 | 3 years | $60 shipping and $30 processing fees. $50 to keep computer at end of term. |
| InterSquid http://www.intersquid.com/ | 333 MHz processor 32 MB RAM 4.3 GB hard drive | $29.99 | 30 months | $60 shipping and $40 processing fees. |

*Minimum configuration available as of October 2000*

ISPs have also tried partnering directly with major retail chains to provide more flexibility in your purchase, especially if you already have a PC. In exchange for a multiyear agreement with CompuServe, Circuit City has offered $400 off anything in the store. Office supply chain Staples has offered similar deals.

# FREE PCS AND MORE  . . . . . . . . . . . . . . . . .

At least two companies have tried interesting twists on the "PC for Internet access." While one will appeal more toward individuals, another is definitely skewed more toward small businesses.

## PeoplePC

PeoplePC has a range of leasing rates for snaring your next PC, depending on which computer package you choose—or you can choose to prepay in one fell swoop. At the lower end, an Intel Celeron 667 MHz desktop system will set you back $24.95 a month for 36 months. An Intel Celeron 700 MHz desktop system is $29.95 a month for 36 months, while a Pentium III 733 MHz laptop costs $39.95 for 36 months. Furthermore, the company has committed to on-site support for the three years of the contract, a nice touch that companies such as Dell typically charge for after the first year.

PeoplePC hopes to leverage its network of "members" to command discounts from vendors, who will in turn deliver special perks to PeoplePC owners. For example, PeoplePC comes with a $100 credit from online broker E*Trade, $20 off every purchase of $50 or more at Art.com, and 5 percent off all purchases at AtYour Office.com. Using straight math, it's hard to see the PeoplePC proposition making sense, but if you're going to hitch your wagon to one of these schemes, you may as well milk it for the perks.

PeoplePC has also struck some major deals with some of the nation's top employers recently, such as Ford Motor Company and Delta Airlines. These deals provide free computers to employees in exchange for heavily subsidized Internet access. The days of the company town may be back in the global village.

URL: http://www.peoplepc.com/

**Contact:**   info@peoplepc.com

## Everdream

If PeoplePC has made support a differentiator, Everdream and competitor Center-Beam have made it their focus. Designed specifically for small businesses, Everdream calls its plan "subscription computing." For a monthly fee, the company supplies Pentium PCs and Internet access through Concentric Networks, but under its own ISP. It offers both dial-up and high-speed ADSL access.

Everdream claims it can support the hardware better because it retains control of the configuration. With a simple remote command, Everdream's technical support team can restore the PC's configuration to its original pristine state. Don't worry about losing your files, though; they're backed up and encrypted on the company's servers. Everdream's service starts at $150 per month per PC for dial-up access. Discounts apply as you add PCs. In addition to Microsoft Office, Everdream supplies ACT!, a program popular with salespeople.Through a partnership with Netopia, Everdream precodes its customers' PCs with a template that will enable them to create a Web site to publicize their business. Customers can then work through Everdream to add increased functionality to their online stores as their business needs grow.

URL: http://www.everdream.com/

**Contact:**   info@everdream.com

## CenterBeam

Through an alliance with Microsoft, CenterBeam lives slightly more on the cutting edge than rhyming competitor Everdream. It supports laptops and wireless networking technology from Lucent. CenterBeam's service starts at $165 per month. The key components of CenterBeam's technology service include a wireless LAN solution, Dell PCs and servers, Microsoft Windows and Office 2000, Hewlett-Packard printers, high-speed Internet connectivity, daily data backup and recovery, comprehensive security, hardware and software upgrades, and dedicated customer support.

Paying $150 per month and up may seem like a huge premium above more consumer-focused efforts such as PeoplePC, but both Everdream and CenterBeam have invested heavily in their remote diagnostics. These should provide a level of support beyond what consumer-focused players can offer. The fixed fee also alleviates customers' concerns about unexpected downtime, repair costs, changes in personnel, and upgrades.

Also, they must contend with networked environments, which are significantly more complex than standalone PCs. Both companies promise round-the-clock live support and remote diagnostics. Both also realize they may have to contend with existing PCs when they install their workstations. CenterBeam has developed a buy-back program for a small business's existing PCs.

URL: http://www.centerbeam.com/
**Contact:**   info@centerbeam.com

## NadaPC

The founder of NadaPC started out trying to offer something else for free that was "not a PC" in a strict sense. FreeMac.com sought to give away one million iMacs, but the initiative collapsed. Now the company is trying to recover from the cold shoulder with the Icebox.

The device, manufactured by Samsung, looks like a later generation of the Macintosh Color Classic (see Figure 1.2). It integrates many features not found in competitive standalone Internet appliances, like Netpliance's iOpener and Compaq's Home Internet Appliance, that rely on the MSN Internet service provider. The Icebox includes a CD with stereo sound and a DVD player, and the device itself is free when you pay for its Internet service. Most notably, the device's 9-inch screen doubles as a television. It comes with a remote control and wireless keyboard, which can both be washed clean. In fact, it seems that NadaPC threw in everything but the sink in the kitchen, which seems to be the room for which it was made.

**Figure 1.2**
NadaPC's Icebox, an appliance manufactured by Samsung, doubles as a
TV and DVD player. It's free when you sign up for 36 months of NadaPC's
Internet service.

NadaPC charges $21.95 for its ISP service for a minimum of 36 months and re-
quires that you open a bank account with its partner bank. You can also purchase it up
front for $689; while the device may work with other ISPs, there's no guarantee it
will. There's also a nonrefundable shipping and handling fee of $59.99.

It remains to be seen how robust Internet surfing will be in the Icebox, but its
hardware indicates a unique convergence device that compares favorably with other
access-bundled Internet appliances. If what you really want is just a small, integrated
DVD player, though, Chinese manufacturer Konka makes one built into a 13-inch
television for about half the price.

URL: http://www.nadapc.com/

**Contact:**   http://www.nadapc.com/custservice.html

## FreePCTV

If you'd like to recommend something to your less savvy customers, or would like to just have a home page on one of the hosting services listed in later chapters, FreePCTV may be your answer. It also may be handy to have around for checking out how your commerce Web site looks like on the tube.

Like its far better known cousin, WebTV, FreePCTV allows you to use your television and a phone line to access the Net. In addition to free Web access, it supports up to six e-mail accounts. It also comes with a remote control and a wireless keyboard that often costs extra on WebTV models. FreePCTV is even smaller than the original WebTV box (but not Sony's latest WebTV Classic), much less the larger WebTV Plus units from Philips and Mitsubishi that have fancy VCR control and electronic programming guides. That said, FreePCTV's operation is not quite as elegant, and the interface is very "inspired" by WebTV's (see Figure 1.3).

FreePCTV is offered by PowerChannel, Inc. Like the old Free-PC, you have to apply for the device, so there is no guarantee you'll be able to get one. Unlike Free-PC, FreePCTV doesn't take up a lot of your screen real estate with ads. This is especially fortunate, as TV screens display far less than most computer screens, even though in general they are much larger (go figure). You will, however, have to fill out

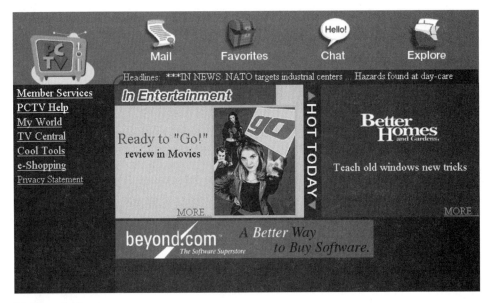

**Figure 1.3**
FreePCTV is a free Internet service accessed through any TV set.

a monthly online survey of your buying habits and product preferences that takes about ten minutes to complete.

URL: http://www.freepctv.net/

**Contact:**  info@powerchannel.net

# FREE ISPS . . . . . . . . . . . . . . . . . . . . . . . . . . . . . . . . . . .

The basic free ISP proposition is that in exchange for Internet access, you agree to watch online advertising. However, unlike advertisements on a Web site, which disappear when you leave the site, free ISPs typically install a banner on your screen that remains active as long as you have your connection open. This banner "floats" atop all other windows and can't be hidden. To do this, they need to install software on your computer, which typically includes a dialing program. Because of this, you may not be able to access your free ISP account if you are working on a PC that doesn't have the software installed.

Table 1.2 provides a comparison of the free ISPs discussed in this section.

## NetZero

NetZero has over seven million registered users, although it's unknown how many of them use it as a primary access vehicle. Its chunk of online real estate, dubbed the ZeroPort (see Figure 1.4), is indicative of two major trends in free ISP access, providing utility and transaction capability in what was previously a window that served only ads. The ZeroPort may be docked to either the top or bottom of your screen. Your personalized My Z Start page includes news, sports, stocks, financial services, and weather. Since NetZero is also the ISP and provides free e-mail accounts, it can alert you when you have new e-mail. The NetZero Free service includes 40 hours of free Internet service per month. Fee-based programs—referred to in these pages as "big spender" services—include the $9.95-per-month NZ Platinum service (which removes banner ads) and the NetZero Professional Extended Access Pass, in which you pay $9.95 for unlimited access for the remainder of the month.

The first time you connect to NetZero, you'll receive a brief tour of NetZero's features as you're connecting. It includes a ticker that can be extensively customized—including one of the most innovative interfaces for selecting company stocks to track—or turned off entirely. Underneath and to the right of the banner ads are buttons. Most take you directly to Web sites, although some branch out into a menu of buttons.

URL: http://www.netzero.net/

**Contact:**  instantanswers@netzero.net

**Table 1.2**   Comparing Free ISPs

| Company | Speed | Availability | POP e-mail? | Advertising |
|---------|-------|--------------|-------------|-------------|
| NetZero | 53.3 Kbps. | Across the U.S. and Canada. 40 hours of free usage per month. | Yes | Configurable 800×88-pixel banner, dubbed the ZeroPort. Your surfing patterns are tracked. |
| FreeLane | Up to 56K. | Across the U.S. | Free Web-based e-mail accounts only—no POP accounts. | Persistent 800×60-pixel banner can be anchored to your Windows Start menu. |
| Juno | Up to 56K. You're asked to choose three access numbers: One to log on, one for the Web, and a third for e-mail. E-mail access requires a separate logon. During e-mail logon, a dialog box sits atop all your applications. | Across the U.S. | Yes, using Juno's e-mail software. You can also have your own free 12 MB Web site. | This movable 632x81-pixel banner bar cannot be anchored to the top or bottom of your screen. |
| Winfire | 14.4 Kbps (higher for premium plans). | Service is available in selected U.S. cities, including Chicago, Atlanta, Dallas, and Los Angeles/ Orange County. | Web-based e-mail account. | Banner ads appear on the Winfire toolbar (which do not appear for pre-mium Winfire plans). If you ter-minate service in less than 13 months, Winfire charges a $200 cancellation fee. Winfire may also add promotional messages to your e-mails. |

**Figure 1.4**
The ZeroPort viewbar, ever-present for users of NetZero's free Internet service, may be docked at the top or bottom of your screen.

## FreeLane

To use Excite's FreeLane free Internet service, you'll need to download and install its Windows-only software. You'll then be able to take advantage of unlimited 56K Web access across most of the U.S. The service also provides access to free e-mail, online communities, and voice chat (see Figure 1.5). FreeLane's requests for personal information—from hobbies and interests to the name of your current long-distance carrier—are more intrusive than the other free Internet service providers in this roundup.

FreeLane's obligatory advertising banner bar measures 800x60 pixels and can be docked to your Windows start menu. FreeLane also offers 60 free voice mail messages and 10 free faxes a month.

**Excite Inbox**
You now enjoy a FREE email, voicemail and fax account, accessible from any computer with Internet access. Let everyone know your new email address with 100 free business cards courtesy of Excite. Create your cards now.

**Excite Planner**
More than a personal calendar, Excite Planner provides free access to Web-based versions of your contact lists, appointments, notes, and tasks, plus full integration and synchronization with personal information managers.

**Excite Clubs**
Create your own place on the Web and invite anyone you like to share photos, files, a calendar and fun information. We offer FREE photo scanning with Seattle Filmworks.

**Excite Chat**
Make friends and find people who share your interests. Join over 14,000 simultaneous chatters talking about everything from the hottest celebrity gossip to how to play the stock market.

**Excite Message Boards**
Exchange ideas on any subject you can think of. Share jokes, stories and advice with people from around the world.

**Excite Member Directory**
Find old and new friends on Excite. Update your personal profile, and share it with others. Your profile is at: http://members.excite.com/directory/emullin

Download Freelane 2.0 Now

**Figure 1.5**
At registration, FreeLane shows you the Excite community portal services of which you can take advantage.

The site includes straightforward, step-by-step installation instructions. If you have already registered at Excite's Web portal, you can use your Excite username and password when you begin the registration process at FreeLane.

URL: http://freelane.excite.com/
**Contact:**    info@excite.com

# Juno

If you can't lead 'em, beat 'em, and if you can't beat 'em, join 'em might describe the history of Juno, which began as a service that offered only free e-mail. It then offered full Web access but at full price, and then finally became the only major ISP to offer both paid and free access.

Juno retains much of the simplicity of when it was just an e-mail program, which is now integrated into the Juno Web program (Figure 1.6). Large tabs marked Read and Write allow you to see and send e-mail; the Juno program has an address book and even a spell-checker built in. Clicking Web prompts you to dial out and then offers full Web functionality. If you sign up for Juno's premium Web service, you can eliminate the banners.

URL: http://www.juno.com/

**Contact:**   http://www.juno.com/corp/contact/

## Winfire

Like the somewhat better known cable modem, DSL is about ten times faster than the average dial-up connection, but it is persistent, which means that it is always on. In theory, anyway, you never get disconnected and never have to dial up. (In reality, connections can drop off, but reconnecting typically happens in less than a second.) DSL

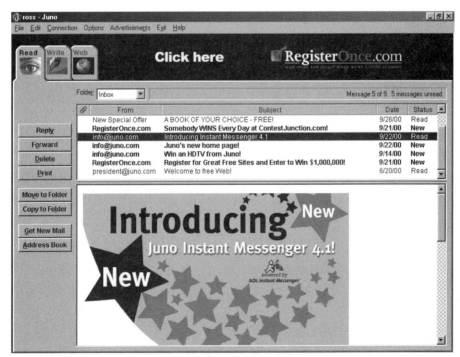

**Figure 1.6**
Juno has expanded from providing free e-mail to free Internet access.

also lets you use your existing phones and lets you talk and use the Web simultaneously. One of the problems with DSL, though, is that you must live a certain distance from a central phone switch in order to receive it at all, and the farther you are, the slower you can go.

There are some stipulations. Winfire uses a browser assistant of the same name to help you navigate the Net. It includes such features as a built-in MP3 player that lets you listen to digital music and a novel bandwidth-on-demand feature that lets you crank up the speed for tasks like downloading files. While Winfire's basic level of service is far slower than most varieties of DSL and usually requires the purchase of a $199 DSL modem or rental for $10 a month, many DSL providers either give away the modem or subsidize it. In addition to greater speed, the premium versions of the service remove the banner ads from the Winfire toolbar.

URL: http://www.winfire.com/

**Contact:**   http://www.winfire.com/company/contact.asp

# GOING SOFT . . . . . . . . . . . . . . . . . . . . . . .

Now that you managed to score a PC and free Internet access (or they've managed to score you), you'll come to quickly discover that a computer without software is like a body without a soul. (Think of your least favorite politician.) Most computers include an operating system like Windows, which controls the basic functions of the computer, like launching programs and storing files, and a number of programs or applications, including those needed to create office documents, send e-mail, surf the Web, and create Web pages.

If you'd rather not shell out for those products, though, and would like to try some free alternatives or go beyond the basics, this section will clue you in on great, free software to enable your enhance your online experience.

## Linux

Linux is a free operating system that runs on a variety of different types of computers, including PCs and Macs. It's similar to Unix, a very powerful operating system popular in scientific, engineering, financial, and telecom industries. Many leading Web sites run on Unix, in particular the commercial version sold by Sun Microsystems, called Solaris.

Linux is developed and distributed under a license that's called *open source,* which basically means that developers are free to enhance it as long as they share how they did it by releasing the underlying source code. There are many different distributions of Linux that package together parts of it differently or run on different processors. Linux.com lists 15 such distributions. Among the more popular commercial ones for the

PC are those from Red Hat, Slackware, Caldera (OpenLinux), and TurboLinux. For PowerPC-based Mac, there's Yellow Dog Linux, MkLinux, and LinuxPPC.

While the hardware demands for Linux are modest for a modern operating system, Linux may be one of the largest software products you can download from the Internet. According to Red Hat's Web site, it can take 27 hours to download its distribution of Linux over a modem connection so, ironically, it could take less time to order it and have it shipped by overnight courier. You can order it on CD-ROM from Red Hat; it's also included with many books on Linux, although typically those books include older versions.

If you're used to Windows or the Mac, Linux is a different beast. It is a very powerful operating system that is built by and for technical types, but it doesn't have the breadth of mainstream applications available for other operating systems. For example, Microsoft Office, Photoshop, and other Web development staples are not available for Linux. However, as more people use Linux, it is being increasingly considered for development; a version of the popular computer game *Quake* runs on Linux, and more user-friendly interfaces are being built for it. One of the friendliest to date is the KDE, or K Desktop Environment, with which most Windows or Mac users will feel pretty comfortable (see Figure 1.7).

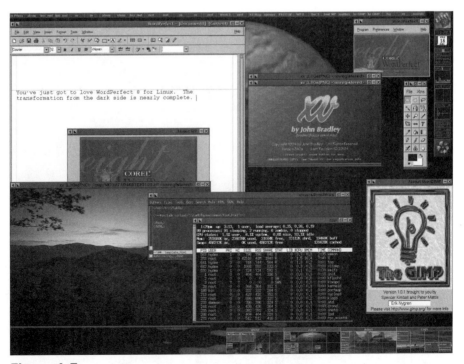

**Figure 1.7**
KDE is a graphical desktop interface for Linux workstations that will seem fairly familiar to Windows or Mac users.

Even with KDE, you can spend plenty of time fiddling with text files and adjusting obscure parameters to avoid glitches in Linux, but once it's running, it's very stable. Linux may not be your mainstream desktop, but it can serve other uses around your office. For example, it makes an excellent and reliable file server, or can serve as a gateway for linking multiple computers to the Internet.

Stay tuned, though. The popularity of Linux has inspired many talented developers to improve the operating system. Eazel (http://www.eazel.com/) is working on improving Linux's user interface and file management to make it even easier for everyday users.

URL: http://www.linux.org/
**Contact:**   http://www.linux.org/about/contact.html

## StarOffice

In 1999, Sun Microsystems purchased Star Division GmBH, which produced StarOffice, a perennial also-ran in the office suite space. Available for Linux and Windows (a Mac version is under development), StarOffice is actually a fairly complete yet compact office suite that consists of several components:

- StarOffice Writer, a word processor
- StarOffice Calc, a spreadsheet
- StarOffice Draw, a graphics program
- StarOffice Impress, a presentations program
- StarOffice Base, a database
- StarOffice Mail and Discussion, for reading e-mail and Internet newsgroups
- StarOffice Chart, for creating charts and graphs
- StarOffice Schedule, a planner

StarOffice can be used for a wide variety of office productivity tasks, such as creating sales presentations (see Figure 1.8), writing business plans, creating a customer or product database, tracking expenses, and creating appointments. Note that while StarOffice is not as large as, say, Red Hat Linux, it can consume 80 MB or more of disk space before it is installed, which also makes it a product you should consider getting on CD-ROM from Sun.

URL: http://www.sun.com/staroffice/
**Contact:**   http://www.sun.com/products/staroffice/contact.html

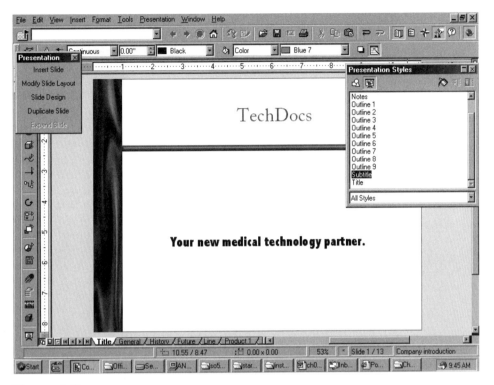

**Figure 1.8**
You can create presentation slides with the StarOffice Impress program.


# FreeDesk

In addition to 50 MB of free storage space, FreeDesk.com provides a full-featured application suite of common PC office tools. You can access spreadsheets, graphics, or dash off text files with the Web versions of these applications. The business model calls for displaying ads that are seen at logon, though not in the applications. A future $4.95-a-month version is intended to let users remove the ads entirely.

The site's application suite is called Applix Anyware Office, and is comprised by a word processor, an HTML authoring tool, a spreadsheet, a program for creating presentations, and a database (see Figure 1.9). Each is reminiscent of its Office 2000 counterpart, although performance is abysmally slow.

The word processor, Applix Words, even includes recordable macros, columns, tables, footnotes, borders, and outlining. Similarly, the multipage spreadsheet sports over 300 functions and charting features that will likely go unused by all but power users.

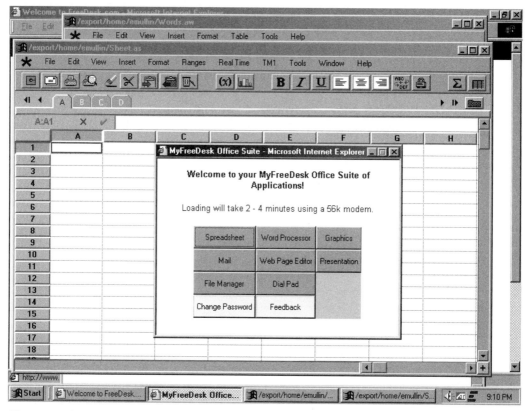

**Figure 1.9**
When you access FreeDesk.com, you can readily open multiple windows for working on Web-based versions of text files, spreadsheets, or presentations.

Your files are saved on FreeDesk.com's server in a proprietary format that unfortunately cannot be read by any other application. In order to use your document on your own local hard disk, you'll need to first export that file to Microsoft Word or WordPerfect, then use a separate file manager applet to download it. In the same vein, in order to use FreeDesk to edit a Word file on your hard disk you'd need to upload the Word document to the file manager, then run a complex Import Wizard to open it in the suite. For this reason, FreeDesk.com lends itself better to creating documents on-the-fly thanks to spontaneously bursts of energy—if you're traveling, for example, and don't have ready access to a laptop—rather than continuing to work on documents that you began editing at home or at the office.

URL: http://www.freedesk.com/

**Contact:**  info@freedesk.com

# FREE BROWSERS · · · · · · · · · · · · · · · · · · · ·

There are many browsers available for both PCs and Macs, but the two most popular are free: Netscape Navigator and Internet Explorer. While Microsoft has beat Netscape in a vicious market share battle, the two products are similar in many respects. For example, they both include shortcut features to make it easier to enter a Web address or get past a login screen with less typing.

There are three main ways to navigate around the browser. The first is by following "links" embedded on the Web page. These typically appear within text, in which case, the text is underlined. They can also appear within buttons or graphics. A browser's Back and Forward buttons let you trace your steps, returning back to pages from which you've linked.

A second way is by typing Web addresses in the Address field. These are the near-ubiquitous URLs (Uniform Resource Locators) plastered over everything from shopping bags to television commercials. For example, typing http://www. prenticehall.com/ will bring you to the publisher of this book.

A third way is by saving your favorite pages. Netscape calls these saved locations "bookmarks"; Microsoft calls them "favorites." Selecting these links from a menu or a toolbar palette can be a great time saver. Bookmarks can be saved in folders, and both Internet Explorer and Netscape Communicator offer facilities for managing them. There are also Web sites, such as Backflip at http://www.backflip.com/, Blink at http://www.blink.com/, and HotLinks at http://www.hotlinks.com/, that allow you to store your bookmarks online. A program that lets you synchronize your bookmarks across multiple PCs is Bookmark Sync at http://www.bookmarksync.com/.

Table 1.3 compares each browser's feature set.

## Netscape Navigator

Netscape, now a subsidiary of America Online, has released Netscape 6 as a more full-featured, standards-compliant program for Web browsing, e-mail, and instant messaging (see Figure 1.10).

Netscape 6 sports a customizable left side panel known as the My Sidebar feature for conducting extensive searches and integrating a buddy list for instant messaging. You can also modify My Sidebar to view stock prices, news headlines, and any of hundreds of content tabs offered by Netscape or its content partners.

Another nifty feature is Smart Browsing, which lets you reach a Web page by typing in a single keyword instead of an entire URL. Type in *prenticehall,* for example, and your browser fills in the *www.* and *.com.* Netscape also supports multiple user profiles—so if you share your computer, each of you can maintain separate

**Table 1.3** Comparison of Netscape and Microsoft Internet Explorer

| Feature | Netscape 6 | Microsoft Internet Explorer 5.5 |
| --- | --- | --- |
| System requirements | Windows 95, Windows 98, Windows 2000, or Windows NT 4.0, Pentium, 133 MHz, 64 MB of RAM.<br><br>Mac OS 8.5, Mac OS 8.6, or Mac OS 9 with PowerPC, 200 MHz PowerPC 604 or G3, 64 MB RAM, with virtual memory turned on (or 48 MB dynamic RAM) or later. | 16 MB RAM for Windows 95 or 98, 32 MB RAM for Windows NT, 64 MB RAM for Windows 2000; 45 MB to 111 MB hard drive space to install; 27 MB to 80 MB after restart.<br><br>At press time, the most recent Mac release of Internet Explorer was IE 5. |
| Security features | Provides encryption option for all Web and e-mail passwords. A new menu option called Privacy and Security gives users access to managing new cookies, password and form managers, as well as the standard security manager. | Includes support for 128-bit encryption. You can use security zones to specify how you want Microsoft Internet Explorer to download applications and files from different Web sites. |
| Password and form management | Password and form managers simplify letting users automatically fill in forms on sites. | AutoComplete feature lets users automatically enter username and password as they begin to fill out online forms. |
| E-mail capabilities | Lets users define and use more than one SMTP server to send mail. Lacks the handheld sync capabilities that had previously been in Netscape Communicator. | Integrates seamlessly with Microsoft's Outlook Express. |
| Supports XML | Yes | No |
| Supports Cascading Style Sheets 1.0 | Yes | Yes |
| Distinguishing features | Automatic translation of Web pages. | Extended DHTML capabilities through proprietary extensions. |

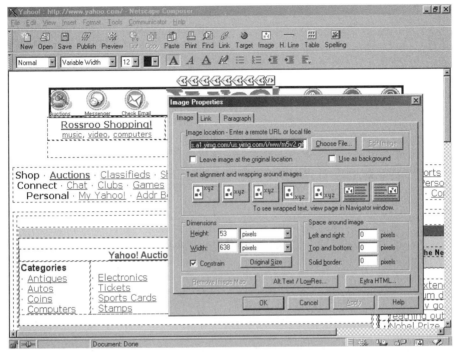

**Figure 1.10**
Netscape 6's new Forms Manager helps you fill out and submit Web forms more quickly. Here, Netscape Composer is used to create your own Web page.

bookmarks and settings. The browser can fairly easily be customized even by new users; bookmarks can be arranged in folders via dragging and dropping. The browser includes a Quality Feedback System feature for automated incident reporting when your browser unexpectedly crashes.

Netscape has made its search feature accessible and powerful: Just enter your search term in the URL field and click Search; the Google-based search technology quickly delivers relevant results. Password Manager and Cookie Manager are two features designed to give you greater control over your privacy.

Netscape has added a novel and sophisticated translate option under its View menu. The language of the Web page you were viewing will be automatically selected for you as the source language. You can then choose the language you'd like for this Web page to be translated into; the service will remember your preferences for future translation requests. Click the button to start AutoTranslate, and in seconds the text in the browser window will appear, translated into the language you selected. If you then follow any links in the translated page, the service will translate that page for you into the target language you chose in the setup screen. Supported languages include translating from English into Portuguese, Italian, German, Spanish, French, Japanese, Traditional Chinese, and Simplified Chinese. You can also translate to English from Portuguese, Italian, German, Spanish, French, and Japanese.

URL: http://www.netscape.com/browsers/

## Internet Explorer

Microsoft's strategy has focused on achieving seamless integration of the PC and the Web—after all, it was Microsoft's bundling of Internet Explorer with Windows that was at the heart of the government suit against the software company. IE is flexible and readily customized either by users or developers (see Figure 1.11).

The browser is integrated with the Outlook Express mail client, FrontPage authoring tool, Microsoft Office Suite, and just about everything else Microsoft produces. It uses IntelliSense technology to help automatically complete the entering of informa-

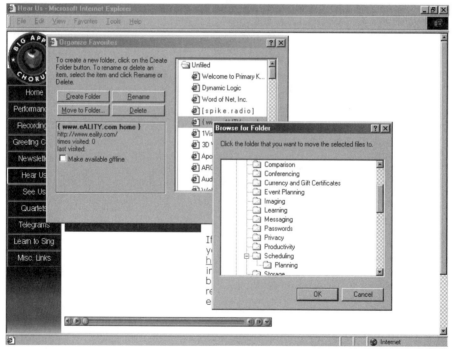

**Figure 1.11**
Like Netscape, Microsoft also emphasizes its brower's timesaving features. Here, the Organize Favorites feature lets you store the addresses of your favorite Web sites. (Screen shot reprinted by permission from Microsoft Corporation.)

tion on online forms and logon screens (known as AutoComplete) and automatically install Web browser components when you come to a Web page that requires them (through AutoInstall). You'll also be able to save pages for off-line viewing. The Install-On-Demand feature installs any component as required by the Web page you're visiting—so if you're browsing a Web page in Japanese, for example, Internet Explorer will download the character set you need to view the page correctly.

Microsoft has used proprietary extensions to DHTML (dynamic HTML) to add features such as colored scroll bars, color gradients, and zooming to the browsing experience. One nice new feature will probably go unnoticed by most users—there's now a print preview option, which shows how many pages are needed to print a site. Better support for Cascading Style Sheets 1 is now added, which should be seamless to end users but is a good plus for Web developers.

URL: http://www.microsoft.com/ie

# FREE ONLINE ACCELERATORS . . . . . . . . . . . . .

Most of the products and services we've discussed so far enable the basics of going online, but there are many products out there that make going online just a bit more sophisticated.

## NetSonic

NetSonic is by far the most popular Internet speed accelerator. The free version is a subset of the professional version. NetSonic uses two techniques for speeding up Internet access. One is by keeping a version of frequently used Web sites on your hard disk. This can dramatically speed access, but if you're not careful, you can be viewing an older version of the site. NetSonic will let you know if you're not viewing the most recent version of a page. The second way NetSonic speeds Web access is through a technique known as "prefetching." The software will look at links where you might click next and start downloading them while you're reading the first screen. Of course, there's a good chance it will guess wrong. Prefetching is controversial because it can cause undue load on a Web server. Imagine the drain of lots of visitors sucking down huge video files that no one will actually watch.

NetSonic's benefits are worthwhile, but it is certainly not shy about reminding you of its value. Your frontmost browser window will include a short line of text in a button that takes you to one of their sponsors. NetSonic also displays a floating toolbar that shows you how much it's speeding access and allows you to turn certain features on and off. Opening NetSonic's interface will invariably pitch you the commercial version of the product, and at startup, the product will provide ads for other, typically free products.

URL: http://www.web3000.com/

## GoZilla

If you've tried to download any of the software mentioned until now, you've noticed that downloading files can be a monstrous chore. Enter GoZilla. When you start to download a file, GoZilla springs into action, automatically checking out sites where the file is available. Once it finds them, it rates each of them in terms of how quickly they're responding. Sites that were closer, less busy, hosted on faster hardware, or that took advantage of faster connections were up to 50 percent faster than our average throughput. GoZilla can also seamlessly switch sites in the middle of a download if the site you're downloading from happens to slow down.

GoZilla includes a file manager (see Figure 1.12) for software you've downloaded, and it can schedule downloads for time that has less traffic or when you're online. It even has its own channels for popular download sites. If you have your sound set high, GoZilla's roar can be quite alarming, but generally, the software stays out of your way much better than NetSonic.

URL: http://www.gozilla.com/

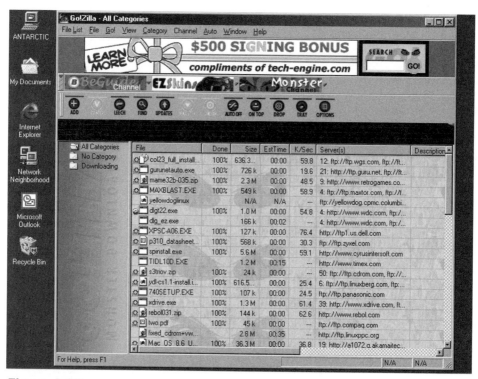

**Figure 1.12**

With GoZilla, you have a behind-the-scenes view of how well your file downloads are going.

## Atomica

Atomica, formerly known as GuruNet, is a service for finding out more information about any given word or selected words on a Web page. After you install it, just hold down the Alt key and click on a word in your browser, and Atomica's window will display related links and other information (Figure 1.13). Best of all, Atomica appears as a taskbar icon and does not show ads.

The options intelligently change depending on what has been selected. If you click someone's name, like George Washington, Atomica will find a biography. Clicking a ticker symbol like IBM will display company news and a stock quote. Clicking a city name like Seattle will provide geography information and weather. Many words and names will bring up encyclopedia entries, definitions, or an option

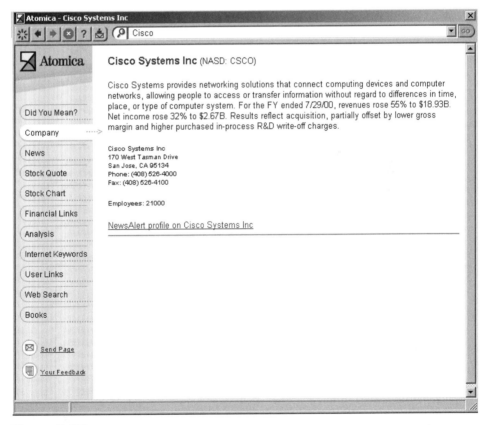

**Figure 1.13**
By involving the Atomica pop-up window, shown here, you can access reference information about any term or proper name on a Web page without leaving that site.

to translate English words into other languages. While Atomica requires you click on only one word at a time, you can type phrases into a search window in the box. The system tray icon allows you to choose different preferences, such as what combination of keys will call up Atomica.

URL: http://www.atomica.com/

# FREE INFORMATION ASSISTANTS · · · · · · · · · · ·

As programs such as Outlook Express and NetMeeting have shown, there's more to getting on the Net beyond the browser. Apart from a proclivity for exotic names, such as Odigo, Obongo, and Zadu, they are all available only for Windows. They're described here in three categories, although some have feature sets that would place them in multiple groups.

Information accessories are typically thin strips (see Figure 1.14) that float on your screen, similar to the ones that are provided by some free ISPs. They typically

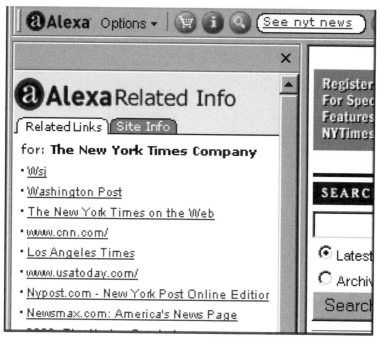

**Figure 1.14**
By clicking a button on Alexa's toolbar, you can find information related to the topic on the Web page you're reading.

provide tickers on news, stocks, and sports, and integrate with "wallets"—software that lets you purchase items online without having to fill in your credit card information every time.

Some examples are

- Alexa (http://www.alexa.com/)
- Desktop News (http://www.desktopnews.com/)
- Infogate (http://www.infogate.com/)
- Iware (http://www.iwareinc.com/)

Communication accessories typically provide a forum to comment on or to communicate with other Web site visitors about content on the Web page being viewed (see Figure 1.15). In general, they are only as good as the number of people using them.

**Figure 1.15**
Odigo is a free tool for instant messaging and online chats.

Some examples are

- Cahoots (http://www.cahoots.com/)
- MessageVine (http://www.messagevine.com/)
- Odigo (http://www.odigo.com/)
- Third Voice (http://www.thirdvoice.com/)
- uTOK (http://www.utok.com/)
- Zadu (http://www.zadu.com/)

Finally, form accessories remember your user IDs and passwords, streamlining the process of logging in to countless sites (see Figure 1.16). Like information accessories, they are often integrated with or serve as wallets.

Some examples are

- Gator (http://www.gator.com/)
- v-Go (http://www.passlogix.com/)
- Obongo (http://www.obongo.com/)

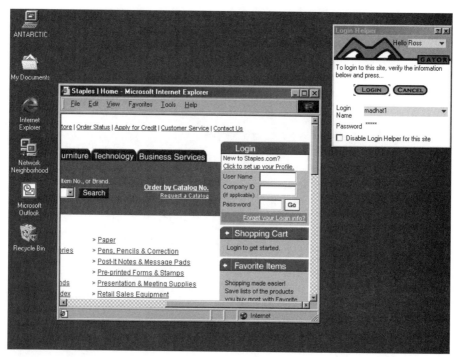

**Figure 1.16**
Smart online companion Gator fills in forms and remembers passwords.

# WHAT'S AHEAD . . . . . . . . . . . . . . . . . .

Here's a brief introduction to the types of services for your small business or home office that you can acquire for free—or almost free—covered in the chapters ahead. You may not have a need for all, but gaining familiarity with the underlying concepts—and even a couple of technical definitions—will help you assess whether these capabilities would help you in your work.

In Chapter 2:

- **E-mail.** Would you like to access your e-mail over the Web? Do you need another account to separate your business e-mail from your personal correspondence?

- **Redirection.** Do you worry about missing your e-mail messages every time you need to switch e-mail addresses? With an e-mail redirection service, all messages coming to your forwarding e-mail account will be redirected to an existing e-mail address.

- **Voice mail, fax, and answering machines.** These voice mail services provide free phone numbers to receive and sometimes send voice and fax messages via e-mail.

- **Translation services.** In a global economy, you may sometimes need to communicate in an unfamiliar language—these free services help you get by.

- **Spam filtering.** Besides slow connection speeds, the main complaint of today's Internet users is the exasperating amount of unsolicited e-mail, better known as spam, that they receive. These services help keep the spammers out of your e-mailbox.

In Chapter 3:

- **Scheduling, appointments, and collaboration tools.** Get organized with free Web-based schedulers that provide address books, e-mail reminders, event tracking, appointment scheduling, to-do lists, messaging features, and more.

- **Webtops.** These virtual desktop sites store the files and applications you use everyday on a Web server so that you can access your information anywhere, anytime.

- **Mobile services.** These services can help you receive financial news and the latest stock quotes, and can even help you create Web pages on your personal digital assistant (PDA), such as a PalmPilot.

In Chapter 4:

- **Site hosting.** You're ready to hang out your shingle on the Web, but how can you do so most inexpensively? These hosting services give you free server space and often easy-to-use tools for posting your content.
- **HTML templates and graphics.** Even if you have dedicated Web production resources, you may need some divine inspiration or a quick boost for designing your pages more quickly. These resources include freely distributable HTML code to underlay your pages, as well as graphics you can use as-is or modify for your specific buttons, icons, or navigation bars.
- **Content.** Keeping a Web site continually updated is a challenge for any Webmaster. These content services arrange licensing deals with third-party content providers, who let you post their interactive headlines or search boxes in exchange for publicity.
- **Surveys, polls, and chat forums.** Letting your audience tell you want they want and what they think is a good way to keep them coming back to your Web site. These services let you quickly add interactivity to your Web site without any Web development on your part.

In Chapter 5:

- **Affiliate programs.** By placing ad banners and links to other online merchants on your site, you can receive commissions when your visitors click through and make a purchase.
- **Auctions.** Find out how to extend your commerce capabilities through these online auction services, which can bring together interested purchasers and enable the bidding process for you.
- **Escrow services.** For a minimal fee, these services will act as a go-between for buyers and sellers in online auctions.
- **Credit card processing.** Selling online is difficult if you can't process your customers' credit cards. Find out how these services can streamline this step for you.

In Chapter 6:

- **Small business portals.** You're not alone out there! These sites aggregate a wide variety of content and services with a special focus on the needs of small businesses.

- **Product research.** These sites give you the know-how to assess online vendors and products with input from consumers and experts, and even provide questionnaires that let you determine the feature set you need.

In Chapter 7:

- **Online banking.** You'll discover how financial services firms are offering a slew of services from low-cost stock trading to bill aggregation.
- **Shipping services.** To provide comprehensive customer service you'll need to be able to track the goods you ship and receive—these services make it easy.
- **Legal services and information.** These sites offer a wealth of legal information and advice if you're on the road to seeking legal representation.
- **Travel services.** Online reservations, bookings, and fare comparisons were key applications in the growth of the Web's popularity—find out what discounts and promotions you can take advantage of the next time you're traveling on business or for fun.

# 2

# Managing Communications

..........................

**I**n the last chapter, we discussed how you can get a free computer, free ISP service (but usually not both), and free software to get you on the Net, and how you can access rich media, and even enhance your browsing experience. Now that you're all outfitted for the Web, the rest of the book will focus on Web sites that offer free business services. In broad strokes, the Net is about three things—communication, information, and transaction. This chapter will focus on communications. Long before you reach out and build your online empire, you can start by responding to queries via e-mail, sending messages to your suppliers, or even consolidating your many different points of contact into a single Web site.

The services in this and all subsequent chapters are designated as appropriate for either small office/home office (SOHO) use or for small businesses. Additional fee-based or subscription services are listed in each site summary as "big spender" options.

## FREE REDIRECTION . . . . . . . . . . . . . . . . . . . .

One tool that Internet service providers use to retain customers is their e-mail address. If you have the e-mail address jsmith@netzero.net, then you must inform everyone of your new e-mail address if you leave NetZero. Web-based e-mail can help with that problem because it's ISP-independent, but what if you decide you want to find an e-mail site that integrates better with your calendar or offers more features?

In this way, one major advantage of Web-based e-mail is "ISP independence." To truly isolate yourself from any ties, redirections simply point to another e-mail address, an alias. If you change e-mail providers, you simply change the address to which you're forwarding your e-mail.

Table 2.1 shows how the leading services in this area compare against one another.

**Table 2.1**  *Comparison Chart for Redirection Services*

|  | Mail.com | Bigfoot.com |
|---|---|---|
| Pros | Large number of domain names to choose from for your e-mail address, such as doctor.com, engineer.com, japan.com, or many other available domain names. | Includes URL redirection. Offers autoresponders (e-mails that are automatically sent to your visitors in your absence). Reminder services provide a heads-up about upcoming birthdays, appointments, and other events you schedule. |
| Cons |  | Cumbersome registration. |
| Filters junk mail? | Yes | Yes |
| Supports POP mail? | Yes | Yes |
| Supports Web-based e-mail? | Yes | Yes |

## Mail.com

Formerly known as iName, Internet messaging services company Mail.com's free e-mail service lets you forward all your incoming messages to another e-mail address (see Figure 2.1) or collect messages from all of your external e-mail accounts into one location.

You can choose from hundreds of fun domain names (e.g., usa.com, techie.com) for your own personalized, permanent e-mail address that you can check from any Web browser.

Mail.com powers the e-mail services offered by other Internet e-mail services, such as Email.com and other partners. The service also generates revenues through sales made through the Mail.com Marketplace, a one-stop shopping service users can access from their e-mail inbox.

**Getting started:**

After you log in with your username and password, click Tools in the left-hand navigations to activate e-mail forwarding, add a signature to your outgoing messages, filter junk mail, change your password, or manage external e-mail collection. You can also append your own custom signatures to outgoing mail. Signatures are the lines of text that fall below the message that often include contact information or a quote.

Required information includes

- full name
- your desired e-mail address (includes choosing domain name) and password

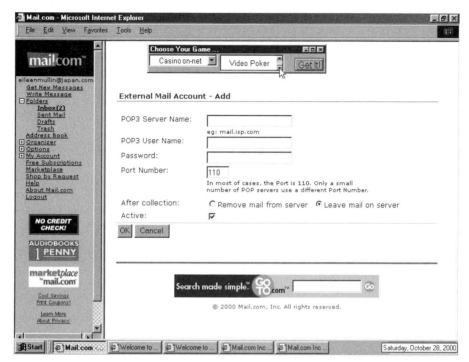

**Figure 2.1**
With Mail.com, you can forward all incoming messages from one e-mail
account to another.

- birth date
- mailing address
- occupation

When you register, you're asked if you want to opt in to receive merchant promotions
in a number of broad categories (from adventure/outdoors to consumer electronics) or
from specific retailers.

**Big spender:**

MailPro increases your mailbox storage capacity to 20 MB and the size limit for incoming and outgoing attachments to 4 MB. It includes 4-hour turnaround time for
customer service. The cost is $29.95 per year or $2.95 per month.

Upgraded (POP3) access lets you use access your Web-based e-mail on
Mail.com using any standalone POP3-compliant email program, like Eudora or
Microsoft Outlook. This will enable you to read your e-mail offline, which may help
you save money on phone and Internet service charges. This will run you $39.95 per
year or $3.95 per month.

URL: http://www.mail.com/

**Contact:**   http://www.mail.com/cgi-bin/mailcom/noframes/support/

   _X_  SOHO                            ____  Small business

## Bigfoot.com

E-mail company Bigfoot offers a service called Bigfoot for Life, which redirects Bigfoot e-mail addresses when users change their e-mail provider. You choose one of
three free customized e-mail delivery options.

- Forwarding. All your Bigfoot mail is sent to another e-mail address of
  your choice. Multiple forwarding addresses are allowed (see Figure 2.2).
- Distribution. Copies of all your incoming Bigfoot e-mail are forwarded to
  up to five other e-mail accounts you may have.
- Filtering. Based on specific criteria you set up, Bigfoot will send or reject
  your incoming e-mail to multiple e-mail addresses you may have.

**Figure 2.2**
Bigfoot.com offers free e-mail forwarding.

Additional services include the company's Bigfoot Directory, a Web-based white page directory. Bigfoot also has a free reminder service; you'll receive e-mails to remind yourself about upcoming holidays, birthdays, and other occasions you specify. The service lets you set up an autoresponder for whenever you are unable to check your e-mail. Bigfoot's PermaWeb is a free URL redirection service that can give you a permanent Web address for your home page. Even if you change service providers or alter your URL, visitors to your site will still find you if you promote http://www.bigfoot.com/~yourname/(where "yourname" is your username on Bigfoot) as your site's URL.

**Getting started:**

Registration at Bigfoot is a multiple-screen process that seems much more cumbersome than that at many of the other free e-mail services. If you want to change any of your e-mail options once you've registered, return to the Bigfoot site, click on Members Entrance, and follow instructions for making changes.

Required information includes

- full name
- e-mail address
- state
- country
- zip code
- gender

You'll also be asked to choose your Bigfoot for Life e-mail address (in the format anyname@bigfoot.com) and a password for your account. You'll be asked if you want to opt in to receive promotional materials from Bigfoot and its partners. You then indicate whether or not you want your e-mail address to be included in the Bigfoot directory.

**Big spender:**

Premium services include consolidation: Use Bigfoot as the base for receiving messages from multiple e-mail accounts to your Bigfoot for Life address. This service comes with a one-month free trial and costs $19.95 per year.

URL: http://www.bigfoot.com/

**Contact:** help@bigfoot.com

  X  SOHO                ____  Small business

# FREE E-MAIL . . . . . . . . . . . . . . . . . . . .

As popular as the Web is, there's an even more popular use for the Internet—e-mail. E-mail has become a crucial way to communicate with just about anyone on the Internet. There are already more e-mails sent per year than there are U.S. postal letters. Let's look first at a free program you can use to receive your e-mail on your PC; next, we'll cover free Web-based services that let you check your e-mail at any time, from any machine.

## Outlook Express

It may have a similar name to Outlook, the full-fledged group-scheduling program from Microsoft, but Outlook Express is a relatively lightweight, full-featured, and free e-mail client (see Figure 2.3).

E-mail clients typically let you compose a message, address it to multiple recipients (usually stored in an address book), and send it. To send mail, you need to know

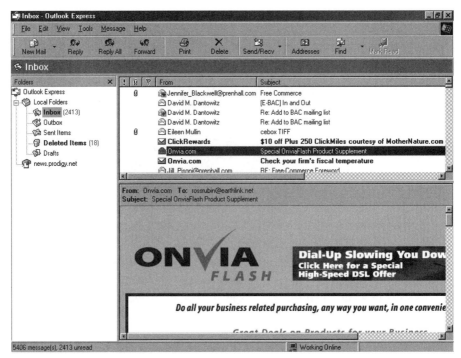

**Figure 2.3**
Outlook Express is a free but full-featured e-mail program.

the name of your SMTP (Simple Mail Transfer Protocol) server. To receive mail, you need to know the name of your POP (Post Office Protocol) server. Your ISP can give you this information, but a good first guess is to place the word "mail" and a period before the ISP's full name, for example, mail.earthlink.net.

Once you've received mail, you can treat it like you treat mail in the real world. You can delete it, forward it, file it, or reply to it. Outlook Express also has extensive filters. For example, you can take any e-mail that has the subject "Payment Due" and make it high priority (or dump it in the trash). Outlook Express even has a filter that can screen out unsolicited e-mail, typically called spam. Outlook Express also ties into MSN Hotmail, the free Web-based service discussed a little later in this chapter.

URL: http://www.microsoft.com/windows/oe/

URL: http://www.microsoft.com/mac/oe/

# FREE WEB-BASED E-MAIL . . . . . . . . . . . . . . . . .

Having your e-mail on the Web allows you to retrieve it from virtually any computer. Even if you already have an e-mail account, free Web-based e-mail can be enormously helpful to separate your personal e-mail from your business correspondence, receive critical files from someone else's PC when your office network is down, or stay in touch when you're on the road.

With Web-based e-mail, you connect to the free e-mail provider's site with your Web browser and then log in with a username and password. The e-mail provider stores all your messages for you, but usually limits you to a relatively small amount of storage space. As a result, you'll eventually need to start deleting your old messages after you read them in order to make room for new ones. You can obtain extra mail storage space from some of these e-mail service providers, if you're willing to pay for it. You won't have to buy such extras when you sign up for the free services, but may significantly improve the quality of your experience in using them. Many services offer extra functions, such as online spell-checkers, personal address books, and distribution lists. An overview of several popular services' features can be found in Table 2.2.

The most useful free Web-based e-mail services also let you check POP mail accounts, which are what most Internet service providers offer. You wouldn't receive a new POP account with a free Web-based e-mail service, though. POP stands for Post Office Protocol, which refers to how e-mail software, such as Eudora, gets mail from a mail server. This lets you tap in to an existing or primary e-mail account you have with an Internet service provider—say, EarthLink or RCN—while you're on the

**Table 2.2**  Comparison of E-mail Services

|  | **Hotmail** | **Yahoo! Mail** | **Hushmail** |
|---|---|---|---|
| Pros | Easy-to-use interface. Enhanced security features. Includes reminders, message searching, and address book capabilities. | Easy-to-use interface. Includes spell-checker for composing messages. Provides access to an online calendar, chat, games, classifieds, and message boards. | Web-based encrypted e-mail system for assuring secure and private communications. |
| Cons | Requires cookies. (Unpopular with privacy-minded users.) |  | Recipients also need to be Hushmail users. |
| POP mail support | Can retrieve POP3 mail. | Can both access and retrieve POP3 mail. | No |
| File attachments | May attach any number files to an outgoing message as long as the total file size is less than 1 MB and no one file is more than 500K. | Up to three files may be attached to an outgoing message, totaling less than 1.5 MB in file size. | Yes |
| Available space for message storage | 2 MB | 3 MB | 3 MB |
| E-mail forwarding | No | Yes | No |
| Filters for removing junk e-mail | Yes | Yes | No |

## Cookies and Your Privacy

First implemented in 1994 in version 1.1 of the Netscape browser, cookies are tiny files that are placed on your hard drive by the Web sites you visit. Cookies give Web sites a means of recognizing return visitors in order to offer customized information or services.

Let's say you frequent a news-oriented Web site. While there, you may choose to look up your local weather report, check out the closing price of certain stocks, and leaf through the automobile classifieds. By enabling a cookie, the site may note your interests for future reference. The next time you visit, the site queries your Web browser to see if a cookie is stashed there. If one exists, your browser automatically sends it over, and your preferences—the city for your local weather forecast, the stocks you're tracking, and your interest in cars—are all imparted to the site in question. Many Internet advertisers now use cookies so that they recognize you when you come to a page containing one of their ads. In this way, they know what ads you've most recently seen and make sure you don't see them again.

But what if you'd rather not have anyone know that much about you, or if you'd at least like to decide who knows what about your browsing? There are four good ways to control cookie consumption:

- Set your browser to limit or stop cookies

- Delete your cookies manually on a regular basis

- Install a free cookie-manager program, available over the Web. Two examples are AdSubtract (http://www.adsubtract.com/) and IDcide Privacy Companion (http://www.idcide.com/)

- Use an anonymous browsing program like Anonymizer (http://www.anonymizer.com/) or Privada (http://www.privada.com/)

road. When you configure your free Web-based e-mail to access your POP account, you'll decide whether to delete your POP mail after you read it. Otherwise, you can choose to keep your POP mail on your Internet service provider's server after you read it through your Web-based e-mail account, then download it later from the primary machine where you usually check that e-mail account.

Free Internet e-mail services typically show you banner advertisements when you collect your mail. Many also append a short tag line to each message you send that identifies the service you used. If you'd rather avoid advertising that you use a free e-mail service, you'll need to take this into consideration when deciding which service to use. If you're plagued by junk e-mail, you'll want to ensure you choose a free e-mail service that lets you filter your incoming messages. In this way, you can identify and block e-mail addresses or domains from which you want to block incoming mail. The free e-mail service itself may also identify and automatically remove messages whose origins are suspect.

There are literally hundreds of Internet services that hawk free e-mail accounts—you'll find a continually updated listing at http://www.emailaddresses.com/—but all are not created equal. In the following sections, you'll find our favorites, along with their differentiating factors.

## Hotmail

Now owned by Microsoft, Hotmail is the original and most popular free e-mail service. It sports an easy-to-use interface and enhanced security features, as well as advanced options like filtering, instant messaging, and support for POP mail. Hotmail is also key to MSN Passport, a way of providing a single username and password across a variety of services (see Figure 2.4).

Hotmail recognizes its members through cookies, small bits of information stored by your browser on your hard disk. This is designed to prevent hacker attacks, but is unpopular with privacy-minded users who want to avoid using cookies. Other security-minded features include unsuccessful log-on error delays and the option of having any Hotmail pages you've viewed expire from the browser's cache when you log off. This prevents anyone who uses the same system after you do from accessing cached pages via the browser's History or Back buttons.

You can attach files to your outgoing e-mail messages, as long as they weigh in at less than 1 MB in size. You can expand the service's functionality by taking advantage of features like Reminders, FindMessage, and QuickList Addresses. In addition, Hotmail uses McAfee VirusScan to scan attachments before downloading them. When you receive an e-mail with an attachment, you can click an option to run the virus scan before you download the file. Note that Hotmail scans only the attachments, though, not the contents of any attached compressed files (like a .ZIP or Stuffit file).

You can use Hotmail's filtering features to delete unwanted junk e-mail messages before they ever hit your inbox. You can filter messages based on name, address, and subject, then move these messages to a folder designated for this purpose.

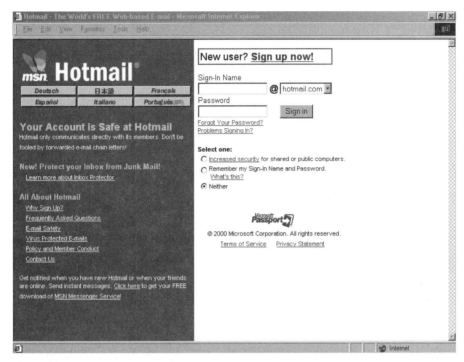

**Figure 2.4**
You can set security features directly on Hotmail's home page. (Screen shot reprinted by permission from Microsoft Corporation.)

You can also type a list of addresses you want to block and add the addresses from spam e-mails that have managed to slip through to block them in the future.

**Getting started:**

To set up Hotmail to check another e-mail account, you'll need to enter your primary account's server name, username, and password. You probably won't need to change the server timeout and port number setting. If you plan to read your messages only from your primary e-mail account on Hotmail then download them later, you can choose to leave messages on the POP server, which means you'll still be able to download them later into your usual e-mail client, such as Eudora or Microsoft Outlook.

Required information includes

- full name
- country
- zip code
- occupation

- time zone
- gender
- birth date

When you sign up, you're asked to select a username and password, then enter a clue to prompt you if you forget your password.

Hotmail's optional WebCourier service lets you sign up for news updates from a variety of sources. If you sign up for one or more of these subscriptions, you'll receive e-newsletters and other news updates from these third-party media sources directly as e-mail messages to your Hotmail account.

**Big spender:**

No premium services.

URL: http://www.hotmail.com/

**Contact:**   support@hotmail.com

  X   SOHO                    ____  Small business

## Yahoo! Mail

With Yahoo! Mail's easy-to-use free e-mail service, you can set up a new free e-mail account—here, the naming convention is yourname@yahoo.com—and you can also access POP mail from an existing account on an Internet service provider if you already have a primary e-mail account elsewhere.

With Yahoo! Mail, you can send messages that contain up to three attachments (see Figure 2.5); you can also open attachments that include audio and video clips, or scripts. A built-in spell-checker is included for use when you compose messages.

Like Hotmail, Yahoo! Mail lets you filter e-mail based on name, address, and common spam phrases (e.g., XXX, babes, FREE) found in the subject line, then move designated messages to a special folder. In addition, Yahoo! Mail filters messages based on text in the body of the message itself. This is a bonus for catching junk e-mail or spam—that is, advertising and e-mail sent to you that you never asked for and that you don't want—more quickly. Yahoo! Mail's options also let you block the address from any junk e-mail that does accidentally slip through, to ensure the sender doesn't reach you again (see Figure 2.6).

Yahoo! Mail also gives you access to an online calendar, chat, classifieds, games, and message boards to encourage users to stick around the service. You'll be preregistered to buy and sell goods in Yahoo! Auctions, send and receive instant messages with Yahoo! Messenger, track stocks using Yahoo! Finance, and choose to use Yahoo! Calendar for scheduling events.

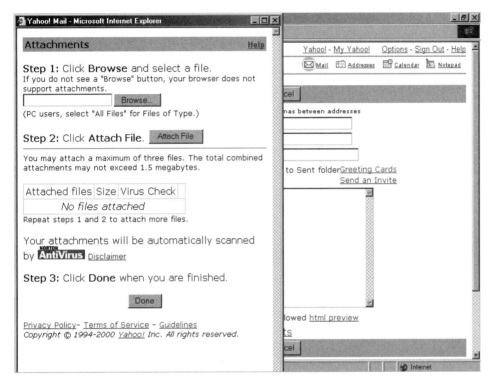

**Figure 2.5**
You can attach files to your outgoing Yahoo! Mail messages via a pop-up
window interface.

### Getting started:

To configure POP mail in Yahoo! Mail, you'll need to provide the server name, your
username, and password. You have the option of choosing to leave the e-mail you've
checked on the server in case you want to use another mail client to download this account's messages to your primary machine. When you want to check your POP accounts, click on Check Other Mail.

Required information includes

- full name
- zip code
- gender
- occupation
- the industry you work in

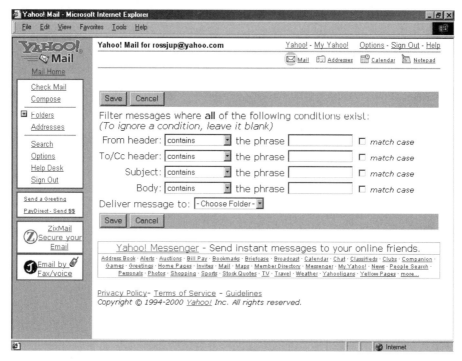

**Figure 2.6**
With Yahoo! Mail, you can filter messages based on several criteria,
including words in the subject line.

You can also choose to enter your interests from a preselected list and agree to receive advertisers' promotions based on your interests.

**Big spender:**

No premium services.


URL: http://mail.yahoo.com/

**Contact:**   http://help.yahoo.com/help/mail/

   X  SOHO                      ____  Small business


# Hushmail

When moving through the Internet, your e-mail can be hijacked and read as it passes
through a number of insecure junctures. That may not be comforting if you plan to
exchange sensitive data with partners or clients. Hushmail provides secure Web-
based e-mail that ensures only your intended recipients receive your message by issu-
ing a special key to them (see Figure 2.7). It protects messages to and from you, using

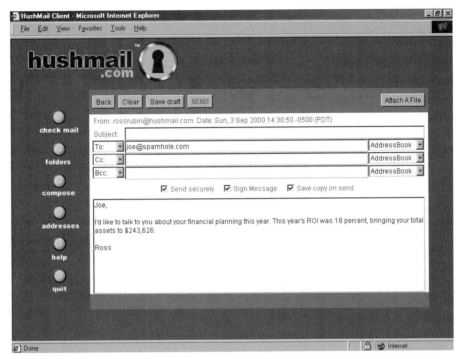

**Figure 2.7**
Encrypt your e-mail messages with the Web-based Hushmail service.

encryption, which scrambles them with a secret code. This kind of secure communications is possible in other kinds of e-mail programs, but usually requires extra confusing steps. In contrast, Hushmail operates like most other Web-based mail. The catches are that the recipient must also use a Hushmail account, which lacks many bells and whistles of other Web mail accounts, and also works only under Windows.

**Getting started:**

The first time you use Hushmail, you'll be required to move your mouse randomly throughout a square to generate a unique identification key for yourself. Subsequently, you need to enter only your password, and then use Hushmail's Compose, Check Mail, and Address Book features as you normally would. The encryption takes place behind the scenes.

Required information includes

- industry
- state or province
- zip code or postal code
- how you were referred to the site

**Big spender:**

If you refer eight other members to Hushmail, your storage space is increased for a year to 7 MB from 3 MB at no charge.

URL: http://www.hushmail.com/

**Contact:**   http://www.hushmail.com/contact.htm

   _X_  SOHO                         ____  Small business

# FREE CONTACTS . . . . . . . . . . . . . . . . . . . . . .

As more and more software products start to be subsumed as services, some users have expressed concern that we won't see the rich capabilities that many of these products have had before. Those skeptics can rest easy in the field of contact management, though. Relegated to an address book feature of an e-mail program for many users, the contact manager has been revived by Contact Networks. The company has produced one of the most full-featured contact managers this side of professional sales management tools, and one clearly in touch with the Internet.

If you'd prefer to stick with your own contact manager, an alternative is Active-Names (http://www.activenames.net/). This free program and service allows e-mail to reach you even if you change your e-mail address. The company offers a server version of its product for businesses.

## Contact Networks

Contact Networks starts out by letting you track more than 50 tidbits of information about your contacts, from the name of their assistant to their grandfather. You can also add multiple data points for many kinds of information. If you need to keep track of three pager numbers for someone, this is the program for you. But Contact Networks goes beyond data. You can also include a contact's picture, their company logo, and a voice sample.

If you're wondering how you can get all of this data, you're not expected to. Contact Networks allows you to "invite" contacts to download the program. Once they've updated their own information, you receive it automatically so you never need to have an out-of-date contact. The company has taken advantage of the Internet in other ways, too. You can instantly view a map of any address or even take advantage of e-commerce links to send your contacts gifts and flowers (see Figure 2.8). The

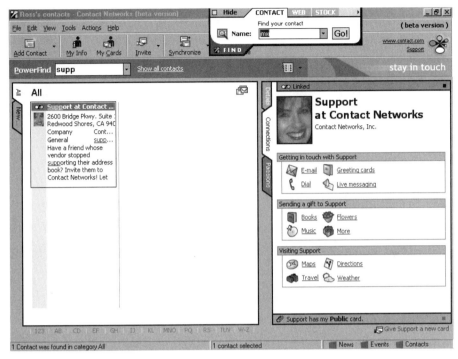

**Figure 2.8**
Use Contact Networks to track details about your acquaintances and store the information online.

software also has a handy Find "drawer" that sits at the top of your screen and allows you to do quick searches for people when you're not in the program.

**Getting started:**

You will need to download the Contact Networks application to register your account. Once you have registered your account, you can set up your Internet-ready mobile phone to access your information.

**Big spender:**

No premium services.

URL: http://www.contact.com/

**Contact:**   http://www.contact.com/files/about_contactus.html

  X  SOHO                     X   Small business

# FREE INSTANT MESSAGING . . . . . . . . . . . . . .

Instant messaging has become an Internet phenomenon. A cross between e-mail and the telephone, "IM'ing," as it's called, combines some of the best elements of e-mail and the telephone by letting you set up private and group chats on the fly. It shares some of its weaknesses, too, though. Since it happens in "real time," there really isn't a good way to answer an instant message if you're not there; a link to a pager or cell phone is sorely needed.

## AOL Instant Messenger

With more than 40 million users, AOL Instant Messenger is one of the most popular software programs in use on the Net today. Its musical tones announcing the sending and receipt of small text messages have become almost as famous as AOL's "You've Got Mail!" sound.

To set up AOL Instant Messenger, you first indicate whether you're a current AOL member. Then you add the lists of your buddies. Whenever a buddy signs on, you hear a door opening sound. When they log off, you hear the door close. You can also choose icons to represent yourself or others; AOL allows you to gradually view the images in case someone has chosen something objectionable. If someone says something objectionable, though, you can issue them a warning. You can use AOL IM to send files directly to someone else on your buddy list (see Figure 2.9). It also automatically converts "smileys" like : - ) into ☺.

Even though AOL IM is the most popular and simplest instant messenger, it's moving forward and catching up with its more sophisticated sister software, ICQ. AOL IM recently added similar links to the Web and is adding the voice chat features of ICQ.

**Getting started:**

Follow the links on the AOL Instant Messenger home page to download the version appropriate for your computer platform. You'll need a screen name to use AIM, but you may already have one reserved if you are a current AOL or CompuServe2000 member. These users have a separate registration page.

**Big spender:**

No premium services.

URL: http://www.aol.com/aim/

**Contact:**   http://www.aol.com/info/feedback.html

    _X_  SOHO                          ____  Small business

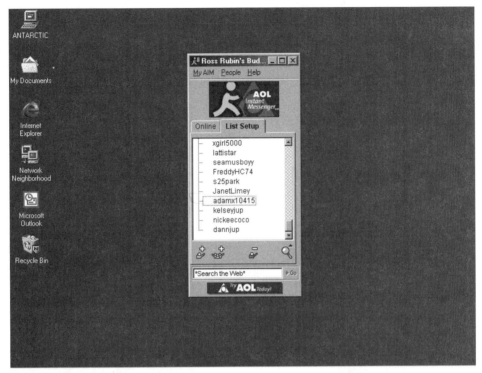

**Figure 2.9**
You can see at a glance whether your friends or colleagues are accessible
via AOL Instant Messenger.

## ICQ

ICQ ("I seek you," get it?) has also attracted millions of users; America Online now
also owns the product. ICQ is more full-featured than AOL Instant Messenger and is
better integrated with other forms of communication, such as the Web and e-mail. For
example, ICQ was first to allow a group of buttons to be added to a Web page that allowed Web users to contact ICQ users through ICQ. You can monitor whether you've
received new e-mail through ICQ. ICQ can also be used to send messages to digital
cell phones that support SMS (Short Messaging Service).

**Getting started:**

Visit http://www.icq.com/download/ to download the installer program appropriate
for your computer platform. Double-click the installer to begin the installation process; when finished, follow the Registration wizard instructions that appear onscreen.
The ICQ program will open in Simple Mode on your desktop with a green online

status icon displaying. You can then begin to add users to your Contact List. More extensive instructions and technical information is available on the ICQ site.

**Big spender:**

No premium services.

URL: http://www.icq.com/

**Contact:**   http://www.icq.com/company/ncontact.html

    X  SOHO                    _____  Small business

Yahoo! and Microsoft (via MSN) also offer instant messaging clients. Yahoo! Messenger and MSN Messenger were somewhat late to the game, and don't have nearly the feature set of ICQ, but they are integrated with their own e-mail sites and other properties. For example, MSN Messenger allows people to invite other people into games that use Microsoft's DirectPlay technology and has ties to its NetMeeting conferencing client. However, AOL has blocked users of these products from communicating with AOL Instant Messenger users.

## NetMeeting

While instant messaging clients are gradually beginning to incorporate other media, such as audio, several higher end software products have been focused on videoconferencing for years. If you're using a dial-up connection to the Net, you'll find videoconferencing quality is so poor that you'll probably forego the video and just use the audio features.

Nevertheless, NetMeeting has many features. In addition to conferencing via audio or video, you can send both kinds of media to an associate who doesn't have a camera. NetMeeting can automatically adjust the sound level so that associates on the other end don't get an earful. It also allows you to manage the tradeoff between video size and performance in the middle of a conference.

There are other collaborative features as well. NetMeeting includes a whiteboard feature that allows you and a colleague to work on the same program simultaneously. You can copy and paste information between other PC programs and the whiteboard, and when you're done collaborating, save the results for later viewing. A file exchange feature allows trading documents among conference participants, and desktop sharing even lets you remotely control your PC!

Unfortunately for Mac users, NetMeeting is available only for PCs. iVisit (http://www.ivisit.com/), a product from Web developer iXL, lets both Mac and Windows users videochat for free with each other. It even supports more than two people talking at the same time. Yakety Mac!

**Getting started:**

Windows 2000 users will find that they already have NetMeeting installed. To use NetMeeting on Windows 2000, just click Start, point to Programs, point to Accessories, point to Communications, and click NetMeeting.

Other Windows users can find a link on the NetMeeting home page to download the latest version.

**Big spender:**

No premium services.

URL: http://www.microsoft.com/netmeeting/

**Contact:**  http://www.microsoft.com/netmeeting/

   X   SOHO                          ___ Small business

# FREE VOICE MAIL . . . . . . . . . . . . . . . . . . . .

Online, it's easy for people to get addicted to e-mail, but the most natural way for people to communicate is by voice. That usually requires that two people be available at the same time, but the Internet has created a few answers to the answering machine. These voice mail services let you keep in touch, even with those who lack e-mail, from just about any phone or, in some cases, Web browser. Some pros and cons of these kinds of services appear in Table 2.3.

## EchoBuzz

For young adults or budding entrepreneurs who don't yet have their own phone lines, Blue Diamond Software has launched a free voice mail service called EchoBuzz. Users can send and retrieve voice mail for free on EchoBuzz in exchange for listening to advertising when they access the service.

You'll need to register online at the EchoBuzz site for your own voice mailbox, which you can use to log in. The registration process includes filling out a personal profile that enables EchoBuzz to send targeted ads tailored to your specific interests.

Note that your callers won't hear any advertisements when they leave messages for you. Rather, you'll be compelled to sit through one or more ads (about 30 seconds worth) when you retrieve your voice mail messages.

In terms of features, the service doesn't stack up well against commercial voice mail services like AT&T's—there's currently no option for recording your own personal message, for example—but the price is right. However, with the ability to save up to 20 messages in your mailbox at one time, the message-storing capabilities are more generous than those available to many employees at large companies via their enterprise-wide voice mail services, and the mailbox is easier to navigate.

**Getting started:**

When you complete the service's registration process, you'll receive an EchoBuzz mailbox number and choose a four-digit security code. You'll then connect to EchoBuzz by dialing a toll-free access number from anywhere in the continental United States. Your voice mailbox will remain active as long as you check your messages at least once every two months.

At the EchoBuzz site, you can listen to tutorial sound files that demonstrate how the service works.

Required information includes

- full name
- mailing address
- telephone number
- e-mail address
- birth date
- gender

**Table 2.3**   Comparison of Free Voice Mail Services

|      | EchoBuzz | eVoice | CallWave's Internet Answering Machine |
|------|----------|--------|----------------------------------------|
| Pros | Can store up to 20 messages at a time. | Can record a personalized message. May send a broadcast message to up to 20 users. | Close to real-time notification of incoming calls. |
| Cons | Cannot record a personalized message for callers. | Uneven customer service. | Requires coordination with your telephone service's call-forwarding feature. Messages that users record are only 30 seconds long. |

You'll also be prompted to create a numeric password that's at least four digits long, and you must also answer a question about where you first heard about EchoBuzz (specific ads are named as choices).

**Big spender:**

No premium services.

URL: http://www.echobuzz.com/

**Contact:**   support@echobuzz.com

    _X_  SOHO                                    ____  Small business

## eVoice

eVoice lets you retrieve messages in one of two ways. Your callers can either call an eVoice access number and enter your designated mailbox number to leave you a message, or you can configure eVoice to work with your local telephone company to enable the service to automatically answer your telephone when you can't pick up.

Local access numbers are being gradually rolled out across the U.S. When you visit the site to register, you'll first be asked for your telephone number. If service is available in your area, you'll be able to complete the registration process.

You'll hear a single 15-second advertisement whenever you call in to check your voice mail, and you'll see an ad display when your messages are delivered over the Web or by e-mail. On the plus side, your callers will not be subjected to hearing any advertising messages. You can currently customize the message that's heard, which is an advantage that eVoice has over some competitors.

One neat feature is eVoice's Message Broadcasting. You can record a single message and send it to up to 20 other eVoice subscribers at once. You can also set up a QuickDial directory that lets you access associates using the service with just a few button presses (see Figure 2.10).

You can also use eVoice to create several private voice mailboxes from a single phone number (in available areas). You choose your own mailbox address and PIN. The eVoice site features a quick online tour to explain the service's features (see Figure 2.11) and plays a sample audio clip so you can hear up front what an eVoice message sounds like.

**Getting started:**

When you call in for your messages, you'll dial a local access number, enter your eVoice mailbox number and PIN, then hear a 15-second advertisement before your private voice mail messages are played. There are a host of different options for controlling the playback and leaving your own messages. You can also choose to receive

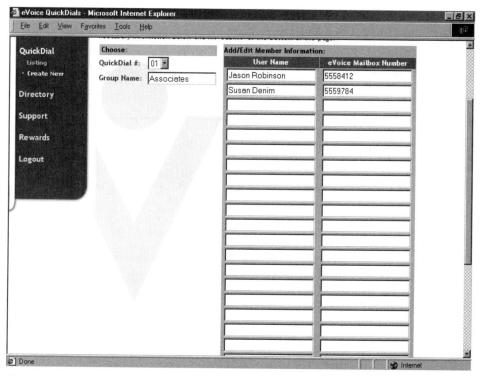

**Figure 2.10**
The QuickDial feature on eVoice is designed to make it easy for you to find others on the service.

your voice mail messages via e-mail notification, in which case you'll retrieve the messages by logging in to the eVoice Web site, or you can have the service send you the actual message as a RealAudio file to your e-mail box.

eVoice will use information you share about your personal interests and demographics with advertisers to target the advertising that you receive. You're first prompted to create your own eVoice mailbox number (at least 7 digits) and a corresponding PIN (4 to 13 digits).

Required information is used for lost PIN retrieval only. Mandatory items include

- phone number
- e-mail address
- birth date
- gender

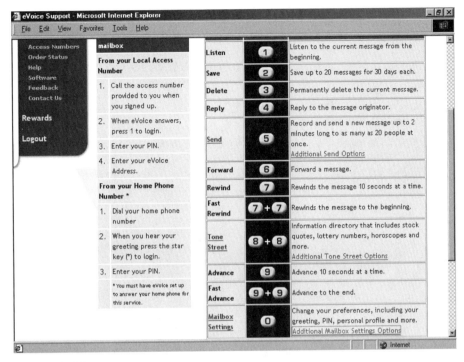

**Figure 2.11**
Step-by-step instructions make it easy to get set up with eVoice's message retrieval.

- zip code
- last four digits of your Social Security number

If you choose to have eVoice answer your phone for you when you can't, you'll be asked to provide the name on the phone bill for this phone and to verify that you are the owner of the phone and allowed to make changes to the service. Once you complete the registration process, it takes eVoice about 3 to 5 business days to connect the eVoice service to your home phone.

There is also a privacy checkbox for indicating that you want your eVoice mailbox number left out of the eVoice directory.

**Big spender:**

No premium services.

URL: http://www.evoice.com/

**Contact:** http://expressresponse.com/evoice/. For comments or questions, write to comments@evoice.com. For subscriber support, write to subscriberservices@ evoice.com.

___X___  SOHO                    _____  Small business

## CallWave's Internet Answering Machine

If you have only one telephone line, the time you spend online may be fraught with worry about missing an important call. Now, with Internet Answering Machine (IAM), you can receive and hear incoming phone messages while you're online. You can even hear your choice of ring tones (see Figure 2.12).

The Windows-based software from CallWave (also the provider of the free FaxWave online fax service) uses the busy call-forwarding feature on your phone line and your PC's audio speaker to answer calls while you're online. IAM displays a small on-screen window whenever you log on. When there are no calls waiting to be processed, the on-screen window displays banner ads.

Anyone who calls you while you're online will be redirected to the Internet Answering Machine message service. After they listen to a brief greeting plugging

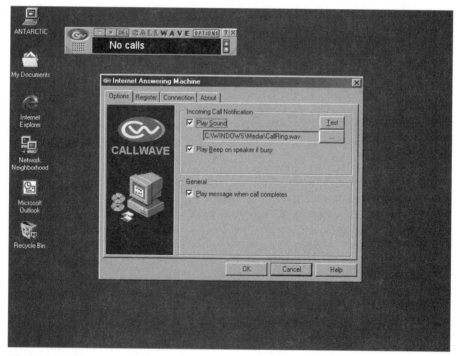

**Figure 2.12**
Setting preferences with CallWave's Internet Answering Machine.

CallWave, callers can leave a message for you. IAM alerts you to an incoming call with a ringing sound—much like an old-fashioned mechanical phone—then plays the message for you over the speakers on your PC. When you hear who has called, you can choose to log off and return the call. There's a lapse of 15 to 30 seconds between the time a message is recorded and when it's played back for you.

You can use the service with any dial-up ISP in the U.S. or Canada, including America Online (with AOL 5.0). Users from other countries are invited to supply their e-mail address so that CallWave can notify them when the service is available to them. IAM works with Windows 95, 98, NT, and 2000; a Macintosh version is in development.

**Getting started:**

If you don't already have call forwarding, CallWave will instruct you on how to set it up when you download the IAM software. If you have call waiting as part of your telephone service, you don't need to have it disconnected. However, when you go online you should deactivate call waiting. Many users do this by preceding the number they dial for their dial-up connection with the access code *70. IAM reactivates call waiting when you go offline.

Required information includes

- full name
- e-mail address
- the phone number that's busy when you're online.

You'll also need to create a numeric password.

**Big spender:**

Using IAM isn't entirely free of charge; you must subscribe to a call-forwarding service through your telephone company.

URL: http://www.callwave.com/
**Contact:**  care@callwave.com

  X  SOHO                       ____ Small business

# FREE FAXING . . . . . . . . . . . . . . . . . . .

Even in this age of e-mail, the lowly, sometimes illegible fax remains a mainstay. It is critical for moving around documents that have strayed far from their original computer file or that contain signatures or other hard-to-reproduce diagrams (as long as they're not in color, of course). If you have access to e-mail and a Web browser, though, you can create a pretty good facsimile of this facsimile machine. Table 2.4 compares the pros and cons of the free fax services discussed below.

## FaxWave

With CallWave's FaxWave, you can have your own free personal fax number that you can print on your business cards or share with your clients and friends, just like any other phone number. You'll receive faxes in your e-mail inbox as attachments that you can view or print in a flash using a Windows-based imaging application.

What's the catch? Each fax you receive will appear with advertising on it. Also, the fax number assigned to you is unlikely to be in your area code, so you'll need to assess if having a local fax number will be necessary for your business. If your FaxWave account is inactive for a 60-day period, CallWave can delete your telephone number and reassign it to another user. On the plus side, with FaxWave you'll be able to receive faxes even when you're traveling. You'll also have the ability to immediately forward faxes to others, via e-mail.

FaxWave lets you receive faxes only, not send them.

**Getting started:**

When you sign up with FaxWave, you can choose from one of several phone numbers that have been generated for you. The service then forwards your faxes to your e-mail with a file attachment. You'll need a program such as Windows Imaging (see Figure 2.13), an application installed on most Windows 95 and Windows 98 machines, to view FaxWave faxes.

**Table 2.4**  Comparison of Free Fax Services

|  | **FaxWave** | **eFax** |
|---|---|---|
| Pros | Provides your own free personal fax number. | Free voice mail services are also provided. |
| Cons | Local numbers are not available in all areas. | Local numbers are not available in all areas. Viewer required. |
| Does advertising display on faxes? | Yes | Yes |
| Send/receive faxes? | Send only | Send only. Receive faxes for a fee. |

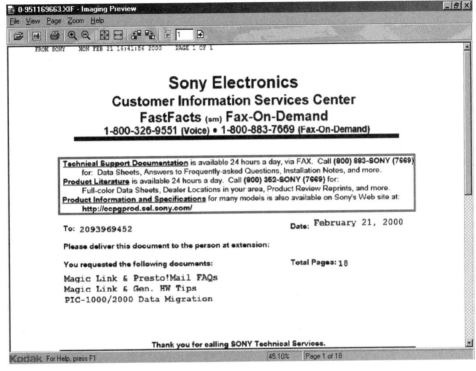

**Figure 2.13**
You'll need an imaging application to view the faxes you receive with
FaxWave.

During the site's registration process, you're asked for personal information—
including your age, occupation category, and annual income—that is used to target
the advertising you'll see. CallWave will also send you several follow-up questionnaires throughout the year and requires you answer at least one a year to maintain
your FaxWave account.

**Big spender:**

No premium services.

URL: http://www.faxwave.com/

**Contact:**   webmaster@callwave.com or info@callwave.com

    X   SOHO                        ___   Small business

## eFax

With eFax.com's free fax service, you can sign up for a fax number that automatically routes inbound faxes right to your e-mail. You'll receive an e-mail message with your digitized fax as an attachment. You'll need to use the service's free Microviewer software to read or print your fax.

When you open a fax attachment, eFax's Microviewer displays the fax along with a small ad window that runs at the top of the window. The company claims its format's compression will produce fax files up to 50 percent smaller than other electronic fax file formats, thus taking up less space in your e-mail inbox and hard disk. The Microviewer is e-mailed to you when you sign up, and you can return to the eFax site to download it at any time.

One nice feature is that if you delete or misplace a fax you've received, you can return to the eFax site within three days and download it again; after that point, it's automatically deleted from eFax's server.

Area codes are assigned randomly from numbers available across the U.S., so some senders will have to fax long distance. Like other free online fax services, you won't have the ability to choose a fax number in your local area code unless you pay for a premium service with a monthly fee.

The Microviewer software is available for both Mac and Windows users. You can use eFax if you have a Unix box or use Linux or WebTV, but the faxes you'll receive are in a TIFF format that doesn't utilize the service's password-protection or compression features.

The free eFax service does not include capabilities for sending faxes. When you sign up you'll be asked if you want to activate eFax's free voice mail services, which include sending, saving, and forwarding electronic copies of your voice mail messages. Voice mails are also played through the Microviewer (see Figure 2.14).

**Getting started:**

When you register, you'll receive a PIN number to view your account information on the eFax.com site. You can use your PIN number to password-protect the faxes you receive and to view an activity log of faxes sent to you over the past three days, which is handy for managing your information and for confirming that faxes were sent.

Required information includes

- full name
- e-mail address
- computer platform
- e-mail software

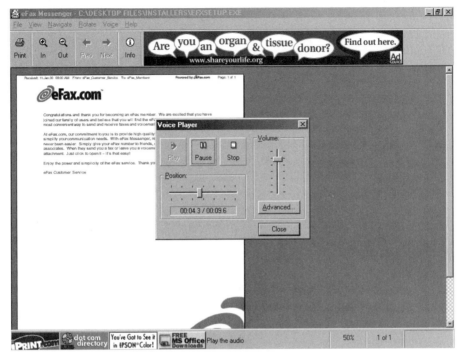

**Figure 2.14**
eFax's voice mail messages are played online via the Microviewer.

- zip code
- country

**Big spender:**

eFax Plus provides toll-free fax numbers, e-mail-based fax sending, fax preview, and online fax storage with access from multiple e-mail accounts or a fax machine for $4.95 a month, plus a 10-cent charge per page and per minute of send time. The site has an easy-to-read chart showing its various services, their features, and pricing.

URL: http://www.efax.com/

**Contact:**   http://www.efax.com/contactus/

 X   SOHO                            ___ Small business

# FREE TRANSLATION · · · · · · · · · · · · · · · · ·

When you're on the Net, you're global, so you must contend with languages you might not ordinarily encounter. Computer-based translation is far from perfect, but it can often give you enough of a gist of what's going on so you have a chance of keeping up.

If you have upgraded to Netscape 6 (see Chapter 1), you may have already seen how you can take advantage of translating Web pages dynamically as you surf. But what if you have additional text—say, an e-mail message or just a phrase—that needs translating? AltaVista's Babelfish is a natural choice.

## Babelfish

If you need something translated fast and no polyglots are nearby, try AltaVista's Babelfish service. AltaVista will translate your text on the fly from English to French, German, Italian, Spanish, or Portuguese—or from any of these languages into English.

The quality of the computer-generated prose won't qualify for a literary award, but it's very serviceable for deciphering foreign correspondence or translating the content on any international sites you may encounter in your Web surfing. You'll also have good results using Babelfish to read international news articles or foreign press releases, or for translating short bits of text, such as welcoming messages, into several languages for your Web site.

There is a 5K size limit on the amount of text you can translate. However, one way you can use Babelfish to translate a long document is to copy and paste sections of your document and just translate each section one at a time.

Babelfish takes its name from a very useful translation device in the Douglas Adams novel *The Hitchhiker's Guide to the Galaxy*. In the book, intergalactic space travelers would insert a little fish (called a babelfish) into their ear in order to understand the languages they heard spoken on distant planets.

The service also provides translation tips, an FAQ, and instructions for placing Add AltaVista Language Translation as a button or bookmark in your Web browser, as long as you have JavaScript enabled (see http://tools.altavista.com/a/s?spage=help/babel_tool.htm).

**Getting started:**

Just type in—or copy and paste—any phrases, whole sentences, or paragraphs into a translator's input box on the Babelfish page (see Figure 2.15). After you select the

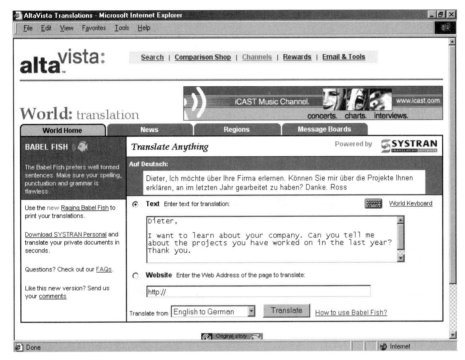

**Figure 2.15**
By copying and pasting text in the AltaVista Translation interactive form, you can translate letters or memos on demand.

language pair you want to use—say, English to French—just click the Translate button.

You can also choose to see an entire international Web site's content translated by entering its URL in the text field window on the Babelfish page, or you can conduct a search for the site from AltaVista's main page (http://www.altavista.com/) and click Translate.

No registration is required.

**Big spender:**

For offline translations, you can order and download Systran Personal translation software (which supports 10 language pairs) directly from a link of the Babelfish service page. You can also order the software on CD-ROM. You can download the program with the ability to translate between two languages for $29.95, or between five pairs of languages for $49.95. A CD-ROM version with the five language pairs is also available for $69.95. The software runs under recent versions of Windows, and needs 20 MB hard disk space per language pair.

URL: http://babelfish.altavista.com/

**Contact:**   http://doc.altavista.com/help/contact/contact_us.shtml

  X   SOHO                X  Small business

# FREE SPAM-FILTERING ................

Spend any amount of time online and you'll find an ever-increasing amount of junk mail—more popularly known as spam—show up in your e-mail box.

If you have a high level of tolerance—and plenty of time on your hands—you may not mind dealing with all the junk mail that floods your inbox. But most spam is commercial advertising—inevitably for dubious multilevel marketing promotions, pyramid or get-rich-quick schemes, or quasi-legal services. For the sender, spam is a very cheap way to put a product or message in front of thousands and thousands of users; most of the costs are paid for by the recipient or the carriers rather than by the sender. For recipients, spam also exacts a cost in the time and effort spent in reading and processing, and obscures the real e-mail in your inbox.

Don't be fooled by junk mail that instructs "To be removed from this mailing list, send a message to somename@somedomain.com." Although you may be removed from a particular mailing list—and there are thousands out there—you'll more often than not be added to another list as someone who at least cared enough about the message to act to get away from it.

## Using Filters Online and in Software

The leading free Web-based e-mail services—including the ones mentioned in this chapter—offer filtering features where you can specify code phrases or domain addresses and automatically forward messages containing those code words to a special folder, like a trash can. The hallmarks of many junk e-mail messages include poorly worded and misspelled copy, fractured grammar, and an abundance of capitalization and exclamation marks—which is helpful in identifying phrases or text for filtering out junk mail.

One of the most popular uses for free e-mail services or e-mail forwarding is to provide users with an e-mail address for use in public forums (like a Usenet newsgroup) that's not their "real" e-mail address. Then when spammers pick up and target these individual e-mail addresses, the free e-mail service can filter out their junk.

Other anti-spam solutions consist of desktop software that's plugged into an e-mail client. You'll then need to identify code phrases or domain addresses found in typical spam messages and write rules for filtering out that junk mail (see Figure 2.16). The following compendium sites for free or shareware software downloads offer a number of desktop-based e-mail filtering programs; conduct a search on "e-mail filtering" or "spam" to see the latest offerings.

Some examples of sites where you can find shareware software include:

- ZDNet (http://www.zdnet.com/downloads/)
- cNet's Download.com (http://www.download.com/). Search for spam or e-mail filter

All the solutions for beating spam thus far, though, place a certain burden on you, as the recipient, to keep spam at bay. See our profile of Brightmail for one site aimed at keeping spam in check at a higher level—namely, when it first hits your ISP's mail servers.

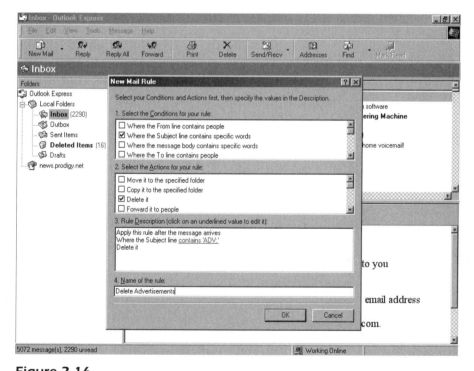

**Figure 2.16**
Your e-mail software may already include options you can take advantage of to filter out junk e-mail.

## Brightmail

Brightmail is a free online service that detects and removes e-mail messages it determines are spam or junk mail from your inbox. These messages won't ever appear in your e-mail inbox, but you can log onto the Brightmail site to check the e-mail that has been caught (see Figure 2.17) and filtered out of your inbox in the last 30 days to confirm that nothing useful has been removed.

It's a real eye-opener to see how much junk mail Brightmail can intercept for you. While Brightmail probably won't catch all the spam that makes its way to your e-mail address, it can catch dozens of messages a week or month for you—which means you'll be saved the trouble of seeing, reading, and deleting that many junk mail messages.

Brightmail offers a small program that makes the appropriate changes to your e-mail configuration, but you can make the change manually from other platforms.

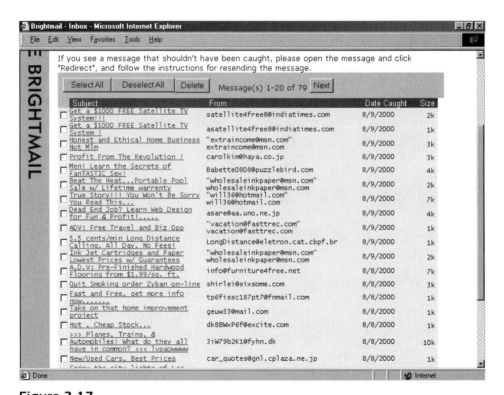

**Figure 2.17**
After you sign up for Brightmail's e-mail filtering service, you can marvel at the volume of e-mail messages it has extracted if you wish.

Brightmail will work with most ISP e-mail accounts and some corporate e-mail accounts. If you're behind a firewall, check with your system administrator. The company has also made its service available to other ISPs, like EarthLink (see Figure 2.18) and AT&T WorldNet, which offer it under their own names and don't require you to make changes to your e-mail settings.

**Getting started:**

You'll need to verify that your e-mail account and software are compatible with Brightmail by entering and submitting your e-mail address; Brightmail checks to see that this is a POP3 account. Next, you register and set up your e-mail software. When you enter your e-mail address, you'll also need to enter your POP username and POP server name. If your e-mail address is jane@yourdomain.com, your POP username is *jane* and in most cases the POP server is *yourdomain.com.* If you are unsure of these settings, you should check the mail server settings for your e-mail program or ask your ISP for this information.

**Figure 2.18**
As an EarthLink customer, you can register to take advantage of its e-mail filtering solution.

Required information includes

- e-mail address
- POP username
- POP server name

**Big spender:**

No premium services.

URL: http://www.brightmail.com/
**Contact:**   http://www.brightmail.com/support/fbm/contact/

   _X_  SOHO                              ____  Small business

## Spamhole

As you've probably started to note, many free Web sites ask for your e-mail address. Once you give it, you open the door to all kinds of contact by the Web site and sometimes its partners, depending on the site's privacy policy. Some Web users try to address the problem by setting up a separate e-mail account for these kinds of registrations, or even a phony one altogether. The sites have countered by sending an authorization code necessary to use the site to an e-mail address to ensure a valid e-mail address. Furthermore, extra accounts designed to attract spam can attract so much that it can be hard to track down messages from the Web site.

Spamhole tries to create an alternative to separate dedicated e-mail addresses. This simple Web site allows you to create a temporary e-mail address that forwards important information like activation codes to your regular e-mail address (see Figure 2.19). After an amount of time that you can set (the default is two hours), the link is broken and the e-mail address disappears. One problem with Spamhole is that many sites will e-mail users a forgotten password, so the temporary e-mail address you have provided them will have expired if you ever need to have such information sent to you again. To get around this, you can always create a new Spamhole address to reestablish the connection.

**Getting started:**

After clicking Create a Spamhole on the home page, enter a name for your temporary Spamhole address. Then enter your real e-mail address and how long you'd like the link to be active. The temporary address will then forward any mail to your real e-mail address.

No registration is required.

**Big spender:**

No premium services.

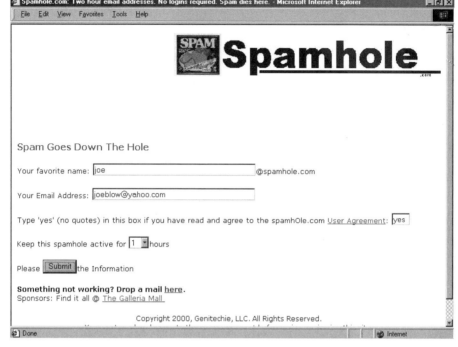

**Figure 2.19**
With Spamhole, you create a temporary e-mail address that remains active
for only a couple of hours.

URL: http://www.spamhole.com/

**Contact:**    http://www.spamhole.com/comments.html

  _X_  SOHO                          ____  Small business

# FREE E-CARDS . . . . . . . . . . . . . . . . . . . . . .

Whether you're sending a quick thank-you note, an invitation, or a holiday newsletter, electronic greetings can help you express yourself to your clients and customers. Like paper greeting cards, these sites offer e-cards for all occasions—but unlike paper ones, these are offered for free.

For small businesses, e-cards can be an inexpensive and effective marketing tool. You can use cards to generate traffic and attract new customers to your site, where you could then try to pique their interest in other products.

## Egreetings

At Egreetings.com, you can pick from thousands of digital greeting cards embellished with graphics, animation, and music that you can personalize and send for free. You can search by occasion (birthday, anniversary, thank you, and so on), category (kids, gay and lesbian, business-oriented, etc.). There are animated cards, Spanish cards, and a number that feature TV show themes, popular actors, or performers.

One noteworthy feature is that you can pick a future date and time to send out your cards—so, for example, you can plan your Christmas cards ahead of time but not actually send them until a day you designate in December. An address book feature lets you store the e-mail addresses of people you send digital greetings to frequently, and a reminder service sends you e-mail to ensure you don't forget special occasions. Your outbox keeps track of when your recipients open the cards you've sent, so you'll know when your messages are received. A "My Egreetings" page tracks your favorites and your outbox, and provides reminders (see Figure 2.20).

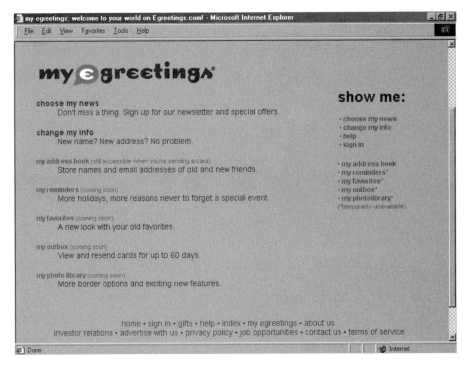

**Figure 2.20**
A central account page helps organize your Egreetings correspondence automatically for you.

You can also send electronic greetings that use what Egreetings.com calls Living Letterhead. These designs feature animated borders, and the Web page expands to include however much text you enter. The design avoids the text limitations of most electronic greetings cards that allow just a few sentences—so it's a good choice for sending out an electronic family or business newsletter.

Finally, you can add one of your own digital photos to add even more of a personal touch to cards you create. Samples and a help file are available on the site to walk you through the uploading and design process.

**Getting started:**

After you select a card and type a message, Egreetings.com will notify the card's recipient via e-mail to fetch the card at a unique Web address.

If you want to embed a personal photo in your e-greetings, you'll need more preparation. You can use any digital photo—it can be one that you've scanned, downloaded from a digital camera, or retrieved from a photo CD. For optimal display, it should be saved as a small JPEG or GIF file. The Egreetings form will prompt you to click a Browse button to search your computer for the file to upload. You can even choose to add a border to your photo. Add a message as you would to any electronic card, indicate when it should be sent, and submit your information.

Required information includes

- full name
- e-mail address
- zip code
- year of birth

You'll also be prompted to choose a password for logging onto the site. If you choose to, you can set up a cookie so that the site will recognize you so you won't need to enter your password on return visits. On the registration page, you can also sign up for an e-mail newsletter on Egreetings products and services, or opt in for notification about promotions and offers from Egreetings and its sponsors.

**Big spender:**

You can order gifts for all occasions through the site's shopping services.

URL: http://www.egreetings.com/

**Contact:**   http://www.egreetings.com/e-products/m_main/cgi/forms?form=cs

  _X_ SOHO                              ____ Small business

## Blue Mountain Arts

Now a part of Excite@Home, leading greeting card site Blue Mountain Arts is the best known, with over 2,000 free e-cards available and 11 million monthly visitors to its site. It specializes in serving up a wide variety of greetings for every kind of occasion, religion, and culture. In addition, you can browse and send cards in Chinese, Japanese, French, Spanish, Italian, Dutch, Portuguese, and Korean.

Each card's designer is prominently identified with each greeting; most have music and animated effects included. Bluemountain.com has recently debuted a voice attachment option for several cards that adds senders' voices to e-greetings. You can even send an associate a screen saver.

You're prompted to preview your card before you send it so you can see the full effect, including any animation or music included with the card. When you send a card, you can take advantage of a return receipt feature, so you'll know when your recipient has viewed the card you've sent. Bluemountain.com will also provide you the URL for the card you've sent so you can return to view it yourself.

**Getting started:**

Filling out and sending an e-greeting on Blue Mountain Arts is most straightforward—unlike many free online services, there's no need to register at this site. The interactive form will ask for the recipient's name and e-mail address, the sender's name and e-mail address, any additional personal message you'd like to add, and whether you'd like to be notified when your recipient views the card.

No registration is required.

**Big spender:**

Related shopping and e-commerce offerings, such as cross-marketing promotions with Proflowers.com, are available through the site.

URL: http://www.bluemountain.com/

**Contact:**   postoffice@bluemountain.com

   _X_  SOHO                    ____  Small business


# FREE UNIFIED MESSAGING . . . . . . . . . . . . . . .

Are you juggling multiple telephone numbers, mobile phones, or e-mail accounts? If you're tired of having to check different places for important messages, read on to find out about unified message services. These all-in-one services aim to bring together fax, e-mail, voice mail, and messages sent to a pager into a single Web mailbox that can be accessed by phone or PC.

If you're on the road frequently for your job, for example, you may have experienced missed faxes or voice mail messages that arrived too early or late at your hotel. These online messaging services offer a solution in aggregating your faxes and voice mail messages to a central location that can be checked by e-mail, Web browser, or phone.

Typically, the companies running such services buy huge blocks of telephone numbers in cities around the world, and assign each subscriber a private number or extension and an e-mail box. If you ever find yourself without a ready way you can be reached, consider using one of these numbers as a secondary phone number or as a central messaging center for your business.

Most of these start-ups offer a free service, allowing customers to receive faxes and a limited number of voice mails. Advanced services, such as added messaging storage space, are then available for a fee.

## Onebox.com

Onebox, a service of Phone.com, lets you listen to voice messages, read e-mails and receive faxes through the Web for free.

When you sign up, you'll receive a telephone number (with extension) and e-mail address. Distribute the telephone number to your clients, friends, and colleagues to leave you voice mail messages and send you faxes. You can then check your messages over the Web, over the phone, and/or automatically receive voice mails and faxes through any e-mail account. Onebox offers several options for viewing faxes (see Figure 2.21).

Onebox offers unlimited messaging, but there's no toll-free service available. The phone number assigned to you by Onebox is the same one you'll dial to check your messages. Local calls are free; normal charges apply to long-distance calls. If you're unable to snag a local Onebox number, you'll probably want to check your voice mail over the Internet rather than pay long-distance charges to check your messages on a regular basis with Onebox. Callers outside your area code will pay long-distance charges to send you a voice mail or fax.

The voice mail messages you receive in e-mail are stored as WAV file attachments that show the phone number of the originating call. You can view your fax attachments online, save the files, and/or print them out. If you really want to crank up the gee-whiz factor, you can even record your own voice mails, using a sound-enabled PC equipped with a microphone, and send them online.

Onebox doesn't yet offer integrating paging service, but bills it as a "coming soon" offering. If you use ICQ instant messaging—an easy-to-use instant messaging

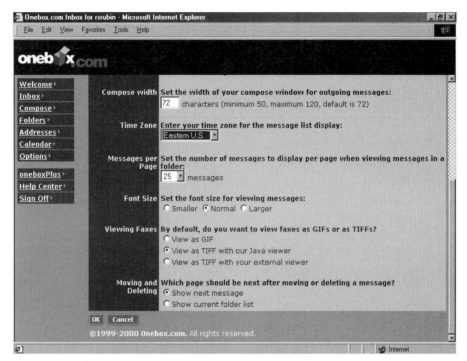

**Figure 2.21**
Onebox gives you several options for viewing and saving faxes sent to your
e-mail account.

program similar to America Online's Buddy List and Instant Messenger programs—
you can have the service instantly notify you when you have messages. Onebox will
automatically build an address book for you, based on the messages you receive.

The company generates revenue through advertising—so that in the future
you'll hear ads when you call your Onebox number to retrieve messages—and
through revenue-sharing deals with other sites. Onebox also controls costs by routing
its calls through the Internet instead of through traditional long distance networks.

**Getting started:**

Fill out the online interactive form to sign up to receive your Onebox telephone number and e-mail address. When you sign up, you can choose to supply a list of e-mail
addresses of people you want to inform about your new contact info; Onebox will
then send them all a notification e-mail with your info.

You'll need to have at least version 4.0 or higher of either Internet Explorer or
Netscape to use Onebox's features. If you want to listen to your voice mail using your

computer, you'll need computer speakers. If you'd like to dictate e-mails through your computer, you'll need a microphone as well.

Required information includes

- PIN for picking up your voice mail messages over the phone
- birth date
- zip code
- full name (displayed in outgoing e-mail messages)
- e-mail address
- gender
- home area code
- occupation
- how you were referred to the site

**Big spender:**

The company says that fee-based premium services are on the way.

URL: http://www.onebox.com

**Contact:**   http://www.onebox.com/company/contact.html

  X  SOHO                      ____  Small business

## uReach.com

uReach.com will give you your own toll-free number you can use to receive voice mail, faxes, pages, and ICQ messages. You'll also get an e-mail address with text-to-speech capability so you can check your e-mail by phone. From the Web, you can read your faxes, hear your voice mail (saved as QuickTime files), or check your e-mail. Also included is a free calendar with text-to-speech reminders you receive by phone or e-mail, or both, or by pager, a public Web page that your correspondents can access, and an address book you can update by phone or the Web. Like some collaboration sites discussed in the next chapter, uReach provides for shared rooms in which you can have private discussions (see Figure 2.22).

Call your uNumber to check voice mail messages, have e-mail read to you over the phone, manage incoming faxes, and access your calendar and address book. You can even automatically transfer incoming calls from your uNumber to any phone and turn your home phone, cell phone, or pager into an instant hotline, or you can have messages sent straight to voice mail. One of the most exciting parts of the service is

**Figure 2.22**
*uReach.com offers a shared chat room feature.*

uReachMe, which tries several sequential phone numbers to track you down (see Figure 2.23).

Since this is a toll-free service, its basic use is limited and funded by advertising. Currently, you receive 60 free minutes when you sign up and then receive 30 free minutes each month on the anniversary date of your registration; you'll have unlimited free Web access.

**Getting started:**

When you first log in to uReach.com, you'll see three messages in your Message Center Inbox: a text message, fax message, and voice message. You can click on each of these messages to see what accessing each of these kinds of messages online is like. Dial the toll-free number assigned to you or log on to uReach.com to send, receive, and manage your voice mail, e-mail, and faxes.

You're prompted to create your own uReach.com ID—you'll use it to sign on, and it doubles as your e-mail address—along with a password and PIN. You'll need the

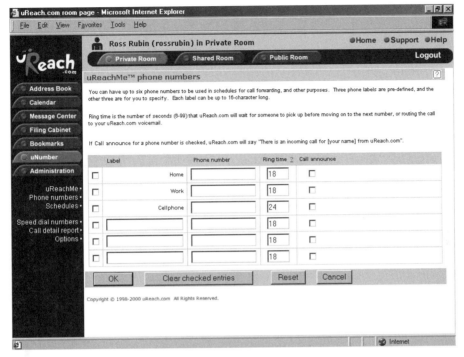

**Figure 2.23**
If at first it doesn't succeed, uReachMe tries and tries again to contact you.

password to log on to the uReach site, and the PIN for accessing your account by phone.

Required information includes

- alternate e-mail address
- first and last names
- birthday
- gender
- zip or postal code
- country
- time zone

**Big spender:**

No premium services are currently offered.

URL: http://www.ureach.com/

**Contact:**   http://www.ureach.com/home/about_contact.htm

  _X_  SOHO                                    ____  Small business

# SUMMARY . . . . . . . . . . . . . . . . . . . . . . . .

In this chapter, you discovered a number of sites that can actually make it easier and
more efficient for you to stay in touch with your colleagues, friends, and family—and
can save you money while doing it. Next up, you'll learn about making the most of
the quality time you spend interacting with others on your task-oriented projects,
from free mechanisms for distributing shared documents to scheduling meetings for
an entire team.

# 3
# Managing Projects

..........................

There are three components to getting your business online—automating your internal business processes, communicating with your suppliers, and dealing directly with your clients and customers. This chapter deals with the first. Whether you are a sole entrepreneur or a small group taking on the world, you have to stay on top of your business to stay in business. These sites can help you manage your time and information, and even schedule meetings. Finally, we go beyond the desktop, and even the Internet, to talk about free services that can keep you in the know when you're on the go.

## FREE SCHEDULING . . . . . . . . . . . . . . . . . . . . .

The following free Web-based schedulers give individuals and groups a variety of services including address books, e-mail reminders, event tracking, appointment scheduling, to-do list management, profiling, and messaging features. Table 3.1 compares these services' features at a glance. While almost anyone could benefit from the centralized coordination of a broad range of daily activities, you should note the importance of choosing your service carefully. Once you commit a substantial amount of personal data to a specific online scheduler, switching to another provider can be tiresome at best.

### Excite Planner

Excite Planner tracks your schedule, contacts, to-do items, and notes online. It can synchronize your calendar and address book with Microsoft Outlook and a number of personal information managers, including palm devices. Indeed, like Outlook, it has a summary screen so you can summarize with different modules (see Figure 3.1).

**Table 3.1** Comparison of Online Scheduling Services

| | **Excite Planner** | **MyPalm** | **Interplanner** | **ScheduleOnline** |
|---|---|---|---|---|
| Distinguishing features | The personal notepad lets you store notes that you can exchange with other users on the Excite Message Board. | You can publish your calendar online so nonmembers can see it. The event directory will let you drop the schedule of your favorite teams or TV shows into your calendar. | Includes news and weather information, e-mail capabilities, real-time stock quotes, portfolio tracking, and cultural event and trade show listings. | Powerful and flexible group scheduling capabilities. |
| Group calendaring | No | Yes. You may create both private and group calendars, publish calendars, or just individual meetings to other users, and select from several formats to print your calendar. | Yes. You can create separate calendars for multiple groups in one of four categories (Office, Home Office, Personal, or School). | Yes. You can add participants to your meeting, check for conflicts, and send e-mail invitations, with a carbon-copy option, to everyone on your group list. |
| Address book/ contact lists | Yes | Yes | Yes | Yes, but address book is not group-enabled. |
| To-do list | Yes. You can set priority levels when creating to-do lists, although items can't appear on your calendar. | Yes | Yes | No |
| E-mail reminders | Yes | Yes | Yes | No |
| Can synchronize with handheld organizers? | Yes | Yes. Supports WAP (Wireless Application Protocol). | No | With Palm devices only. |
| Filter tools | Yes | Yes | No | No |
| Field mapping | Yes | Yes | No | No |

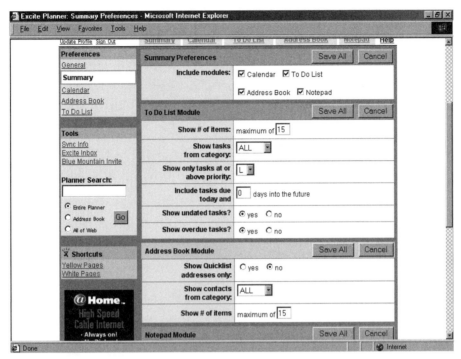

**Figure 3.1**
Set your Excite Planner preferences on a single screen.

With Excite Planner, you can store your appointments and recurring events on-line and have e-mail and pager reminders of them sent to you. If you remember to synchronize regularly, it can serve as a useful backup if you ever forget or lose all your data in your handheld organizer.

When you sign up with Excite, you can also use Excite's home page as a portal to see stock quotes, weather reports, horoscopes, TV listings, or other customized features. Excite also has its own message boards, chat rooms, and Excite Clubs. It also gives you a free Web page for designing and building your own Web-based community.

**Getting started:**

After you register, your Excite Planner page defaults to a day-at-a-time calendar view; you can also view your appointments by week (see Figure 3.2) or month. By clicking other tabs in the local navigation, you can see views for your to-do list, address book, notepad, and a summary page.

You'll find Excite Planner more useful if you take the time to customize it. Click the link Update Profile on any of the standard views, then Personalization

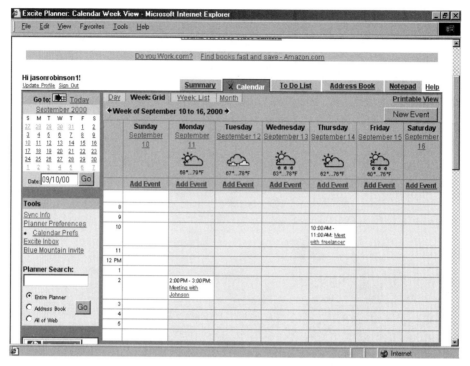

**Figure 3.2**
You have several views in Excite Planner for browsing your calendar.

Manager to get to a page where you can choose the features you want to see displayed. You'll also see a link for Planner Preferences that takes you to a main page for updating content or the display for your calendar, to-do list, address book, notepad, and summary page.

When you sign up, you're asked to provide the following information:

- full name
- street address
- e-mail address
- birth date
- gender

You can opt in (or out) when it comes to sharing your contact information with Excite or its partners for promotional offers. If you choose to, you can receive periodic solicitations from Excite advertisers or Harris Poll Online.

**Big spender:**

No premium services.

URL: http://planner.excite.com/

**Contact:**   http://www.excite.com/feedback/FYI/

   X  SOHO                       \_\_\_\_  Small business

## MyPalm

Like other free online calendars, MyPalm, owned by Palm Computing of pocket organizer fame, solicits information about your daily schedule and personal preferences
and presents it in a personalized calendar accessible from anywhere you can connect
to the Web. Formerly known as Anyday.com, the service is advertising-driven; you
can also choose to receive information on advertisers' promotions directly.

The service includes a full-featured calendar with several views, and a contacts
section for scheduling appointments and automatically sending out e-mail confirma-
tions or reminders to others attending your meetings. An event directory lets you plug
the schedule of your favorite sports teams or TV shows into your calendar. You can
also create your own personal reminders and to-do lists (see Figure 3.3). Besides

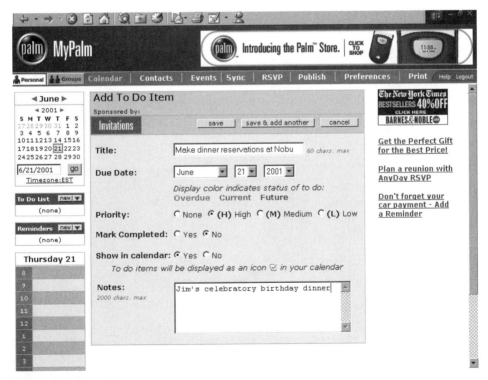

**Figure 3.3**
With MyPalm, you can assign a priority and display preference to your to-do
items.

using the Web, you can also retrieve information wirelessly through the MyPalm downloadable Web clipping application. With this application, your data is formatted specifically for handheld screens, so you can wirelessly update a Palm VII.

Another great feature of the service is its group functionality for scheduling office or community events. For example, you can set up private calendars on MyPalm for affinity groups like clubs, a special project at work, or a sports league. Once you set up a new group, you can invite your group members automatically. Unlike other services, though, MyPalm can publish your calendar online so nonmembers can see it (see Figure 3.4) or it can prepare a print version.

**Getting started:**

When you create a new account, you'll be asked to choose an account name and a 4- to 12-character password. You can have birthdays, anniversaries, legal and other holidays, and local sports team schedules appear on your calendar.

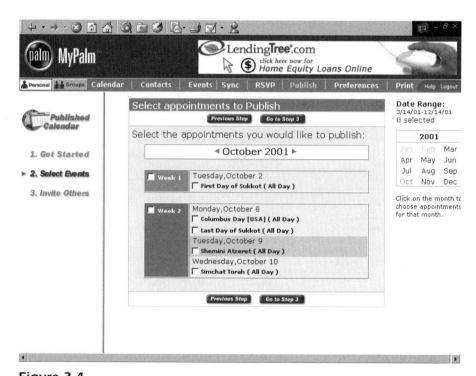

**Figure 3.4**
You can pick and choose which holidays, events, and to-do items are published on your online calendar.

Required information includes

- full name
- gender
- e-mail address
- birth date
- zip code
- local time zone

**Big spender:**

No additional services.

URL: http://www.my.palm.net/

**Contact:**   http://www.my.palm.com/about/contacts.html

  _X_  SOHO                    ____  Small business

# Interplanner

Interplanner is a Web-based personal information management service that includes calendaring services, contact lists, appointment entry and tracking, notes, and to-do lists.

If you frequently need to swap files back and forth with one or more colleagues or friends, Interplanner can be a helpful service. You can send calendar reminders for appointments or tasks on an individual or group basis via e-mail and directly to e-mail enabled pagers and cellular telephones. Interplanner also lets you schedule on-line meetings (see Figure 3.5), but its chat feature is still not operational.

**Getting started:**

After you log in, click the Customize button in the left-hand navigation to refine the display of your calendar and content information.

After choosing a member name and password, you're required to enter the following information:

- full name
- time zone
- current e-mail address
- city, state, and zip code
- marital status

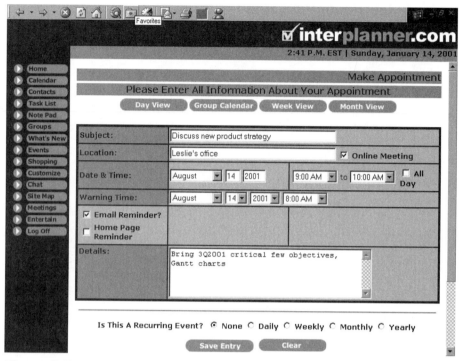

**Figure 3.5**
You can set up e-mail reminders of upcoming meetings using Interplanner's free service.

- occupation
- income level
- education
- birthday (not including year)

You can also choose whether or not you'd like an Interplanner e-mail account.

**Big spender:**

No premium services. The site has a gateway to its own advertising-laden online shopping mall.

URL: http://www.interplanner.com/

**Contact:**   http://www.interplanner.com/contactus.shtml

   X   SOHO                                     ____ Small business

## ScheduleOnline

If you need help scheduling group events or managing shared resources, try ScheduleOnline for checking members' calendars to find available time slots or to track who's using what group equipment.

When you sign up with ScheduleOnline, you become the administrator for your organization's online calendar. You can add new members and the departments they belong to, and identify group resources like meeting rooms and shared company cars.

Group members can create three kinds of events: meetings, tasks (which are time-based and may involve resources), and to-do items. Relevant items appear on each member's calendar, which displays in either a daily, weekly, or monthly view.

When you schedule a meeting, the service automatically checks all invitees' schedules and determines whether requested resources (say, a particular conference room) are available (see Figure 3.6). If there is a conflict with a time you chose, the

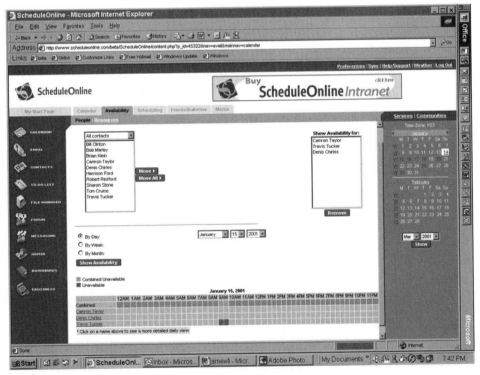

**Figure 3.6**
When you schedule a meeting with ScheduleOnline, the availability of all invited parties is automatically checked.

program lets you view the problematic schedules to find a better time slot. You can also choose to send reminders of upcoming meetings to members via e-mail. Invitees, in turn, can choose to accept or reject the meeting invitation; ScheduleOnline lets you see the status of who has accepted or declined the meeting. Another nice feature is that any member can also invite nonmember guests.

The advertising-supported site has a largely text-based interface. Although it lacks the personalized content of services like Excite (e.g., horoscopes or weather reports), the no-frills look enables the service's pages to load very quickly. Still, ScheduleOnline is branching out, and features the ability to designate documents for approval by other group members.

While you can save new members' phone numbers and e-mail addresses, there are no fields for alternative telephone numbers, such as fax numbers or pagers, which limits the service's functionality for managing contacts. ScheduleOnline Sync has been tested on Palm Pilot III and V devices.

**Getting started:**

Since ScheduleOnline is really a group management tool, it's important to set up online representations of the departments and their members. Click the Administer Departments tab in the local navigation's masthead to create a new department. Similarly, click the Administer People tab to create a new member. When you create new members, you'll need to assign them usernames and passwords. You'll also want to assign people to specific departments as necessary. Oddly, there's no automatic notification sent to your new members about the service you're inviting them to join; you'll need to inform them yourself about your organization's account name on ScheduleOnline and what usernames and passwords they'll need to use.

While most personalized sites prompt you to choose a username and password when you sign up, here you also have to choose an organization name and enter that at log-in. Required information includes

- full name
- e-mail address
- organization name

**Big spender:**

No premium services.

URL: http://www.scheduleonline.com/

**Contact:**   support@scheduleonline.com or feedback@scheduleonline.com

   _X_  SOHO              ____  Small business

# FREE COLLABORATION . . . . . . . . . . . . . . . . .

Web-based collaboration services act as virtual offices that can help streamline interactions between individuals in remote offices, working from home, or on the road. Most services offer document management, group calendars, e-mail, bulletin boards, contact lists, chat rooms, instant messaging, and online conferencing. If this is starting to sound like an intranet to you, you're on the right track—the following Web sites provide a central online hub, much like a full-blown intranet, for managing projects and for helping team members share information and to-do's with one another. Consider one of these services if your small business doesn't have the resources to install large-scale enterprise groupware applications. Table 3.2 summarizes the main features of the services profiled below.

## iTeamwork

iTeamwork is a Web service that gives managers a central place to organize to-do items for projects and teams. By tracking the daily progress of each team member iTeamwork offers a very step-by-step, task-focused approach to project management (see Figure 3.7).

For each project you create, you can manage any number of tasks and assign them to one or more people on the project's team. You can then choose to send e-mail notifications or reminders to each assignee. The service shows you at a glance the ongoing to-do list for each member and the target dates for completion of every task at hand. Each team member, in turn, can use the service to notify the rest of the group about their latest accomplishments and achievements.

One helpful feature is the ability to include multiple companies in a single project, which is most handy for projects involving one or more external vendors. You can also delegate tasks to others. The service, though, lacks a contacts database and appointment scheduling, though, which are necessities for many projects and tasks. As a result, the exclusive focus on tasks and their completion may make it difficult to intuitively use iTeamwork to notify team members about upcoming meetings.

**Getting started:**

Once you've successfully registered and logged on to the site, your main view displays all projects you're involved with by name. You'll see the number of total and open tasks for each project, as well as the name of the team member who created the project.

Refer to the left-hand navigation at all times for the actions you can take and available views within each project. At the top level, you can create a new project or, if you've drilled down to look at a specific project, you can create a new task. The list

**Table 3.2**  Comparison of Collaboration Services

| Feature | iTeamwork | QuickTeam Express | OfficeTool.com |
|---|---|---|---|
| Distinguishing features | When you create a project, tasks are assigned to a team member; e-mail notification reminders can be set up to outline open tasks. | Chat room.<br>Threaded discussions.<br>"Issues" area for raising topics for discussion among the group. | Wireless access to productivity tools, e-mail, and calendars.<br>In/out board tracks status and location of team members.<br>Online file viewers are available for viewing and printing MS Word, Excel, PowerPoint, and Adobe PDF files. |
| Contact manager | None | Not available at press time. | Can synchronize with Outlook. |
| Document storage and version control | None | Document manager provides capabilities for storing documents in folders, adding notes, viewing a document's history. Version control is enforced by checking documents in and out. | You can upload multiple documents to the company using folders or subfolders, or place in a personal briefcase. You can upload new versions of documents with version-tracking dates. |
| E-mail capabilities | No e-mail accounts are included. Users can be notified by e-mail when tasks are completed. | No e-mail accounts are included. You provide users' e-mail addresses when you invite them to join your QuickTeam site. Users can be notified by e-mail if they forget their passwords. | Free e-mail account for each user. |

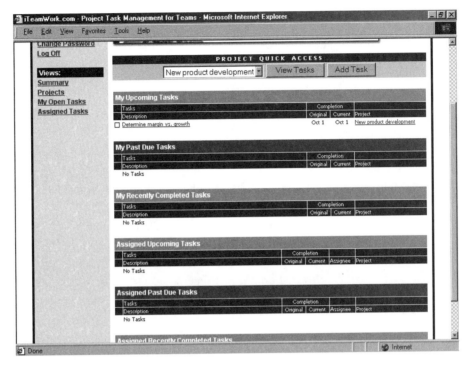

**Figure 3.7**
Your task list on iTeamwork shows both what's coming up and what's past due.

of views in the left-hand navigation shows which of your tasks are still open, your overall assignment list; you can also choose to see all users who have had tasks delegated to them and an overall task list.

In addition to creating a username and password, required information includes

- full name
- e-mail address
- nickname

When you register, you're also prompted to indicate which days you'd like to receive your e-mail of current open tasks—so you can take weekends off or, if you're a workaholic, you can continue as usual!

**Big spender:**

No premium services.

URL: http://www.iteamwork.com/

**Contact:**   http://www.iteamwork.com/feedback.html
    X  SOHO            ____  Small business

## QuickTeam

Now owned by iManage, QuickTeam provides work teams with communication and collaboration tools that can be accessed using a Java-capable Web browser. The service features a collection of tools to facilitate project management, including document sharing, team calendaring, and task management.

The service's most impressive features include multiroom chat capabilities (see Figure 3.8), online polling, threaded discussions, an interactive whiteboard, Gantt chart capabilities, and a contact organizer.

QuickTeam's crowded online interface could use some streamlining to enable users to get to their documents faster. In our experience, the Java-based tools that

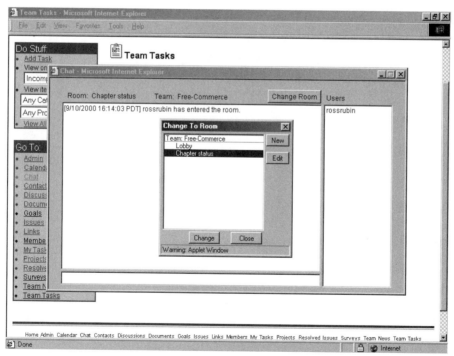

**Figure 3.8**
Chat rooms display in pop-up windows for QuickTeam users.

power some of the site's features perform unreliably for Macintosh users. The site is also riddled with dead links to many of the online help files and documents.

**Getting started:**

After you submit your QuickTeam registration, a new team site is created for you. You can then invite others to join your team room by going to the Admin My Team Rooms link.

You'll need to create a login name and password to use QuickTeam. Other required information includes

- full name
- e-mail address
- occupation
- local time zone
- number of employees at your company
- location (U.S. or non-U.S.)
- year of birth
- gender
- a name and description for your team site (if you're the administrator)

You're also asked to choose if you want to receive the QuickTeam e-mail newsletter and if you'd like to opt in or out of sharing information with third-party vendors.

**Big spender:**

The free online version of QuickTeam is a scaled-down evaluation version of Quick-Team Professional, a commercial product. Among other features, QuickTeam Professional includes Palm VII integration and 128-bit SSL security. The full-featured QuickTeam Professional version can be leased (or vendor hosted) for $12.95 per user per month; the one-time purchase price for on-site use is $899.

URL: http://www.quickteam.com/

**Contact:**   http://www.quickteam.com/feedback.html

  _X_  SOHO                 ____  Small business

# OfficeTool.com

OfficeTool.com provides a range of free productivity tools, such as project management and file sharing applications, e-mail, and calendars, that would enhance any corporate intranet.

OfficeTool's wireless capabilities distinguish it from other Web-based collaboration services. Using a Web-enabled phone, OfficeTool.com users can access their company's OfficeTool intranet at any time or from any location using the service's Wireless OfficeTool. Users can find other employees or indicate their own location using an in/out board (see Figure 3.9), check messages, and access an address book and calendar.

When competitor RedGorilla closed its doors in October 2000, OfficeTool.com licensed RedGorilla's Web-based and wireless applications such as its time tracking and expense application, Gorilla Time, and resumed that site's operations.

**Getting started:**

When you first register, you're prompted to create a unique company code for your company, and a username and password for yourself. A series of screens with sample data are provided to guide you in setting up your office's online settings.

Required information includes

- full name
- company size

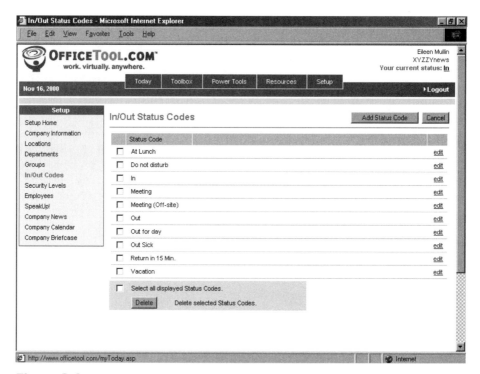

**Figure 3.9**
The online in/out board at OfficeTool.com could be used to track colleagues' whereabouts.

- industry
- age (choose a range)
- gender
- position within company
- e-mail address

**Big spender:**

A private label version of the productivity applications can be licensed at a premium.

URL: http://www.officetool.com/

**Contact:**   support@officetool.com

  <u>X</u>  SOHO               <u>   </u>  Small business

# FREE WEBTOPS . . . . . . . . . . . . . . . . . . . . . . .

Have you ever forgotten an important e-mail or electronic file on your home computer when you needed it at work, or vice versa? When you back up your files on a virtual desktop—or Webtop, as it's sometimes called—this doesn't have to happen anymore. These sites provide Web-based, server-stored versions of the files and applications that run your life, from your e-mail to memos in progress, so that you can access your information anywhere, anytime. Unlike collaboration tools for sharing files, Webtops simply aim to make your personal files accessible to you no matter where you are, if you're just as likely to work from home as at the office or from a cybercafe while traveling. Most of the services also offer the kind of integration that you would expect from a company network: You can share your appointment calendar, book meetings and invite others to them, and create discussion groups. Table 3.3 compares the services described below across a range of popular features.

## MagicalDesk

MagicalDesk is a free calendar and document management service that lets you store and synchronize your documents online. In addition to 30 MB of free file storage, you get an online calendar, address book, e-mail (with 30 MB more disk space), to-do list, and Internet bookmarks.

     You link to many of the built-in applications—called MagicalDesk Objects— from the start page, which is called Desktop. An Edit Desktop (see Figure 3.10) menu lets you customize your virtual desktop completely, down to its background; it includes drop-down lists with the most common search engines and other popular sites.

**Table 3.3**  Comparison of Webtops

| Feature | MagicalDesk | Visto | Zkey |
|---|---|---|---|
| Wireless access | Yes | Wireless access to e-mail, address book, calendar, and tasks. | Wireless access to address book, calendar, and to-do list. |
| File storage | 5 MB | 15 MB for personal files; 25 MB for each group you create. | 30 MB |
| Address book? | Yes | Yes. Synchronizes with PIM/PDAs. | Yes |
| Bookmark storage? | Yes | Yes | No |
| Calendar? | Yes | Synchronizes with PIMs. Personal and group calendaring. E-mail reminders. | Yes, private, shared, and group. |
| E-mail? | Yes | Yes. Includes attachments, filtering. | Web-based e-mail account. |
| To-do list | Yes | Yes | Yes |

The applications—known as MagicalDesk Objects—are well-integrated, but their features are not as rich as those on Visto and Zkey.com. While you can share the calendar, your time is shown as busy or free but doesn't display to others the details of your appointments. While this might suffice for users who want to ensure privacy, it won't help if you want to let your colleagues or an assistant know where to reach you at any given time.

You can send reminders to yourself or others using both the calendar and to-do list. When you create a calendar entry, for example, you can specify who needs to be reminded and when.

The latest version of the desktop provides support for Palm VII users, as well as a light version called q.MagicalDesk, intended to be open even as you visit other Web sites. There's also a Mac-only version of the service available, called iMagicalDesk. This version lets you search your e-mail for key words and phrases. Information from

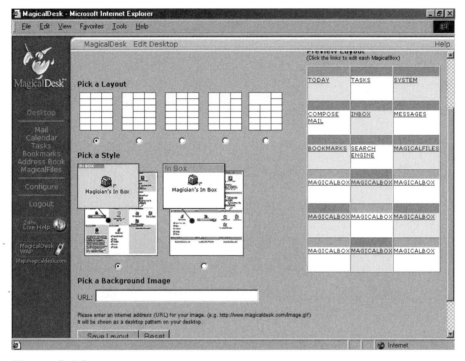

**Figure 3.10**
You can customize the display of your virtual desktop on MagicalDesk.

several online Mac sources, such as Macworld.com and MacWEEK.com, is also pushed to your virtual desktop.

**Getting started:**

You can rely on the service's online tutorial to learn how to use the applications and see how they work together.

Required information includes

- full name
- username and password

**Big spender:**

For $5 a month, the MagicalViewer file viewer lets users view a document in any of 250 different file formats, such as Excel and WordPerfect—regardless of whether you have a copy of the program that created the file. You can also sign up for three additional external POP accounts ($2.50 per month) or choose extra storage space ($10 per month for 50 MB).

URL: http://www.magicaldesk.com/

**Contact:**   help@magicaldesk.com

   X  SOHO                              ____  Small business

## Visto

Visto provides a clean, easy-to-understand interface, bringing together standard desk-top functions on the Web. It can synchronize and import your calendar and address lists from Microsoft Outlook or the Palm desktop. Best of all, you can share files or open your calendar to others who are not Visto members.

Your start page, called MyVisto.com, presents you with your inbox, news head-lines culled from iSyndicate, and the number of appointments, messages, and overdue tasks you have, as well as a list of your active groups, for which preferences can be set. You'll receive 15 MB of free file storage and free e-mail forwarding to your Visto.com account.

Like many Web sites, Visto is making its services available on smart cell phones through the Wireless Application Protocol (WAP) (see Figure 3.11).

**Figure 3.11**
Visto's services are available over the Web or through wireless access.

**Getting started:**

When you register, you're asked to choose a member name, which will double as part of your e-mail address (using the convention yourname@visto.com).

Use the left-hand navigation to move among your applications: e-mail, calendar, tasks, address book, and other modules. The tabs along the top of this page—Overview, My Start Page, Import/Sync, Phone/PDA, and Share—take you to advanced features and to advertising.

Required information includes

- full name
- primary e-mail address
- time zone
- zip or postal code
- daytime phone number
- birth date
- gender

**Big spender:**

An additional 25 MB of storage space costs $25 per year.

URL: http://www.visto.com/

**Contact:**   support@visto.com

   _X_   SOHO                         ____   Small business

# Zkey.com

Zkey's integrated Web suite of desktop applications presents you with a customizable home page where you can search your address book, view a summary of your calendar, get the weather and stock quotes, or search the Web. Zkey can maintain extensive personal information (see Figure 3.12) about your preferences, which may be a factor for those concerned about their privacy.

Zkey's calendar displays a daily, weekly, and monthly glance at upcoming items. You can categorize an item as a meeting, appointment, conference, or business trip, or as a personal item such as birthday or anniversary. You can give your contacts varying levels of access to your calendar; for example, you may want some users to see all your appointments but let others see only the times you're busy. Unfortunately, there's no way to tag appointments as private. You can give access to users who have not registered with Zkey.

**Figure 3.12**
With Zkey.com, you can customize exactly who among your contacts has access to specific types of information.

The collaboration features let you create groups for specific purposes and assign users to one or more of them. The Zroom feature lets you invite contacts into a private conference area and record a transcript of the conference, and the Zdrive feature allows you to store your files online, and integrates with the program's e-mail feature. You can choose to see dynamically updating headlines from a variety of media sources appear on your home page too.

**Getting started:**

When you sign up, you're first asked to choose a username that will also be the beginning of your Zkey e-mail address. You'll also need to actively agree to the terms of service before you can register.

Required information includes

- full name
- e-mail address
- time zone

**Big spender:**

No premium services.

URL: http://www.zkey.com/

**Contact:**  contact@zkey.com

  X  SOHO                 ____  Small business

# FREE MOBILE SERVICES . . . . . . . . . . . . . . . . .

Free services can take you beyond time management and even beyond the desktop, but they can also take you beyond the computer itself. As business people take advantage of increasingly sophisticated cell phones, pagers, and personal digital assistants (PDAs), they increasingly want to take their content with them.

PDAs are handheld devices that combine computing, telephone and fax services, and networking features. A typical PDA can function as a cellular phone, fax sender, and personal organizer. Many PDAs (like the Palm Pilot series or Handspring Visor) are pen-based, using a stylus for input, while Windows CE devices (such as the HP 320LX, Vadem Clio, or Sharp Mobilon) use a keyboard for input.

Many mainstream Web sites, such as Amazon.com, Ameritrade, and MSN, are reaching out to these devices, but new players are on the scene as well. These services can help deliver the latest stock quotes and financial news on your Blackberry pager, or even allow you to create Web pages on your PDA!

## AvantGo.com

AvantGo has two businesses. One is developing mobile channels for enterprise data, but the one that more people will find useful is a series of channels. The heart of AvantGo's offering is a pint-sized Web browser for Palm and Windows CE handhelds. Downloading the AvantGo browser gives you access to dozens of channels in nine key areas—business, entertainment, news, sports, weather, city and regional, lifestyle, sci-tech, and travel. The business category (see Figure 3.13), for example, has over 120 channels, including those developed by FedEx, *Business Week, Financial Times, Wall Street Journal, The Economist,* and TheStreet.com.

**Getting started:**

Installing AvantGo can be a bit daunting. After registering, you have to install the AvantGo software on your PDA and desktop. AvantGo also includes a program for your PC or Mac called Mobile Link, which is key for transferring data onto your

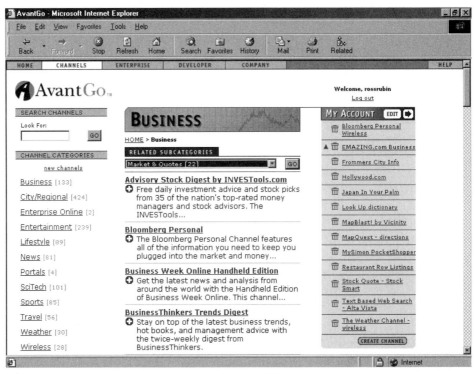

**Figure 3.13**
Choose to view the latest headlines on a variety of subjects when you access
AvantGo's channels.

PDA. After you choose a channel, Mobile Link remembers to update information on
it the next time you synchronize your PDA. Be mindful, though. While AvantGo is
compatible with a wide variety of PDAs, older ones may lack the memory to run
AvantGo, or may only be able to accommodate a small number of channels. AvantGo
even allows you to create your own wireless channels through a wizard interface.

If you have a wireless PDA, like a Palm V with an OmniSky modem, the
AvantGo's wireless channels offer information anywhere you can access your wireless
service. They allow you to get the latest information in real time, without having to sync
to your desktop. AvantGo has almost 30 wireless channels, including services that provide maps by MapBlast!, directions by MapQuest!, white and yellow page lookups by
InfoSpace, and weather by The Weather Channel. And if you're searching for the right
words to describe your excitement, one of the member-contributed wireless channels is
a dictionary that can look up words from a wireless connection to the Net.

You're prompted to create a username and password. Required personal information includes

- full name
- e-mail address

**Big spender:**

No premium services.

URL: http://avantgo.com/channels/

**Contact:**   http://www.avantgo.com/help/contact.html

  _X_  SOHO                                    ____  Small business

## PageInfo

In some ways, PageInfo is a throwback to the days of DOS, where you would type an instruction to the PC and it would spit back the output (see Figure 3.14). The difference is that with PageInfo, the requests travel through wireless networks. Indeed, it's

**Figure 3.14**
PageInfo's commands are explained on the service's Web site.

no coincidence that the home for PageInfo is hz.com. The domain name is short, which makes it easy to type on the generally cramped keyboards and keypads of wireless devices, and it's the abbreviation for Hertz, the unit for measuring wireless spectrum. PageInfo's services range from checking the weather to checking the status of packages.

**Getting started:**

Designed for cellular phones and pagers, PageInfo lets you retrieve quick snippets of data from online services via wireless networking. It usually takes about a minute to receive your information. The e-mail address is always the same to get the data; it's pi@hz.com. Hz.com has partnered with SkyTel, a leading paging provider, and Glenayre, one of the world's largest paging equipment manufacturers. Many paging companies, such as SkyTel, already offer services where they regularly update you on information, but that information is "pushed" to you. Hz.com lets you "pull" information when you need it.

Hz.com has software available for Motorola's PageWriter 2000x and its predecessor, the PageWriter 2000, and it is also working on software for the RIM Inter@ctive Pager. Otherwise, the trick is to remember the right phrases to send to the service in the Subject line of the phrase. If your memory ever fails you, you can send an e-mail to the address with the subject "help" and a whole list of commands will be sent to you.

**Big spender:**

No premium services.

URL: http://www.hz.com/

**Contact:**   http://www.hz.com/feedback.html

   X   SOHO                          _____ Small business

# LifeMinders Mobile

The Wireless Application Protocol promises to transform future generations of cell phones and pagers from just communications to information devices. But is there hope for users of phones that don't have the advanced microbrowsers that WAP requires? LifeMinders Mobile (formerly SmartRay) is a service that can deliver content to just about any device that can receive e-mails. This includes most alphanumeric pagers as well as cell phones that support SMS (Short Messaging Service).

Often, the service providers of these devices offer the ability to have certain kinds of information delivered automatically to them, but there is sometimes a charge associated with it. LifeMinders Mobile may offer greater control over your preferences than does your service provider, as well. However, if you get charged on a per-message or per-character basis for your device, LifeMinders Mobile's messages will count toward that limit.

**Getting started:**

After registering, pick the services that you'd like to automatically receive. In addition to setting up reminders, LifeMinders Mobile offers several different kinds of news, sports scores from professional leagues and college teams, stock quotes, weather, and lotteries. While LifeMinders Mobile is noteworthy for its automatic delivery to less capable devices, you can also "pull" information, as with PageInfo, but with a WAP-compliant phone. First, though, you must go through the tedium of entering "mobile.smartray.com" on your mobile phone's keypad.

When you register, you're required to submit the following personal information:

- full name
- e-mail address
- gender
- birth date
- zip or postal code
- time zone

**Big spender:**

No premium services.

URL: http://www.smartray.com

**Contact:**    customerservice@smartrayinc.com

   X   SOHO                              ____   Small business

# Halibot.com

Halibot is a keyword-based information retrieval agent for wired or wireless e-mail users. Since the service is based on standard e-mail protocols, mobile users can gain instant access to answers and information using any e-mail-capable device without downloading or installing any software.

Halibot has categorized its information in over 80 broad-based topic areas. The service can be accessed by sending e-mail from cell phones, PDAs, and two-way pagers.

**Getting started:**

Pick the desired topic and combine it with @halibot.com to create the address where you are sending your e-mail message. Next, enter the information required by the topic selected to retrieve your answer as the subject of the e-mail. Send the e-mail; Halibot will respond nearly immediately with a detailed description of the requested topic with instructions, examples of use, and sample results.

If you send an e-mail to help@halibot.com without specifying a subject in the message, Halibot will e-mail you a reference guide for all topics.

**Big spender:**

Fee-based premium services include Virtual GPS, scheduled delivery, shortcuts, and query compositing.

URL: http://www.halibot.com/

**Contact:**   info@halibot.com

  X   SOHO                     X   Small business

# BeVocal

1(800) 4BVOCAL (1(800) 428-6225) is a gateway to information such as turn-by-turn driving directions, traffic reports, weather forecasts, business locations, flight information, and stock quotes. You can even locate the address of your nearest FedEx drop-off box with BeVocal's service. The information is then delivered by voice. Users can also visit the company's Web site to personalize the service for their specific needs.

BeVocal is currently available across the U.S. only. Services include Business Finder, which combines the convenience of dialing 411, the *Yellow Pages,* and nationwide driving directions into one easy-to-use service. The Driving Directions service is powered by MapQuest.com. BeVocal can recognize addresses, street names, and landmarks accurately, using voice input. You can also get up-to-the-minute flight information for major U.S. airlines, traffic reports, weather, and stock quotes.

In practice, it's fairly easy to navigate by using your voice; however, BeVocal's automatic detection of your location may be a little off, and the computer's voice for some information is clearly mechanical.

**Getting started:**

To get to a particular service from the main menu, just say the name of the service. "BeVocal home" gets you back to the beginning. To jump from one service to another, say "BeVocal," then the name of the service. For help, say "BeVocal tips" for general information or "What are my choices?" for contextual help.

Registration on the phone or through the Web allows you to customize features when you call, such as favorite stocks (see Figure 3.15). This is especially important because company names can be difficult to decipher for speech recognition.

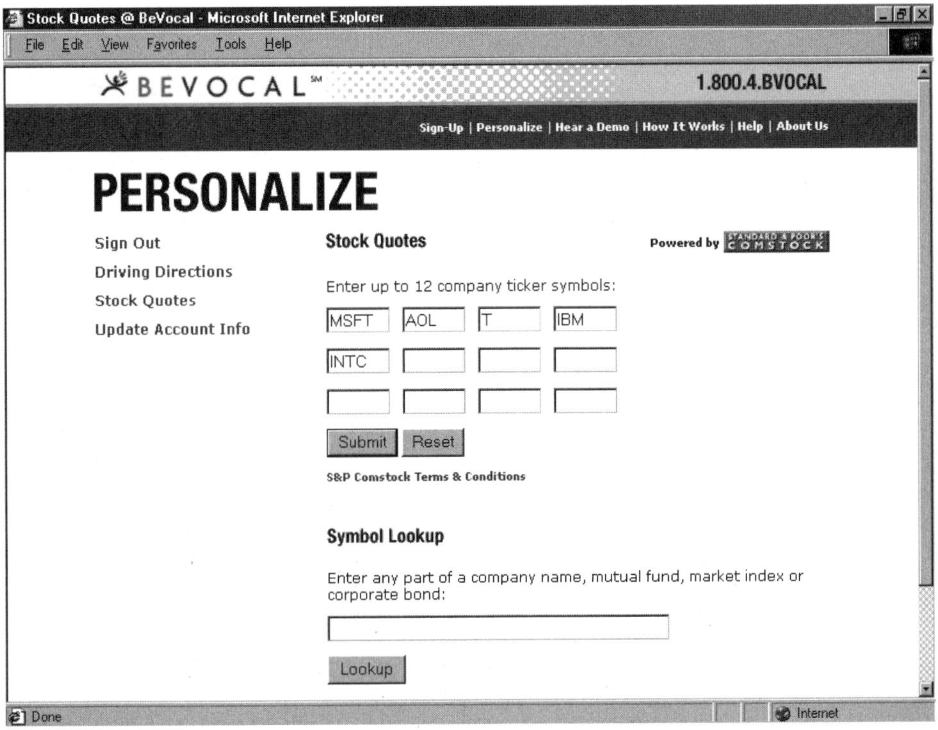

**Figure 3.15**
Sign up over the Web to track your favorite stocks using the BeVocal voice
portal.

Required personal information includes

- telephone number
- e-mail address
- zip code

**Big spender:**

No premium services.

URL: http://www.bevocal.com/

**Contact:**   feedback@bevocal.com

   X   SOHO                  ____   Small business

## TellMe

Calling 1(800) 555-TELL (1(800) 555-8355) leads you to a menu of voice prompts that offer information on restaurants, sports, movies, weather, traffic, and other topics, either for your local area (which TellMe automatically detects, based on the phone you're calling from) or anyplace in the U.S. The voice recognition is good, but gets confused by coughs and other noises. The computer's voice is clear and nonmechanical.

No membership is required to use this service, although members who register through the Web site may customize the information they receive, including favorite items, when they call in (see Figure 3.16).

One of TellMe's best features is a taxi pickup service. Saying "taxi" will refer you to a local car service that can pick you up if you're stranded. This was a lifesaver for us when we were stranded in a strange city.

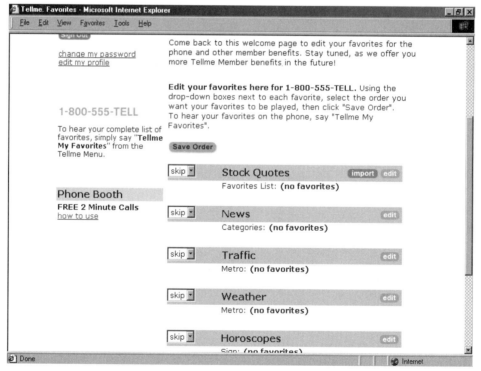

**Figure 3.16**
You can use TellMe's Web site to personalize the information you'd like to receive on its voice-recognition information portal.

**Getting started:**

"TellMe menu" gives you the list of available information. Saying "help" gives a tutorial about whatever section you're in. Each section has a sponsor, which is mentioned in an ad a few seconds long. There are also frequent, quick trivia facts.

You're prompted to create a username and password. When you register, you're required to submit the following personal information:

- phone number
- e-mail address
- full name
- zip code

**Big spender:**

No premium services.

URL: http://www.tellme.com/

**Contact:**   feedback@tellme.com

　X　 SOHO　　　　　　　　　　　_____ Small business

# SUMMARY . . . . . . . . . . . . . . . . . . . . . .

Keeping your projects on track can be difficult, whether you're on the road, working at home, or at the office—or trying to do all three at once. The tools you've encountered in this chapter can help with one or more of these environments, as well as with sharing tasks and projects with your team members.

Straight ahead, you'll learn about valuable resources and remotely hosted free Web applications that can help you avoid the pitfalls of getting started with Web design.

# 4

# Building Your Site

..........................

In the last chapter, we learned how the Net can help organize your business, but to use the Net to its fullest, the Internet must be part of your business. Especially for individuals, a simple Web page can be an excellent promotional tool, working for you 24 hours per day. This chapter highlights the key Web sites that can help you build and find a home for your Web site. Whether you're looking to keep your site simple, to spruce it up with graphics, to add interactivity with counters, guest books, and search capabilities, or to check it for glaring errors, free Web sites can launch you—even if you're a novice—into the Internet without the bill for rocket fuel.

## FREE SITE HOSTING  . . . . . . . . . . . . . . . . . . . .

For many businesses, the purpose of a Web site lies less in the selling than in the servicing. Simply presenting your services to the world can be reason enough to move to the Web. Basic information such as hours of operation, rates, and services offered don't demand the hottest commerce server. For these sites, a number of free Web sites can get you started. Table 4.1 outlines how the sites profiled below compare to each other. You can visit FreeCenter (http://www.freecenter.com/homepages.html) for an extensive set of user reviews of dozens of sites that offer free home pages. If all goes well, though, these free sites can only serve you up to a point—you'll outgrow what these sites can offer you when you're ready to take advantage of full-scale e-commerce capabilities like transaction processing, security, and payment handling.

**Table 4.1** Comparison of Free Web Hosting Services

| Service | Distinguishing features | Domain name hosting | Server space | Online Web editors | Search engine submission? | Host site places advertising? |
|---|---|---|---|---|---|---|
| Angelfire | Angelfire's library of JavaScript and CGI scripts lets you add games, scrolling text, and more to your site. | Yes | 50 MB | Basic and advanced. | Yes | Yes |
| TreeWay | Offers interactive audio and video content feeds. | Yes | 25 pages | Yes | Yes | No |
| Tripod | Supports message boards, chat rooms. Provides Web Gems, forms-based tools for adding interactive elements to your page such as message boards, chat rooms, and stock quotes. You can also join affiliate programs and Lycos's banner exchange. | Yes | 50 MB | QuickPage, Tripod-branded version of Trellix. | No, but offers tips. | Yes |

| Homestead | Includes over 400 editable templates. Includes some e-commerce capabilities. Supports streaming video, audio, access to visitor statistics, polls, guestbooks, online chat. | Yes | 16 MB, but freely expanded for additional storage. | SiteBuilder | Yes | No |
|---|---|---|---|---|---|---|
| NBCi.com | Includes e-commerce capabilities, clip art library. | No | Unlimited | ZY Page Builder | Yes | Yes |
| Bootbox | Supports database backends, dynamic content, e-commerce capabilities. | Yes | 10 MB (35 MB for premium accounts). | No | No | No |

## Angelfire

Angelfire's free Web hosting service provides 50 MB of storage for members to host their Web sites. The service offers a number of interactive applications you can add to your own pages, from online games to polls and simple forms.

The service provides a file uploader it calls a Transloader to move files from your hard drive to Angelfire's servers. You can edit your site's files online with either an advanced editor or a simple version that requires no knowledge of HTML (Hyper-Text Markup Language, the simple coding language that describes the layout of any Web page). An online image editor, GIFWorks, lets you edit and crop images for your Web site, and animation libraries are available. Angelfire will even submit your site to a number of search engines on your behalf.

Angelfire will embed banner ads on your pages. Note that in the site's terms of services, Angelfire reserves the right to delete any page at any time for any reason or for no reason at all. Like sister site Tripod, Angelfire partners with Commission Central to feature affiliate programs on your Web site. You make money when visitors to your site click through these ads to the resulting commercial sites and make purchases there. Angelfire has also teamed with a company called VideoShare to allow you to create, post, and even edit videos on your site (see Figure 4.1). It gives you 10 MB of space for videos, two of which start out occupied by a Lycos commercial.

**Getting started:**

When you register, you're prompted to create a URL that lives off of a subdirectory page of http://www.angelfire.com. The directories that you can choose to place your page in are named after U.S. states or hobbies and interests.

After you successfully log in, you're taken to a Web shell page where you can click on Create/Edit to edit your first page, or Web Shell Guide for complete instructions.

Required information includes

- your name
- mailing address
- gender
- year of birth
- e-mail address

You're also asked if you wish to opt in to receive e-mail advertisements from Angelfire partners, e-mail from Lycos on new services and special offers, and whether to be listed in the WhoWhere? directory.

**Figure 4.1**
Angelfire and VideoShare provide a means for you to publish your own online video files. (© 2000 Angelfire, a Lycos Network Site. All rights reserved.)

**Big spender:**

You can register for a custom domain name through Angelfire.

URL: http://www.angelfire.com/

**Contact:**   http://angelfire.lycos.com/doc/feedback.html

   _X_  SOHO                       ____  Small business

## TreeWay.com

Need a very basic Web site? One of the quickest ways to get up and running online completely free is with TreeWay's Web hosting service. When you register, you're given an 8-page Web site, which you can upgrade to 25 pages just for the asking, plus a free e-mail account.

TreeWay provides Web templates (see Figure 4.2), images, and overall site design schemes with headers, colors, fonts, and other graphical elements you can use to create a consistent look and feel on your pages.

You don't need to know any HTML in order to build Web pages online with TreeWay's service. When you're ready to edit pages, click on Build/Edit in the Site Manager; you edit your text, links, and images using the commands in the toolbars. TreeWay also lets you experiment with Flash animations (see Figure 4.3), one of the hottest features of Web design.

**Getting started:**

A straightforward guided tour on TreeWay's site takes you through each step of building your Web site. You must have cookies enabled on your Web browser.

The only information you're required to enter is your e-mail address and a site name and password of your choice.

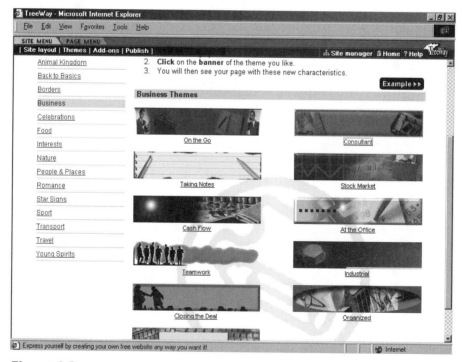

**Figure 4.2**
You can choose from a number of design templates when creating your TreeWay site.

**Figure 4.3**
TreeWay simplifies adding Flash animations to your Web site creation.

**Big spender:**

No premium services.

URL: http://www.treeway.com/

**Contact:**   info@treeway.com

   _X_  SOHO                    ____ Small business

## Tripod

You can use Tripod's online Web page editor to build and edit pages on the fly (see Figure 4.4). Uploading files is easy with an FTP tool. The file manager is slow to load, but provides a ready means to view your online content at a glance. You'll receive 50 MB free hosting space, and can opt for 25 MB free file space through driveway.com. It appears that this service does not provide any type of interactivity other than forms.

You can also earn cash for your site traffic by becoming a member of the Lycos Traffic Affiliate Program. Add one or more of the dynamic Lycos Network content boxes on your site's pages, and you'll collect either $.02 or $.03 every time someone clicks through.

The service provides customizable CGI and JavaScripts that allow members to write their own interactive forms for use on their sites. A number of premade interactive tools, like counters and guestbooks, are already provided. Tripod calls these Web Gems (see Figure 4.5).

Like many other free Web hosting services—but unlike sister site Angelfire—Tripod compels you to display its own advertising on your personal pages. The only option you can choose is whether these ads should appear embedded in your pages or as separate pop-up windows.

Tripod now comes with a short subdomain URL with the format http:// membername.tripod.com/, so your site URL will be more memorable.

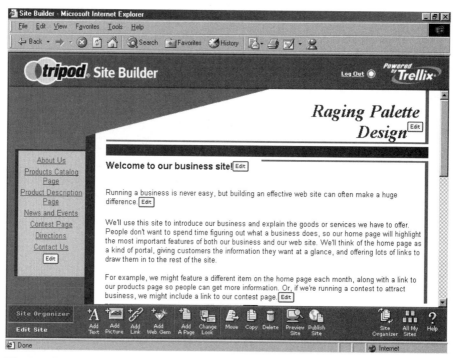

**Figure 4.4**
Tripod offers an easy-to-use Web-based interface for updating your Web pages. (Tripod ® is a registered service mark of Tripod, Inc., a subsidiary of Lycos, Inc. All rights reserved.)

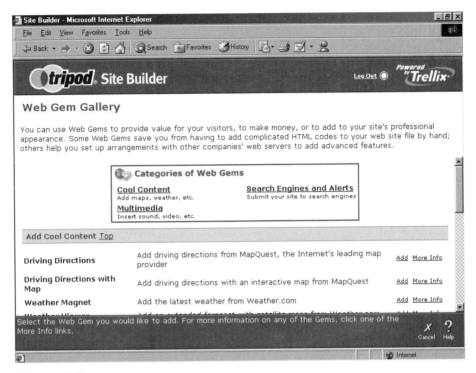

**Figure 4.5**
Tripod's Web Gems provide shortcuts to creating online weather reports and
guestbooks. (Tripod ® is a registered service mark of Tripod, Inc., a subsidiary of Lycos, Inc. All rights reserved.)

**Getting started:**

After you sign up for a Tripod account, upon your return visit you're prompted to
have your Lycos Network Passport stamped. This will enable you to log on to any
Lycos site with your Tripod username and password. You'll also be prompted here to
learn more about Commission Central, the Lycos affiliate center described earlier in
this chapter.

Required registration information includes

- full name
- gender
- birth date
- zip code (for U.S. residents only)

- country
- current e-mail address

You'll also be prompted to create a username and password.

**Big spender:**

Tripod offers domain registration services.

URL: http://www.tripod.com/

**Contact:**   http://help.tripod.com/

   X   SOHO                    ____  Small business

## Homestead.com

Homestead's drag-and-drop tools for building a Web site are as beginner-friendly as any you'll ever find. After you point-and-click your way to designing your own home page, the HTML results will display exactly as expected. Visitors to your site will be spared seeing ad banners display on your pages or enduring the ubiquitous pop-up advertising windows on similar free page-hosting sites like GeoCities or Tripod.

Homestead's business model relies heavily on licensing arrangements: Companies provide content tools that they've already developed, such as search boxes, rotating news banners, or stock tickers, to Homestead, which makes them available as ready-made elements that users can deploy on their own pages (see Figure 4.6). Homestead then receives a fee each time visitors click through one of the branded buttons. This arrangement also offers you, the site developer, instant content you can use to draw and keep users without any expended effort on your part.

The service provides you with 16 MB of space. If you require additional storage space, though, Homestead will simply let you create a second site for free and link it to your first. Through Homestead, you can register your own domain and take advantage of URL forwarding. The company's MoneyMakers Stores Elements let you set up an online store to sell what you want and earn commissions as you do so.

To build a Web page with Homestead SiteBuilder, you must have at least Netscape 3.*x* or Internet Explorer 4.*x* using Windows 95/98/NT. A downloadable version of SiteBuilder is available so you can continue to work on your site offline. Mac users and WebTV users will use Homestead Express, a template-based Web page design tool that is easy to use but doesn't have all the snazzy drag-and-drop capabilities of Homestead SiteBuilder. An online browser test on the site helps you determine if your operating system and Web browser meet Homestead SiteBuilder's system requirements.

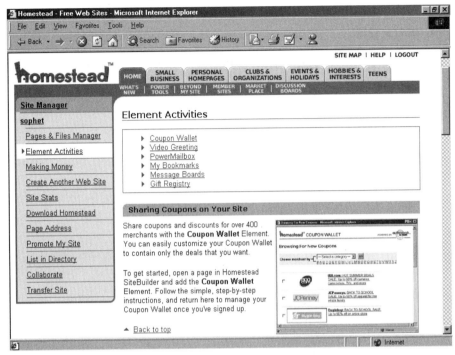

**Figure 4.6**
When you create a site on Homestead, you can incorporate ready-made content elements like search boxes or stock tickers.

**Getting started:**

When you are ready to design your site, Homestead will prompt you to describe the type of site you want to build, such as a small business site or personal home page. The choice you make will determine which sample templates are next presented for you to choose from in building your overall design scheme. When SiteBuilder launches, you'll see what Homestead calls Elements: text and shapes, clipart, graphics files, and interactive items, like a chat room. You can click and drag any of these onto your page, save, and your page is done. Elements can be accurately positioned, resized, recolored, and layered quickly and easily with just a few clicks of the mouse.

When registering, you will be asked to select a URL for your Web site, in the format http://www.yourpagename.homestead.com. You will then be required to enter the following:

- first and last names
- e-mail address
- member name and password
- gender
- year of birth
- country of residence
- zip code (U.S. residents)

You're also asked if you want to sign up to receive e-mail promotions and special offers from third-party merchants.

**Big spender:**

You can sell your own goods online with Homestead's Buy & Sell service, which requires you pay a transaction fee when you complete a sale.

URL: http://www.homestead.com/

**Contact:**   support@homestead-inc.com

   X  SOHO                          ____  Small business

## NBCi.com

The result of the integration of Xoom.com, Snap.com, and other sites into NBCi.com, this service allows you to build your own home page that takes advantage of chat rooms, message boards, HTML-based e-mail, electronic greeting cards, and downloadable software utilities (see Figure 4.7). Moneymaking opportunities include affiliate programs, auctions, or your own online store. You can either create your own HTML pages and upload your Web site files or use an online editor for creating your new site on the fly.

The site's Affiliate Network lets home page builders earn commissions on sales by selling other companies' products on their personal pages. But NBCi is especially targeting small business owners through an affiliated service at Bigstep.com, which lets users build and promote their own online stores (see description of Bigstep.com in Chapter 5). Bigstep.com includes a Web-based application that lets you create a free online store with an unlimited number of pages and 12 MB of free space to store photos and pictures. The service also includes technical support and shopping carts, and allows you to establish an Internet-ready credit card merchant account.

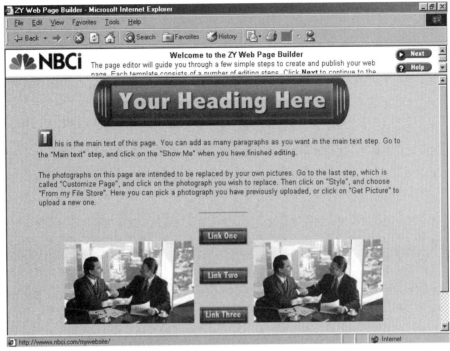

**Figure 4.7**
NBCi.com provides an online Web-page-building utility to simplify creating an interactive Web site.

One great feature allows you to track who's visiting your Web site. You'll also get access to NBCi's online clip art collection of animated GIFs, photographs, backgrounds, textures, and other images that you could use to dress up your site.

**Getting started:**

After you register, the site prompts you through creating your home page via a series of screens that direct you to make decisions about your page's look and feel and content placement.

Required information includes

- member name and password
- your e-mail address
- first and last name
- country
- street address

**Big spender:**

To accept credit cards, you'll pay a $24.95 monthly fee plus an additional fee—which depends on the credit card—for each transaction. For $8 a month, you can create an unlimited number of Web pages; among other features, you'll gain access to over 100 Web page templates and over 350 graphics to choose from.

URL: http://www.nbci.com/

**Contact:**   http://www.nbci.com/helpcenter/EmailUs.php

  X   SOHO                         X    Small business

## Bootbox

Bootbox has one of the more generous free Web hosting services out there—you need not place any banners or advertising on your Web site. You can host your own interactive CGI scripts, upload your files through FTP, and gain up to 10 MB of free file storage and an unlimited number of free e-mail addresses. You can accept credit cards online if you plan to run an e-commerce site.

You'll receive a URL in the format yourname.bootbox.net, or you can use your own custom domain name. Bootbox can help you register for a domain name if you haven't registered one yet. If you use your own domain name, you'll gain access to many additional Web site capabilities, such as database integration and a shopping cart interface that your customers can use. You'll also receive an additional 25 MB of free storage space. You'll appreciate the services provided here more if you're interested in delving into your own Web development. If you already own your own domain name, you must transfer it to Bootbox.net using Register.com, a process that costs $70, but which extends your ownership of the domain name for an additional two years. If you do not already own a domain name, the site's registration process offers a fairly straightforward means of doing so.

When you register, you'll be asked to choose whether you want 5 MB or 10 MB of free file storage.

Required information includes

- full name
- title (if registering as a business)
- company name
- type of company
- mailing address
- phone number

- fax number
- e-mail address
- current URL
- type of Web site
- number of visitors per day
- description of your Web site

You'll also be asked if you own a domain name, and if so, if you bought it through Bootbox. You'll be asked if you need one or more of a variety of high-end Web services. You'll need to say if your site will be an e-commerce site, and if so, what you anticipate your average ticket sales will be.

**Big spender:**

Some services may incur third-party charges. To use the secure server, Verisign Secure ID charges may apply. If you sign up for your own domain name, InterNIC charges will apply.

URL: http://www.bootbox.net/

**Contact:**   info@bootboxcomp.com
  _X_  SOHO                 _X_  Small business

# FREE HTML TEMPLATES . . . . . . . . . . . . . . . . .

Itching to launch a site in a hurry? The free Web templates at the following sites provide striking-looking designs; the template approach helps ensure your site's look remains consistent.

## Free Web Templates

Free Web Templates lives up to its name with dozens of attractive templates that are free for the taking. New Web developers can take advantage of the page markup and graphics to create good-looking Web sites quickly.

You can choose from frame-enabled sites, table-driven templates, site templates donated by visitors to Free Web Templates (use with caution), and a DHTML-based, JavaScript-enhanced set of templates called ExpandoFace. In the ExpandoFace sites, much of the navigation can be expanded or contracted either vertically or horizontally—a very techie touch. Most impressive is Flash Blaster, a Web-based tool for creating your own Macromedia Flash animations without any programming, based on several available templates.

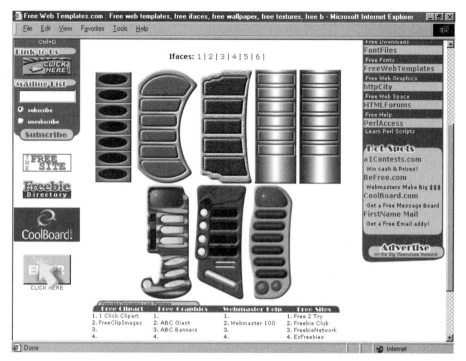

**Figure 4.8**
Pick and choose navigation interfaces based on actual look-and-feel at Free
Web Templates.

The site also provides links to obtain free Web graphics arrayed by function—
(buttons, backgrounds, banners, and more (see Figure 4.8)—as well as site tools, like
a pop-up generator, meta tag generator, and rollover coder, and a number of useful
tutorials for Webmasters.

**Getting started:**

Search for new templates based on one of four categories—frame-based, table-based,
user-donated templates, and ExpandoFace.

No registration is necessary. You can supply your e-mail address to receive notification of when the site has been updated.

**Big spender:**

A premium version of the Flash Blaster service increases your options for creating
personalized Flash animations and splash screens without any programming expertise. These premium templates could run you up to $29.95 each.

URL: http://www.freewebtemplates.com/

**Contact:**   http://www.freewebtemplates.com/contact.shtml

 X  SOHO                    ___   Small business


# netJane

If you or other contributors to your Web site wish to make frequent updates to your content but don't understand a thing about HTML or Web site development, consider using netJane's user-friendly interface to update your pages.

With this service, you can import Web pages to the netJane program window and make text changes, create tables, import graphics, or drag-and-drop content—all without knowing a lick of HTML. You'll need to understand how to connect to your site's FTP server so that you can automatically save your files to your Web site.

To help you get started if you're creating your Web site from scratch, netJane sports an ever-expanding library of themed, prebuilt Web page templates you can fill in with your content.

You'll also find an extensive library of third-party applets (see Figure 4.9) that includes games, calculators, and other gizmos for adding interactivity to your Web site. The site also lets you calculate the download time of your finished pages at various modem speeds so you'll know if your customers will be bogged down or lifted up. You can also sign up to use CashButtons, netJane's way of encouraging your participation in affiliate programs.

**Getting started:**

When you register, you're asked if you have an existing Web site and if so, the name of your Internet service provider. If you don't have a Web site, netJane will prompt you to go sign up for one from NBCi (formerly Xoom.com).

Required information includes


- your hosting provider
- username and password
- e-mail address
- FTP address of your hosting provider
- FTP subdirectory and port


**Big spender:**

No premium services.

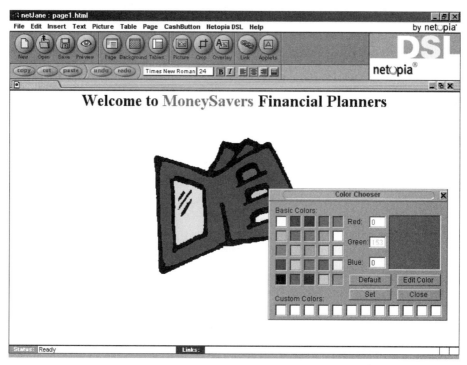

**Figure 4.9**
With netJane, you leverage Java applets to add interactive functionality to
your Web site.

URL: http://www.netjane.com/

**Contact:**   http://support.netjane.com/

   X   SOHO                    ____  Small business

# FREE GRAPHICS . . . . . . . . . . . . . . . . . . . . .

If you're looking for graphics for your Web site, there are many sites that can provide
basic images for every purpose: navigation buttons, bullets and icons, animations
(better known as animated GIFs), lines, logos, and overall interfaces. You may find a
few icons that are perfect for your needs, some that'll inspire you to create better-
looking versions, and a whole bunch that you'd never find a use for.

   If you are creating graphics that are destined for Web sites, you'll want to create
and edit your images in one or both of the two popular Web graphics formats: GIF or

JPEG. Deciding whether you should save your Web graphics as GIFs or as JPEGs should largely depend on what kinds of graphics they are.

The JPEG format is the best choice for photographic-quality images or graphics with a lot of color blends. GIF should be suitable for almost any other kind of Web graphic, from icons to logos to navigational graphics; it's the most widely used format on the Web.

We've listed below several of the more extensive online repositories in the hopes of reducing your search time in order to get your Web site looking beautiful as soon as possible!

## Graphxkingdom

Graphxkingdom is home to thousands of clipart images, icons (see Figure 4.10), backgrounds, bars, interfaces, and other free graphics.

The site doesn't have a search engine for finding specific images, but the graphics are organized into several dozen categories that you can search by topic. For

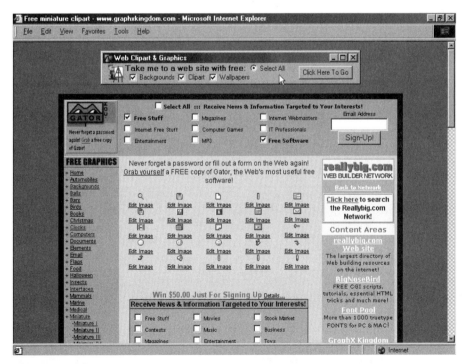

**Figure 4.10**
At the Graphxkingdom site, you can search by category to find free graphics.

example, Cartoons and Christmas have their own categories; you can also readily search for Star Wars images or the broad category Automobiles.

Graphxkingdom is part of the reallybig.com Web builder network of sites, which also includes BigNoseBird (mainly for free CGI scripts), Font Pool (with over 1,000 fonts for PC and Mac users), and Dynamic Drive (free DHTML scripts). As a result, the Graphxkingdom page acts as a portal to useful graphics-related resources on its sister sites. For example, you can link from the main Graphxkingdom page to an extremely useful page on BigNoseBird (http://www.bignosebird.com/sets.shtml) that assembles sets of coordinated graphics ensembles designed for Web pages. If you are looking to create a new overall design for a site, you can come here to find color-coordinated background images, arrow graphics, buttons, icons, and bullets.

**Getting started:**

Use the left-hand navigation to search for images in specific categories or themes. You don't need to register to utilize any of the free clip art resources at this site. You can submit your e-mail address to have a clip art GIF of the Day e-mailed to you every day, or you can sign up to be notified about site updates.

**Big spender:**

No premium services.

URL: http://www.graphxkingdom.com/
**Contact:**   webmaster@graphxkingdom.com

  X  SOHO                    ___  Small business

# FreeGraphics.com

A large, indexed directory to hundreds of Web sites that offer free graphics, Free-Graphics.com organizes its offerings in about a dozen categories (see Figure 4.11). These include Web graphics, holiday-themed graphics, animated graphics, free software for creating graphics, background images, free fonts, wallpaper patterns, and links to sites where you can create buttons and other graphics online for free.

Each listing includes a brief annotation about what distinguishes that site from the others, which makes the listings especially useful when searching for free graphics.

**Getting started:**

No site registration is required. Simply choose your category and begin browsing through to the graphics sites linked off of this portal.

**Big spender:**

No premium services.

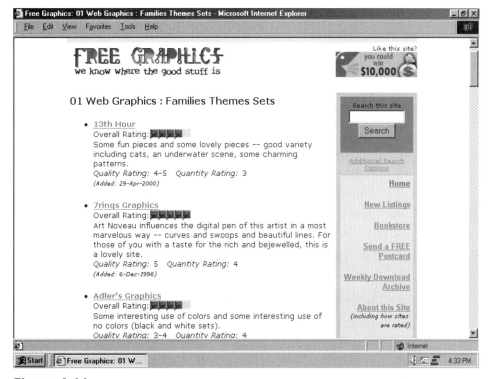

**Figure 4.11**
Each graphics site listed at FreeGraphics.com is rated on both the quality and quantity of its offerings.

URL: http://www.freegraphics.com/

**Contact:**    webmaster@freegraphics.com

   X   SOHO                          ____   Small business

## PhotoDisc

PhotoDisc is one of the best resources for stock photography on the Web. While most of the site's 75,000 images must be purchased, you can download free, nonwater-marked comp versions—useful when a small image is needed—plus find free samples of PhotoDisc's new series of GIF and Shockwave animations.

The site's keyword-based search engine makes it extremely easy to find images on as specific or as broad a topic as you're looking for. Search on the word "object" along with the specific kind of image you want (e.g., "phone") to find silhouetted images—using this example, you'll find cutout photos of telephones and cell phones that could appear on your Web page on top of any kind of background color or texture.

**Getting started:**

You can conduct a search from the main page by entering one or more keywords, or upon return visits to the site, you can retrieve graphics by their unique identifying image numbers. The site also lets you store any number of images online for your personal easy reference in a "lightbox" (see Figure 4.12).

There are separate registrations for U.S. and Canada users and visitors from other countries. Required information includes

- username and password
- place of birth
- name
- telephone number

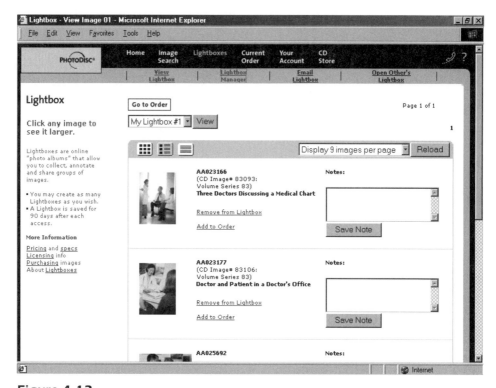

**Figure 4.12**
At the PhotoDisc site, you can reserve images for potential later use by storing them in an online "lightbox."

- e-mail address
- mailing address
- country

Your username and password can also be used on several sister sites that sell stock photography—Energy Film, gettyone.com, and tonystone.com.

**Big spender:**

For purchasing larger, single images, the rates depend on the graphics resolution.

| | |
|---|---|
| 600K 72dpi: | $24.95 |
| 10 MB 300dpi: | $79.95 |
| 28 MB 300dpi: | $149.95 |

URL: http://www.photodisc.com/

**Contact:**   webtech@photodisc.com

  X   SOHO            ____ Small business

## Elated Web Toolbox

Created by a team of Web designers and programmers, the Elated Web Toolbox offers free Web buttons, graphics, animated graphics, clip art, backgrounds, stock photographs, and discussion forums, as well as tutorials on using the popular Adobe Photoshop graphics program and tips for building better Web sites.

Elated Web Toolbox also contains free predesigned, preprogrammed page templates that you can download (in .ZIP format) and alter to build your own page from scratch. All the code and images you need to get started with a great page are included. All that Elated asks is that you mention them and put a link to the Elated Web Toolbox somewhere on your site.

**Getting started:**

No registration is required.

**Big spender:**

No premium services.

URL: http://www.elated.com/toolbox/

**Contact:**   http://www.elated.com/contacts/

  X   SOHO            X  Small business

## ArtToday

While it is only free for a three day trial, ArtToday boasts animated GIFs, photographs, clip art (see Figure 4.13), videos, text, music, and sounds that you can use to create Web pages, advertising, presentations, logos, and other marketing tools.

The free graphics library includes over 43,000 images that you can search by keyword or by type of graphic—for example, clip art or photos. A selection of free fonts and sound clips is available too. Note, though, that many images are just slight variations on other ones.

The site also boasts some community-building features, such as online chat and classified ads. You'll find numerous articles on graphic design from content partners, including Jakob Nielsen's Alertbox and tips for creating special Photoshop effects. There are some popular tools for online graphics creators, including a Web-safe color palette and an RGB-hex converter.

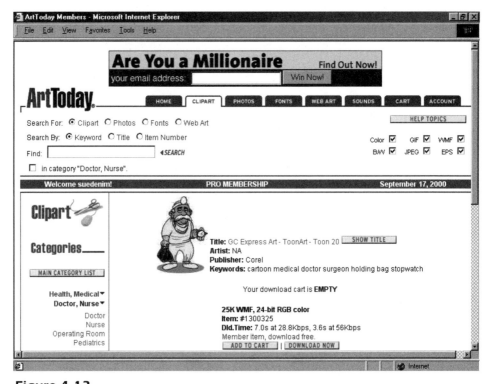

**Figure 4.13**
If you're satisfied with your free trial of ArtToday, you might want to spring for the annual subscription costs.

**Getting started:**

When you register, you're prompted to create a username and password. Required information includes

- full name
- e-mail address
- mailing address

**Big spender:**

Standard membership costs $29.95 a year and includes a broad, searchable selection of graphics—nearly 900,000 images and 1,800 fonts. A $99.95 Professional membership includes over 1.2 million images, 5,800 fonts, and 4,800 sound files. It also includes a powerful image creator utility that you can use to create custom buttons, Web graphics, banners, and logos easily, as well as a powerful image converter that will convert graphic files from and to over 80 different file formats.

URL: http://www.arttoday.com/

**Contact:**   support@arttoday.com/

   X   SOHO                                    _____ Small business

# FREE GRAPHICS CREATION . . . . . . . . . . . . . . .

## CoolText

This free online service will dynamically generate customized logos, buttons, and bullets for you in real time. You're prompted to choose the wording for your logo or button graphic, along with your font, colors, and special effect—ranging from an alien glow to a gradient bevel to a textured display. You can also use the site to create custom bullets and icon graphics from a select number of templates and styles.

**Getting started:**

After you select the type of graphic you want—a logo, button, or bullet—you'll see an online form where you can alter numerical values to change the colors, lighting angle, textures, and shading (see Figure 4.14). If the values for these parameters are meaningless to you, you may want to either stick with the defaults or experiment with one value at a time. A color chart with some suggested values to try is provided through the help page.

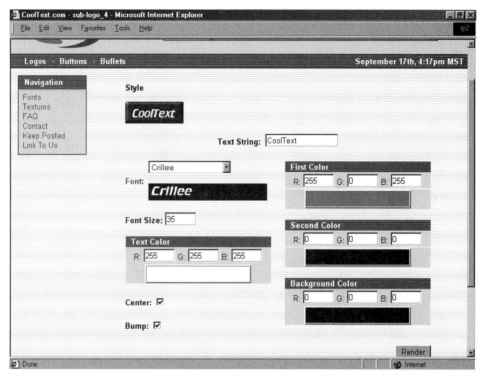

**Figure 4.14**
At CoolText.com, you can create banner text graphics by choosing your font, colors, and effects through an interactive form.

The online graphics generator does have some limitations: you can't create graphics that have transparent backgrounds, and you may find yourself virtually waiting in line for other users' requested graphics to complete before your job can be run.

Once your image is generated, you'll need to right-click on it (if you're using Windows) or just click and hold your mouse over the image (if you're using a Mac) to download the image to your hard drive.

You won't need to register to take advantage of CoolText's services, but you can sign up to receive announcements and updates about the site. When you register, you're asked to supply your e-mail address.

**Big spender:**

No premium services.

URL: http://www.cooltext.com/

**Contact:**   http://www.cooltext.com/email.php3

   X   SOHO                                      Small business

# MediaBuilder

As part of the Andover.net site network for Web-building tools, MediaBuilder acts as a portal to a number of nifty online graphics tools.

- 3D Text Maker. Make your own 3D Web banners with your customized wording. You can choose from dozens of typefaces, colors, and sizes, and add your own special text effects. You can preview the typeface and display before your image is rendered.

- Animated Banner Maker. Create your own custom animated banners online. Choose from one of the animation effects available; these have descriptive titles like Blur and Zoom In With Rotate; all can be previewed before your image is rendered. Enter the text you want to appear on the banner and click the Make Banner button. After the banner is created, you can save the banner to your own computer.

- GIFWorks. Use this online GIF editor for adding and removing transparency effects, cropping images, inserting text, converting to a "Websafe" color palette, and adding filter effects (e.g., warp, offset, sharpness, brightness, and artistic modifications).

- ButtonMaker. Turn any GIF image into a nicely beveled button. The tools work on animated GIFs. To create a button using ButtonMaker, you just need to first provide a starting image that's online or located on your hard drive.

MediaBuilder also provides over 20,000 free graphics files arrayed in libraries according to their function on a Web site. You'll find libraries for background images, borders, icons, line graphics, and fonts.

**Getting started:**

Each of the tools offers step-by-step instructions for entering your custom text and setting values for the tools' various parameters. If you're unfamiliar with any of the parameters you're asked to modify, you can leave the default values alone or experiment with changing one parameter at a time.

No registration is necessary to use any of the MediaBuilder tools.

**Big spender:**

No premium services.

URL: http://www.mediabuilder.com/

**Contact:**   http://www.andover.net/contact.html

  X   SOHO               ____ Small business

# WebGFX

This site offers several online graphics generators that dynamically generate stunning logos, buttons, and navigation bars. Try-O-Mat is the more flexible of the two generators; you can choose from a broad range of fonts, patterns, gradients, and colors. With Log-O-Mat, you choose from a more limited number of predefined logo styles but produce richer renderings. Nav-O-Mat lets you choose from a number of predefined navigation bars to create your own navigation graphics for your home page.

A comprehensive frequently asked questions list is provided, with step-by-step instructions for new users on how to download the graphics that are generated on screen for them. Users will also find helpful the information provided on the differences between graphics file formats, how to create buttons with transparent backgrounds, and tips on creating gradients.

**Getting started:**

Site registration was once required for this service, but you can now use any of the graphics generator tools without registering first.

**Big spender:**

No premium services. Messages on the site indicate that it may charge for services in the future.

URL: http://www.webgfx.ch/

**Contact:**   support@webgfx.ch

  X   SOHO            X Small business

# FREE IMAGE EDITING . . . . . . . . . . . . . . . . . .

For serious graphics editing, you'll probably need to invest in a software program like Adobe Photoshop, PhotoDeluxe, or Microsoft Picture-It. However, for quick or last-minute touch-ups, a number of free Web sites can tune your graphics so that they look better and download more quickly. Optimized graphics can make a big difference in how quickly your Web pages display, which will help prevent your site visitors from becoming impatient with your site's performance.

## NetMechanic GIFBot

GIFBot is a tool for optimizing Web pages by reducing the size of the GIF and JPEG images on the page. Enter the URL of any page on your site containing images, and GIFBot will present a number of optimized variations to your originals. When you view the results, you can select the best tradeoff between image quality and file size, then save the image for your use.

Although you can check just one individual image, the real value of this tool is checking all the images on a given page at once.

**Getting started:**

Enter the URL of either a single online image or a Web page that contains a number of images. Select the type of output you would like—in other words, should GIFBot turn any JPEGs on your site into GIFs, or leave them in their original graphics file format? The results page will list all the images contained in your Web page. Click on an image's file size to reduce it with GIFBot; this resulting page will show you the reduced variations on your original (see Figure 4.15).

You can compare the reduced image to the original by moving the mouse over the reduced image. If you are using a browser that supports JavaScript rollovers, the original image will pop up instead of the reduced image. This allows you to easily perform a better-or-worse comparison between the original and reduced image. Once the desired image is determined, you can click in the image to save it to your local machine.

No registration is required to use this tool. You can provide your e-mail address to have the results sent to you via e-mail instead of waiting in real-time. If you supply your e-mail address, you can also click a checkbox to receive a monthly site tips newsletter.

**Big spender:**

While the GIFBot service is free, the NetMechanic site also heavily promotes its HTML Toolbox tune-up services that start at $69.99 a year.

URL: http://www.netmechanic.com/accelerate.htm

**Contact:**   http://www.netmechanic.com/comp/contact.htm

   <u>X</u>  SOHO                     \_\_\_  Small business

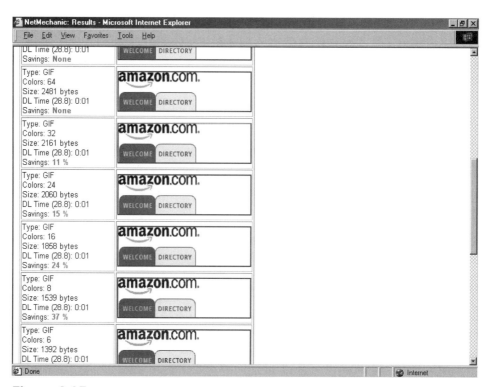

**Figure 4.15**
When you view GIFBot's results, you'll see how much you can reduce your graphics' file size before the quality is affected.

## GIFWorks

Part of the MediaBuilder suite of online graphics creation tools (see previous section, "Free Graphics Creation") GIFWorks lets Web designers select, process, and create animations online using a standard Web browser interface.

You can animate, optimize, and apply special effects to any GIF that you choose. Since all of the processing is done on the remote server, you won't need to download or install any software.

GIFWorks includes some 20 effects similar to those found in professional graphic design applications, including chalk, emboss, oil paint, and watercolor. You can turn any GIF into a Web button (see Figure 4.16) and text using any one of six fonts, specifying the font size and color you want. The "smart crop" feature lets you automatically crop the background out of a GIF, leaving just the image. You may select a color anywhere in the GIF and replace it with another to match a page's border

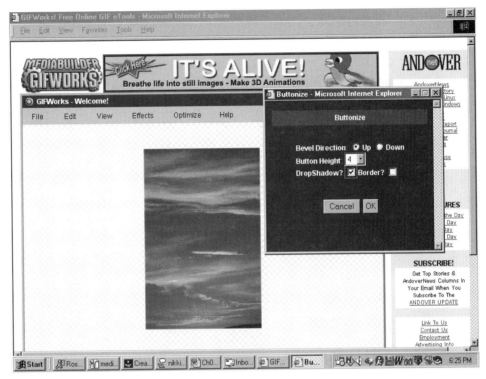

**Figure 4.16**
You can give any GIF file a three-dimensional appearance for use as a button graphic on a Web page.

or background. Additionally, you can click on any color in your image to make that color transparent (so that the background shows through) or return it to its original color.

**Getting started:**

A row of drop-down menus on the GIFWorks home page directs you to choose your file and specify effects to add. Follow the instructions on the home page to load your image and then manipulate it. No registration is necessary to use GIFWorks.

**Big spender:**

No premium services.

URL: http://www.gifworks.com/

**Contact:**   http://www.andover.net/contact.html

   _X_  SOHO                    _X_  Small business

## Spinwave's GIFCruncher and JPEGCruncher

Spinwave's free online utilities can greatly reduce the size and download times of your images, whether they're currently on your Web site or stored on your hard drive. Both products are also available in a desktop version with additional features.

GIFCruncher can optimize the size of single GIFs for you, one at a time, for free. JPEGCruncher image filters clean noise and hard-to-compress information from your images automatically. You can create optimized JPEGs from other formats, like BMP, PICT, and TIFF.

**Getting started:**

Enter the location of your image from the Web or your hard drive, and GIFCruncher or JPEGCruncher will generate several optimizations of your image from which to choose (see Figure 4.17).

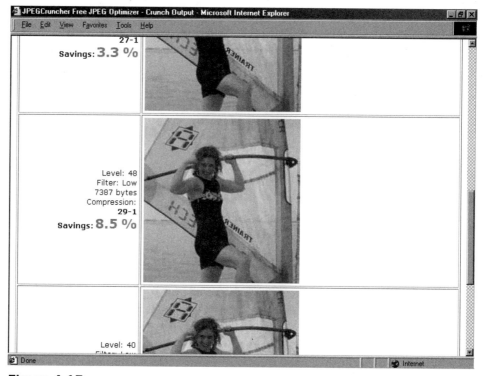

**Figure 4.17**
When you reduce the size of your GIF and JPEG files using Spinwave's utilities, the graphics should display more quickly on your Web site.

If you wish to download any of the images to your hard drive, you may do so by holding down the right mouse button over the image (if you're using Windows) or, if you're using a Mac, by holding the button down for several seconds.

No registration is necessary to use the online Spinwave utilities. You can subscribe to the Spinwave image optimization newsletter for tips and tutorials and product update notifications.

**Big spender:**

JPEGCruncher Desktop is sold for $27.50; GIFCruncher Desktop retails at $49.95.

URL: http://www.spinwave.com/

**Contact:**   info@spinwave.com

    X    SOHO             ___    Small business

# FREE CONTENT . . . . . . . . . . . . . . . . . . . . . . . . .

Many popular Web sites use news feeds from Reuters, Associated Press, and other sources because news gives your site the appearance of always being up-to-date, and keeps users coming back for more. Having the latest news content on your site will keep your users from going elsewhere for the headlines, increasing both your audience and your returning guests. The following sites help you find free news feeds with content that can be pertinent to your audience.

For a more extensive, ever-updated list of services offering free content, see Kresch.com's content resources at http://www.kresch.com/resources/Content/.

## iSyndicate

For Web site owners in search of constantly refreshed content, iSyndicate's Express service provides free access to dynamic story headlines, search boxes, and photos from third-party content providers. Over 1,000 content providers, from *Rolling Stone* to cNet to *Fortune* provide content to iSyndicate.

You can preview and choose to add a number of attractive, prepackaged interactive code snippets to your pages. For example, you can add a weather forecast box in which users enter their zip code or city; users are then directed to a resulting page on an external site to view their personalized results.

Content providers, for their part, pay iSyndicate by the click-through for using its subscribers to drive traffic to their sites. As a result, some of the pages available to link to feature overly prominent advertising or other branding that you may not want on your site. iSyndicate now offers stores where you can customize the banners.

**Getting started:**

After you log on and sign in, you can search the content providers' offerings by names. The JavaScript code for each content offering is provided on-screen (see Figure 4.18) and can also be e-mailed to you directly.

Required information includes

- your name
- e-mail address
- your Web site's URL (and a category describing your site's purpose)

**Big spender:**

A premium service called Network service is designed for larger companies, which pay between $1,000 and $10,000 a month to review and choose syndicated content to

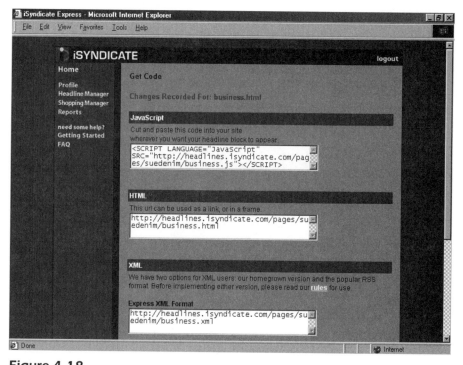

**Figure 4.18**

iSyndicate provides code snippets that you enabled on your Web pages to display dynamic content.

post to their own sites, and to receive detailed traffic reports on what visitors did with the content.

URL: http://www.isyndicate.com/

**Contact:**    http://www.isyndicate.com/company/contact.html

   X   SOHO                              ____   Small business

## Moreover.com

Moreover.com provides Web-based news feeds free of charge that you can add to your Web site. You can choose from 1,500 news sources in dozens of categories (see Figure 4.19), from sports stories to all kinds of industry news headlines to regional news.

After you select your categories, you proceed to an easy-to-use wizard to lay out the design of your news page. In no time, you'll have a complete news page that

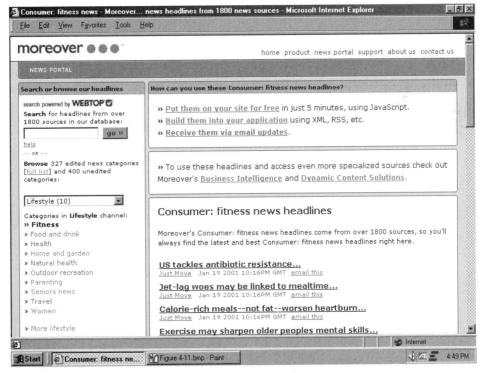

**Figure 4.19**
Moreover.com generates code for generating news headlines that you can copy and paste onto your own page.

you can link from your main Web page—or you can choose to install a piece of JavaScript code or access an XML feed to embed the headlines within your own pages.

**Getting started:**

The three-step wizard prompts you to choose your layout and headline settings, including table width, background color, headline size and font, and whether the source's title and date should be displayed. Once you've made your selections, you preview your settings and can return to the first step if you have any changes.

Required information includes your e-mail address and your site's URL. A copy of the generated JavaScript code for embedding your news feed in your page will be e-mailed to you.

**Big spender:**

No premium services.

URL: http://www.moreover.com/

**Contact:**   http://www.moreover.com/site/about/feedback/

  X  SOHO                         ____  Small business

# FreeSticky

This is a constantly reviewed index of free, automatically updating, embeddable content for keeping your visitors interested in returning to your site. The categories of available content include: cartoons, financial news, games, horoscopes, maps, news headlines, photographs, sports news, syndicated articles, and various tickers.

There is a list in reverse chronological order of the most recent content updates added to the site. A regular newsletter describes new content offerings that you may have overlooked. There are also discussion boards and a number of articles for Webmasters.

Best of all, the sticky content available here is not overtly marked with its own branding, so it will integrate well into your site or intranet.

**Getting started:**

Browse the category list for news feeds or content that sounds like a compelling fit for your Web site. Each content provider listed has a link back to its site, which lists the HTML code that you need to copy and paste into your home page. Some providers offer to e-mail the necessary text to you.

**Big spender:**

No premium services.

URL: http://www.freesticky.com/

**Contact:**  stickymaster@freesticky.com

   X  SOHO             X  Small business

# FREE MEDIA PLAYERS · · · · · · · · · · · · · · · · ·

While much of the Web consists largely of text and graphics, which can be handled
by most Web browsers, mixing in other media, such as audio, video, and animation,
can enrich its communication power. Web video can be created with a number of
products, including Windows Movie Maker, Apple's iMovie, and Avid Cinema. The
following sites are resources for free Web media players. If you begin to offer content
on your site that requires one of these players, it's good to offer a link back to the
necessary player in consideration of users who may not yet have installed this particular add-on.

## RealPlayer

The company was then called Progressive Networks, and the product was RealAudio,
but RealNetworks was one of the first companies to support "streaming" audio and
then video. It is now the market share leader in the category; the latest version of its
RealPlayer product (see Figure 4.20) as of this writing is version 8. Real has a number of other products, including RealJukebox, which can be used for organizing
music, but RealPlayer is all you need to get business news from online news sources
such as cNet, CNN.com, ABCNews.com, ZDNet, Bloomberg, and the *Wall Street
Journal.* Real's Mac version tends to lag the Windows version by a couple of months,
but is reasonably up to date and feature-competitive with its sibling.

**Getting started:**

Follow the link on the Real home page to download and install the free version of
RealPlayer.

**Big spender:**

The commercial RealPlayer 8 costs $29.99. The company also offers GoldPass, an
Internet media subscription service offering premium content, for $9.95 a month.

URL: http://www.real.com/

**Contact:**  http://service.real.com/

   X  SOHO             X  Small business

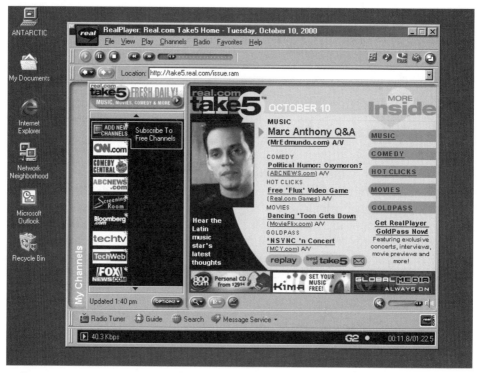

**Figure 4.20**
RealPlayer offers you means for embedding streaming video in your Web
site.

## QuickTime

QuickTime was one of the earliest video formats for any computer. Originally developed for the Mac, Apple has advanced it throughout the years. Long after Real-Networks scooped Apple in bringing streaming video to market, QuickTime 4.1 can finally stream video, and without a dedicated server like Real requires. Apple has also teamed up with Akamai, a company that specializes in distributing content around the Internet, to offer broadcasts online through QuickTime TV. The result has been higher quality video than is typically available online. Some of QuickTime TV's business content partners include ABC News, BBC World, and Bloomberg, the latter of which is a live feed from the television channel instead of the canned video that most sites offer.

On the other hand, QuickTime 4's interface, while pretty, is confusing (see Figure 4.21). To access its channels, drag out the "drawer" from the bottom of the screen

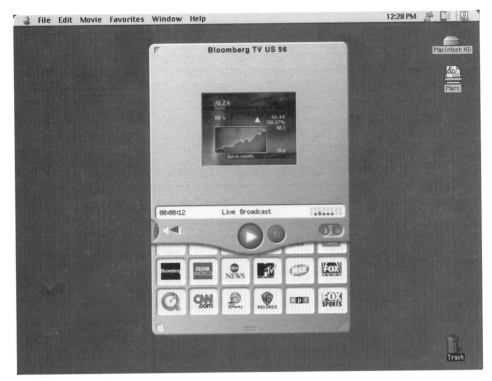

**Figure 4.21**
The drawer at the bottom of the QuickTime player's interface can be
dragged out to reveal channels.

(or double-click it). Those who prefer a more traditional interface can also use the
menu bar to choose channels.

**Getting started:**

Follow the link on the QuickTime home page to download and install the free player.

**Big spender:**

For $29.99, the commercial QuickTime Pro lets you create Internet-ready audio and
video, add special effects to your movies, play back full-screen video, create streaming movies, make presentations and slide shows, and export videos, sounds, and pictures to more than a dozen standard file formats.

URL: http://quicktime.apple.com/

**Contact:**   http://www.apple.com/contact/

  X  SOHO                    X  Small business

## Flash Player and Shockwave

Shockwave content is created in a program called Macromedia Director, a longtime favorite among multimedia developers as a CD-ROM authoring tool. Then Macromedia acquired a product called FutureSplash that it renamed Flash, which lets Web developers create animations that run online much faster than Shockwave ones. As a result, Flash has become very popular on Web sites, much more so than the original Shockwave. You'll find Flash used, for example, to create fancy interfaces to Web sites. If you see lots of text flying around your browser, you're probably in Flash. While some Web multimedia formats have their own viewing applications—Windows Media Player or RealPlayer, for example—a Flash or Shockwave movie will play within your Web browser as long as the plug-in is properly installed.

There are a few hidden tricks for controlling how you play in Flash animations. Right-clicking (or, for Mac users, pressing the Control key as you click) a Flash animation will provide several options such as looping the animation, zooming in on it, or stopping it (see Figure 4.22). The last is especially helpful for cutting short excessively long Flash animations that some Web developer has gone overboard in designing.

**Getting started:**

Follow the links on the Shockwave home page to download and install either free player. If you're looking to start creating your own Flash content, you can download a trial version of the authoring software from Macromedia's site.

**Big spender:**

The full version of Macromedia Flash 5 for developing Flash animations costs $399 from Macromedia's site. Macromedia Director 8 Shockwave Studio is a commercial product for multimedia developers that costs $999 from Macromedia's site.

URL: http://www.macromedia.com/shockwave/

**Contact:**   http://www.macromedia.com/macromedia/contact/

   _X_  SOHO                              _X_  Small business

## Acrobat Reader

Before the birth of the Web, Adobe created Acrobat, which created a file format for distributing high-fidelity copies of documents, regardless of which application created them. Although many documents come from only a handful of programs these days (such as those in Microsoft Office), and the majority of documents online have been converted into the Web's native format of HTML, Acrobat endures as an easy way to send documents through the Internet.

Why does Acrobat remain popular in the Web era? Primarily because it offers a far better representation of what a printed page will look like than most Web

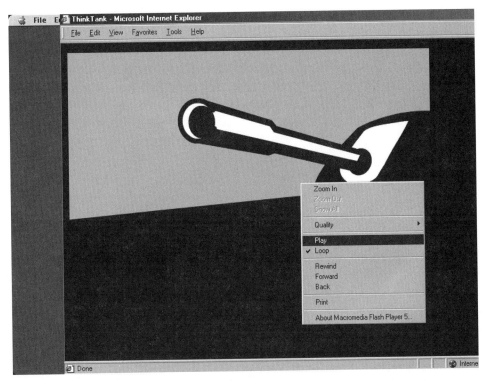

**Figure 4.22**
You can launch a set of controls during the playing of a Flash animation to
rewind or zoom in, among other settings.

"conversions" offer. It's also much better for transferring high-quality documents
(see Figure 4.23). On the Web, most graphics sacrifice quality for speed downloads.
Adobe is spreading Acrobat across a variety of products, but the only one you need
for reading Acrobat files online is Acrobat Reader, the latest version of which, at this
time, is 4.5.

To *create* Acrobat files, you'll need the commercial version of Adobe Acrobat.
There's also a Web page on Adobe's site called Create Adobe PDF Online that lets
you create a number of free PDFs by uploading your files to Adobe's server
(http://createpdf.adobe.com/). Almost all of Adobe's products are available for Mac
and Windows, and Acrobat Reader is no exception.

**Big spender:**

The commercial version of Adobe Acrobat can be purchased from Adobe's site for
$249. There is also a subscription version of the Create Adobe PDF Online service
that lets you create an unlimited number of PDF files online. This service costs $9.99
per month or $99.99 per year.

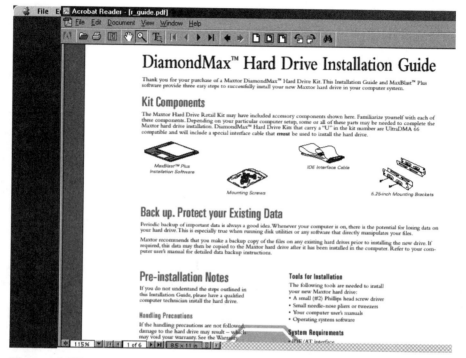

**Figure 4.23**
Adobe Acrobat preserves the original layout and type found in your original documents, but readers won't need the original application you used to create those documents.

URL: http://www.adobe.com/products/acrobat/readermain.html

**Contact:**  http://www.adobe.com/misc/comments.html

_X_  SOHO                    _X_  Small business

# FREE COUNTERS  . . . . . . . . . . . . . . . . . . . . . .

Keeping tabs on how many visitors your site has tracked can be helpful to you, but is also a great way for visitors to gauge the attention to your services. Table 4.2 shows how the free Web page counter services profited here compare on some useful features. A current list of sites that offer free Web counter services is available at http://www.thefreesite.com/freecounters.htm.

**Table 4.2**   Comparison of Free Web Counters

| Service | Styles | Choose starting point for counter? | Displays advertising? | Count unique visitors only? |
|---------|--------|-----------------------------------|----------------------|----------------------------|
| Counter4Free.com | Over 50 designs to choose from. | Yes | No | Yes |
| Freecounter | Two font sizes; any font color. | No | No | No |

## Counter4Free.com

This free service offers over 50 easy-to-install counter styles to choose from, and they're easy to install. Best of all, this service displays no ads on your counter. This counter is outfitted with what the service calls "reload protection," meaning that each unique visitor will be counted only once.

The various styles include a broad range of graphics for the numbers in a variety of colors and type styles. You can even register for as many counters as you like for your different pages.

**Getting started:**

When you sign up, you're first prompted to choose the design that you want. Your password, login, and HTML code will be e-mailed to the e-mail address that you supply.

Required information includes

- e-mail address
- password
- counter value (in case you don't want to start from zero!)

You can also sign up to receive site updates and announcements about other free services through an e-mail list.

**Big spender:**

No premium services.

URL: http://www.counter4free.com/

**Contact:**   support@counter4free.com

   X   SOHO                     ____ Small business

## Freecounter

This free service will host an extremely basic, but advertising-free, hit counter for your Web site.

You can choose between two font sizes and any text color. You will need to include on your own site any explanatory text or formatting you want to appear around the hit counter.

**Getting started:**

After you register and sign in, the service will e-mail you a snippet of HTML code to include on your Web page to keep an ongoing tally of the number of hits your site receives.

Required information includes

- your full name
- e-mail address
- username
- background and foreground colors

**Big spender:**

No premium services.

URL: http://www.freecounter.nu/
**Contact:**   support@freecounter.nu
  X   SOHO                    ____  Small business

# FREE SURVEYS AND POLLS . . . . . . . . . . . . . . .

Adding a poll to your Web site is one of the best ways you can add interactivity to your pages and generate new traffic. The following sites offer quick resources for designing and powering your own online polls—and in some cases, they'll even help you think up the questions to ask! You can also use surveys and polls to help improve your site's products and organization based on visitor feedback. Table 4.3 summarizes the main features in the free Web survey and poll services described in this section.

**Table 4.3**  Comparison of Free Web Polls

| Service | Number of questions | Question type | Styles | Advertising? |
|---|---|---|---|---|
| Alxpoll | 1 | Multiple choice | Four to choose from. | Survey results include a link back to Alxpoll's service. |
| Freepolls.com | 1 to 10 | Multiple choice | Custom designs are available for a premium. | Yes, banner ads display unless you pay a premium. |
| Zoomerang | Up to 20 | Multiple choice, free text, matrix-type questions, free text questions. | Several dozen templates and designs are available. | Zoomerang branding appears after visitors complete poll or survey. |

## Alxpoll

With Alxpoll, you can generate the HTML to place a single-question poll on your Web site. You can present up to 20 responses per question, and best of all, your poll and its results display without any advertising.

The service even gives you the ability to prevent the same users from voting more than once. The poll creation wizard gives you the ability to modify the design scheme: You can set the colors for the text, links, headers, and background image, and set the table border size.

The site's administrative tool gives you options for resetting the poll counters and removing the poll from your account. Your poll responses can be selectable via radio buttons, checkboxes (which allow for multiple selections), or a drop-down menu. You can let viewers click a link to see real-time results before or after they've voted. The results are updated dynamically and display in bar chart form.

**Getting started:**

The site's step-by-step wizard will prompt you to first create a question, then supply each of the possible responses (see Figure 4.24). You're then shown the HTML markup for adding a table-based poll box on your Web site, plus the URL if you just want to link directly to the form on Alxpoll's server.

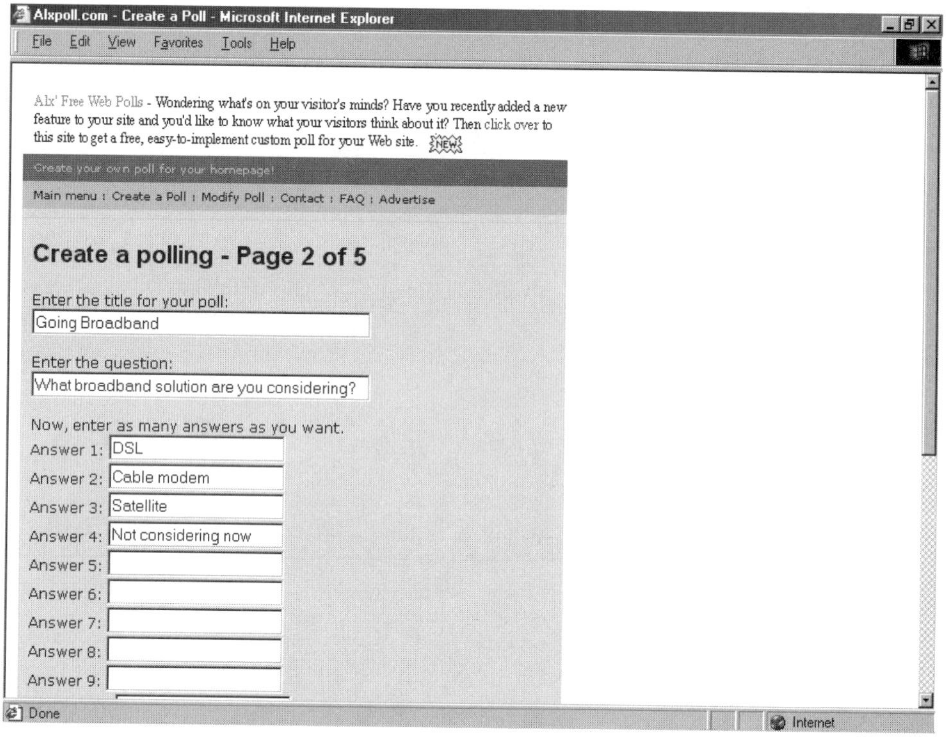

**Figure 4.24**
To create your own online poll with Alxpoll, you fill out a Web-based form with your questions and answers.

Required information includes

- e-mail address
- your home page's URL and title
- a content category that describes your site (choose from a list)

**Big spender:**

No premium services.

URL: http://www.alxnet.com/

**Contact:**   http://www.alxnet.com/company/contact.html

    X  SOHO                    ____  Small business

# Freepolls.com

This site offers two free poll services. One is for creating an instant, single-question poll; with the other, you can create up to 10 questions with up to 15 answers. A number of colorful examples are provided, along with straightforward links for continuing on to either create or modify a poll. When you're finished creating your poll, the HTML code that you'll need to add to your Web page to display your poll is automatically generated.

**Getting started:**

The site's step-by-step wizard will prompt you to first create a question, then supply each of the possible responses. You can preview what your survey will look like at any point during the survey creation process. A number of initial template questions are provided to help you get started.

Required information includes

- e-mail address
- your home page's URL and title
- a content category that describes your site (choose from a list)

**Big spender:**

You'll pay a premium to remove the banner ads from both your poll and results pages. The service charges $10 per 1,000 pages served.

URL: http://www.freepolls.com/

**Contact:**   info@freepolls.com

   X   SOHO                          X   Small business

# Zoomerang

Zoomerang is a Web-based service for creating, deploying, and managing your own online survey from scratch within minutes. You can ask up to 20 questions in each survey, with up to 100 response choices for each question and different question types allowed.

Each survey is hosted on Zoomerang's Web site; an e-mail message containing the survey's URL is sent to your target audience. Through the service's extensive list management capabilities, you can create and manage e-mail lists for your target audience, and you can also use Zoomerang's panel of volunteer respondents. You're asked if you want to receive such surveys from others when you register at the site.

The service includes a number of prebuilt surveys in four categories—Business, Community, Personal/Social, and Education—which you can edit and use as your own. The templates and question types provided let you include multiple choice, free text, matrix-type questions, and other common survey question types. You have limited formatting capabilities, mainly in terms of changing the color scheme.

The e-mail message that your survey respondents will receive includes a long disclaimer from Zoomerang. After they complete the survey, users will see an ad inviting them to sign up with Zoomerang as panel members or survey creators. The site will continue to track responses to your survey until you use the site management tools to close the survey. Once you close a survey, you're unable to access it for later reference or re-use it as a template in building future surveys.

Unfortunately, there are some features desirable in an online survey manager that are not supported. If you decide to change a question after the survey is deployed, you'll need to resubmit the survey all over again. You cannot limit users to respond only once, and you cannot designate any questions as mandatory or validate data as it's submitted. You also can't include images or ask branching questions, in which users see different followup questions based on their answers to a given question. If you hope to mine some serious data analyses from your online surveys, Zoomerang's parent company, MarketTools, offers a commercial solution called zTelligence. If you're looking for an easy way to solicit instant feedback from your site visitors about their experiences or poll their opinions on a variety of current topics, Zoomerang will add a great deal of entertainment value to your site.

**Getting started:**

After you register and log in, you're prompted to click a New Survey link to create your own. At this point, you can choose one of the sample surveys from the four categories or create a new survey from scratch. When you choose a preexisting survey, you'll see the questions display as they would to your target audience. You can choose a new color theme—mainly for the background tables, buttons and headers—and choose to modify or delete a question by clicking Edit or Delete.

Once you finish creating a survey, you can launch your survey immediately or take it on a practice run. You're also prompted to supply the e-mail addresses for the target audience and supply text for the e-mail message sent to survey respondents. Return to My Surveys on the Zoomerang site to locate your survey, and click on View Reports to monitor the results.

Separate registration forms are provided for U.S. and non-U.S. residents. Required information includes

- full name
- zip code
- gender
- e-mail address

You'll also be prompted to indicate if you'd like to sign up to receive the Zoomerang e-mail newsletter, and if you'd like to take surveys on topics of interest to you.

**Big spender:**

For a $200 fee, you can have results to any Zoomerang survey sent to one or more e-mail addresses at any time in a spreadsheet format, which is useful if you do not have other means to conduct analysis or reporting. A premium service called zTelligence includes extended data storage; branching questions; private label branding; the ability to upload images, audio, and video; and more complex data analysis.

URL: http://www.zoomerang.com/

**Contact:**   customerservice@zoomerang.com

    X   SOHO             ____ Small business

# FREE CHAT, GUESTBOOKS, AND MESSAGE BOARDS . . . . . . . . . . . . . . . .

It's good to have customers, better to have clients, and best to have community. Communities provide a way for you to tune your product mix and services, and the excitement around a community can create a powerful network to build businesses. Of course, criticism is always an issue whenever you let your customers speak out, but generally, most people are quite impressed if you take the time to listen, and they can turn around completely if you make the effort to act on their suggestions.

## BeSeen.com

Part of the LookSmart search portal, BeSeen.com offers free chat rooms, guestbooks, and bulletin boards. These services are all remotely hosted on BeSeen's servers, so there are no CGI programs to configure on your end.

When you create a chat room facility, you'll have the ability to require usernames and passwords. You can add your site's own look and feel to the chat room, but an advertising banner displays in a top frame over the chat interface.

Similarly, the bulletin board feature can sport your site's design, but will display a constant banner ad at the top. Threaded discussions can be viewed by topic or by date; links to access the guidelines or contact the administrator are also included.

Advertising is also present when visitors view the guestbook or add their own comments. Visitors can include their own home page name and URL.

One recent addition to the site's hosted services is Quizlet, a tool for providing online polls that dynamically update in real time. The site can also create a

QuickNav, which is a pop-up menu that lets you quickly move to different Web pages on a site (see Figure 4.25).

**Getting started:**

After you register, BeSeen.com will send you an e-mail containing your account information and instructions on using your new online tools. Required information includes

- your name
- e-mail address
- a category description for your site

**Big spender:**

No premium services.

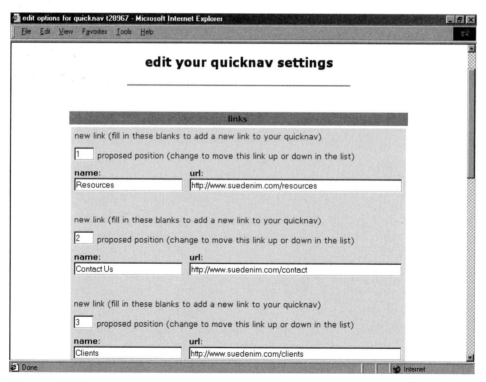

**Figure 4.25**
You can create an instant navigation interface, known as a QuickNav, using BeSeen.com's easy-to-use Web front-end.

URL: http://www.beseen.com/

**Contact:**   http://www.beseen.com/help/

  X   SOHO                    ____   Small business

## Free Gbook

This service will remotely host a guestbook for visitors to your site to leave comments. Best of all, the guestbook pages are entirely advertising-free.

The administration section of the site lets you modify your guestbook's appearance and remove any unwanted messages. You can also edit some features of your guestbook's appearance, including background colors, text size and color, and your guestbook's title. The HTML code you need to insert on your home page is presented on the administration page for you to copy and paste.

**Getting started:**

When you register at the site, you'll be prompted to create a password for accessing your guestbook's administrative features. Your guestbook's URL will then display on-screen and the necessary information is e-mailed to you as well. Required information includes

- e-mail address
- your site's URL
- your site's name
- guestbook title
- language (choose from English, French, Dutch, and Swedish)
- password

**Big spender:**

No premium services.

URL: http://www.freegbook.nu/

**Contact:**   http://www.freegbook.nu/support.html

  X   SOHO                    ____   Small business

## SitePowerUP

SitePowerUP.com provides remotely hosted resources for Web sites to provide interactivity for their users. The site's message boards are the landmark tool.

The service's message boards are extremely configurable, with a threaded message interface to help keep discussion topics together and on track. You can also utilize a suite of administration functions to let you and up to five subadministrators control what topics display and to delete messages. If you want to host multiple discussion boards, you'll need to register multiple times.

Upcoming services include online polls and forms processing.

**Getting started:**

The service has a sign-up wizard to simplify the login process. Your personal user ID is e-mailed to you at the end of the registration process. When you log in upon subsequent visits, you'll immediately see the administrative tools available to you. Required information includes

- full name
- e-mail address
- age
- state and country

**Big spender:**

No premium services.

URL: http://www.sitepowerup.com/

**Contact:**   http://www.sitepowerup.com/help/

  X   SOHO                          ___  Small business

# FREE SEARCH . . . . . . . . . . . . . . . . . . . . . . .

If you're a programming novice or otherwise don't have the ability to install search software on your own Web site, then a remote freeware search engine—hosted and administered on a third-party site—is a good solution for you. These services don't require you to have any programming expertise or access to your Web server. They act like standard robot spiders, following links on your site, rather than using your site's local file system. While all provide simple, straightforward searches, the more sophisticated offer powerful advanced search functions (sometimes for a price), such as proximity operators, date-range searching, and control of the results formats. Users can search your site without your needing to install anything but a few lines of HTML code on your pages to allow a search request to be sent. The search services covered in this section also allow you to customize the look and feel of your search results, at least to a certain extent.

## Atomz.com

Atomz.com's Atomz Search service provides free Web search engine capabilities you can leverage without having to place ad banners on your search pages or results. When a visitor to your site enters a query in the search form on your site, the query goes to the Atomz Search server application, performs the lookup, and formats the results in HTML before sending them back to display on your site.

If you have some knowledge of HTML, you can control exactly how the search results appear and make the transition between your own Web site and the Atomz.com Search site's display of your search results completely seamless. Otherwise, you can choose from a number of ready-to-use templates (see Figure 4.26).

After an initial indexing collects all the words on your site, your site will be reindexed on a weekly basis or upon demand. When you've changed the content of your Web site, for example, you reindex it by going to Atomz.com and clicking the Index panel in the Atomz.com member center. Atomz.com Search will immediately

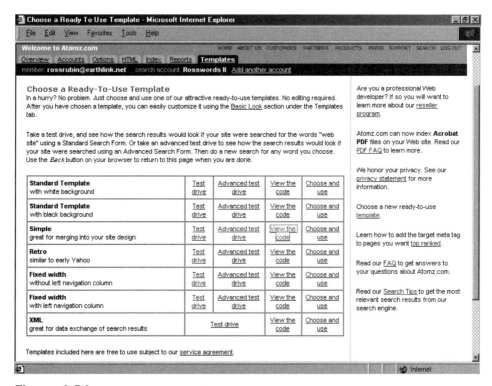

**Figure 4.26**
Atomz.com's free templates provide an extremely speedy means to adding search capabilities to your Web site.

download and index the content that has changed. You can also schedule Atomz.com Search to periodically index your site at a time of your choosing. No advertising appears on your search results, but the Atomz.com logo is ever-present. (Logo-free search results are a premium service.)

The service's options let you limit searching to specific portions of your sites, edit the way your search results display, view the indexing logs, perform test searches of your site, specify synonyms for search terms to improve results returned, and target documents to be returned at the top of search results. You can review statistics for searches made by visitors on your site over the past two months, which can help you glean insights into what users are searching your site for. The service can be used to index and search PDF files on your site, as well as Macromedia Flash content. Another bonus of the indexing feature is that it will point out any broken links it discovers on your site.

Atomz.com is free for indexed sites that total fewer than 500 pages and for fewer than 5,000 user searches per month.

**Getting started:**

An instructions section is shown on every screen of the login process, reminding you what information needs to be provided and what button to push to continue to the next page. After registering to use Atomz.com Search, you need to add a small amount of HTML code to your Web pages—which is e-mailed to you upon registration—so that visitors can conduct searches on your site.

Required information includes

- your e-mail address
- your URL
- a category describing your site's content (from a predefined list)
- first and last name
- street address
- telephone number
- time zone (for reports and index scheduling)

**Big spender:**

This premium service is unbranded and is primarily meant for Web developers who would like to use the Atomz.com Search engine on Web sites they design for paying clients. These sites can be indexed nightly or on demand. Charges are:

250 pages and 2,500 searches/month:   $75 per year

500 pages and 5,000 searches/month: $150 per year

> 1,000 pages and 10,000 searches/month:   $300 per year
> 2,500 pages and 25,000 searches/month:   $600 per year
> 5,000 pages and 50,000 searches/month: $1,200 per year

URL: http://www.atomz.com/

**Contact:**   support@atomz.com

   X   SOHO                              ____   Small business

# FreeFind

As the name implies, the FreeFind search service adds free local site searching capabilities to your Web site. After a quick setup process, you can have your site indexed with an automatically generated site map hosted on FreeFind's servers. Each time you update content on your site, you can send the FreeFind robot out to reindex your site.

FreeFind will automatically e-mail you the HTML you can cut-and-paste to place a search box on your Web pages. You can customize the page display of your search page and results, from background colors to titles and logos.

You're also given the option to choose a time interval to use to reindex your site and track details of visitors' searches. You can receive reports for your FreeFind account that show your site's daily search activity levels, the most common search words used in queries on your site, and the most recent queries.

The service is supported by advertising, which displays as ad banners on your search results.

**Getting started:**

After you register, the FreeFind robot sends further instructions and setup information to your e-mail address. You'll need to revisit the FreeFind site to dispatch the service's spider to index your site.

From the control center (see Figure 4.27), you can also customize your search and search results pages by selecting from a variety of logos and backgrounds or by using your own logo and background.

Required information includes

- your Web site's URL
- your e-mail address
- a category describing your site's content (from a predefined list)
- estimated number of pages on your site

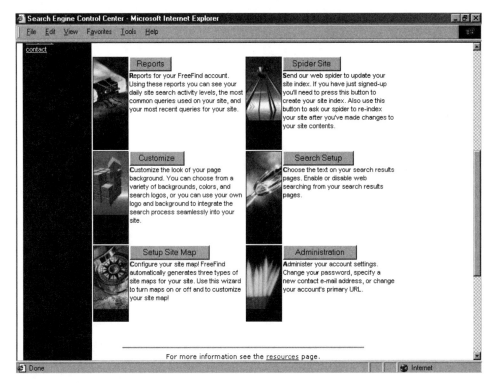

**Figure 4.27**
Use FreeFind's control center to customize how your search results will display.

**Big spender:**

Several pricing plans for ad-free subscriptions are available. An enterprise-wide license allows automatic daily indexing of up to 5,000 pages as well as unlimited on-demand re-indexing for an annual cost of $799.

For smaller sites (up to 2,500 pages), an enterprise-wide license runs $399 per year. The standard site subscription is designed for corporate and organization Web sites up to 1,000 pages and costs $199 per year. If you run a small organization, family business, sole proprietorship, or small nonprofit organization, the economy subscription handles up to 250 pages and costs $59 per year.

URL: http://www.freefind.com/

**Contact:**    http://www.freefind.com/contact.html

    X  SOHO                        X  Small business

## whatUseek intraSearch

This highly customizable, free search service will index up to 1,000 pages on your Web site and revisit them on a weekly basis for reindexing.

whatUseek intraSearch gives you the ability to modify the format of your search engine's results. You can tailor the graphics of the search page to suit your site's layout, and change the colors and headers on your results pages.

**Getting started:**

After you complete the online registration, the service e-mails you instructions for embedding a JavaScript-driven search box on your Web pages. You're prompted to log in to your account in order to activate the service's spider to crawl your site to create a search index. An online FAQ is available at http://intra.whatUseek.com/faq.shtml. Required information includes

- your name
- your e-mail address
- your street address
- your site's subject category
- a title for your Web site
- your site's URL
- an administrative password

**Big spender:**

No premium services.

URL: http://intra.whatuseek.com/

**Contact:**   comments@whatseek.com

  X   SOHO                ____ Small business

# FREE SITE CHECKING . . . . . . . . . . . . . . . . . .

While many easy-to-use Web site builders hide the code behind every Web page, they all use HTML to define the content's formatting and, in a broad sense, the page layout. While HTML is relatively simple, it can contain errors like any other computer language. Errors in your pages can slow down your pages or prevent them from loading. This may frustrate your visitors and creates a bad impression that transcends the site and becomes more generalized toward your products or services. Fortunately, a number of sites can help ensure that your pages are abiding by the rules of the Web.

## Doctor HTML

Doctor HTML is a Web page analysis tool that retrieves an HTML page and reports on any problems that it finds. You can check the markup for any individual HTML page for free and without registering, but there is a limit on the number of page reports you can run on any given day.

If you sign up for an RxHTMLpro account, you can run as many single-page reports as you want with no per-day limits. If you sign up for the premium Site Doctor service, you can map and analyze a bunch of pages at once. For pages that change frequently, you can schedule the Doctor to automatically check your pages for you at given intervals.

**Getting started:**

After you register for an RxHTMLpro account, you will receive an e-mail message with your new account password, which you can use immediately with your five free reports. Required information includes

- username
- e-mail address
- name
- street address
- phone number

Click the Single Page Analysis link in the left-hand navigator whenever you want to validate a single HTML page.

**Big spender:**

You can purchase online reports to run automatically or on demand using the Site Doctor service, which allows you to diagnose an entire Web site at once. For a fee, you can also license Doctor HTML for use on an intranet. Licensing will also give you access to the Site Doctor.

URL: http://www.imagiware.com/RxHTML/

**Contact:**   http://www.imagiware.com/RxHTML/htdocs/docfeed.html

    X   SOHO                    ____   Small business

## WDG HTML Validator

With the WDG HTML Validator, you can check the HTML markup for either a single page or a batch of pages. The validator objectively checks your page's tags against HTML syntax standards. The service has information on troubleshooting common validation problems and offers tips on using the validator.

**Getting started:**

Enter the URL of an HTML document to validate. To quickly validate multiple URLs, try the batch mode. Alternatively, you can validate files on your computer or you can enter your HTML directly. No registration is required.

**Big spender:**

No premium services.

URL: http://www.htmlhelp.com/tools/validator/

**Contact:** liam@htmlhelp.com

  <u>X</u>  SOHO             ____ Small business

# FREE SITE STATISTICS . . . . . . . . . . . . . . . . . . .

The Internet service provider who hosts your site may provide some reports or statistics on who is visiting your site, but what if you're interested in more extensive information? Read on to find out about a third-party service that can provide this service in exchange for a link on your site back to their home page.

## HitBox.com

HitBox is a Web audience-analysis resource center service that can collect and store data from visitors to your site (see Figure 4.28), providing accurate, real-time accumulation of useful data by monitoring the information about trends and online transactions—in laymen's terms, the who, what, when, and where of every visit. HitBox has even begun tracking wireless visits.

Supported through an in-house, network-operating center, data is analyzed, stored, and then converted into relevant information you can use to help redefine and target your strategy.

On the home page, you can check out the top Web sites and access site features, such as a Free Chat and a Tell-A-Friend option. Once you've registered, you visit the Check Stats feature to access a site traffic review that's updated weekly. Additionally,

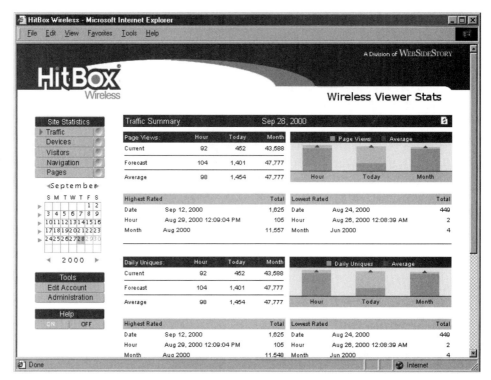

**Figure 4.28**
With HitBox's free Web site traffic reports, you can glean much useful information about your site visitors and how they're accessing your site.

the resources link takes you to a page divided into tabs labeled Building, Promoting, Reviews, and Downloads.

**Getting started:**

To start receiving your HitBox statistics for free, you'll need to display a small button on your pages. You may opt to earn revenue by displaying a larger, paid banner ad. With either option, you'll get traffic back to your site via rankings in HitBox.com and Yep.com. When you fill out the registration form, you'll be asked for the following information:

- Web site name and description
- site-related keywords
- time zone
- zip code

- country
- contact name
- e-mail address
- birth date

**Big Spender:**

For a fee, you can use HitBox's services without displaying a button or banner. Starting at $19.95 per month, HitBoxPro backs up your site statistics and removes the banner requirement. HitBox Enterprise is a high-end service with unlimited scalability.

URL: http://www.hitbox.com/

**Contact:**   enterprise@hitbox.com or comments@websidestory.com

  X  SOHO                  X  Small business

# SUMMARY . . . . . . . . . . . . . . . . . . . . . . . . .

In this chapter, you've learned about free Web design, hosting, and development services that can give your business a boost by helping you launch a good-looking, interactive Web site. These services should help reassure you that even if you've always been intimidated by technology, there's no need to spend a fortune to develop your Web presence.

Up ahead in Chapter 5, you'll learn about services that can help you take your new Web site to the next level of e-commerce through buying and selling your goods online.

# 5
# Selling Online

..........................

**Y**ou've moved on from managing people and projects to assembling the tools needed to build your virtual store, but can you actually sell online? And for free? Absolutely. Web sites will furnish just about everything you need to hang out your cybershingle, from affiliate programs and hosted stores to ways of keeping in touch with your customers. Home office warriors can also track down gigs through a couple of sites just for them.

## AFFILIATE PROGRAMS . . . . . . . . . . . . . . . . . . .

Affiliate programs play upon the old technique of network marketing made famous (or infamous) by such companies as Amway, NuSkin, and Tupperware. The idea is that having many people sell your goods and services is a great way to build exposure.

As a participant in the affiliate program, you place links from the merchant on your site. These links market the merchant's goods or services on your own site. Site visitors who click through on the link are sent to a specified page of the merchant's site, which tracks that they arrived via your site. If the visitor completes the action desired by the merchant—sometimes just clicking on a link, but more often actually making a purchase—then you'll be compensated.

There are significant differences between these online affiliate programs and traditional network marketing, though. You cannot get a cut of the revenue for those you have referred, so no "pyramid effect" can ever take hold. Also, while companies such as NuSkin typically don't sell directly in addition to through their agents (although Tupperware now sells online), virtually all companies that have affiliate programs sell directly from their sites.

In many cases, you'll receive e-mails from each merchant partner you've signed up with, welcoming you to their affiliate program and including links to obtain reports. Even at the collections for affiliate programs listed in this section, you'll need to run individual reports for each merchant partner to see how successful your links are. The trick, then, is to take advantage of these programs without spending an inordinate amount of time tracking what may turn out to be a very small return in terms of commissions. Table 5.1 shows you at a glance what the free affiliate programs described in this section have to offer.

## Commission Central

Commission Central is essentially a clearinghouse for affiliate programs; with a single sign-up, you can join as many of its partners' affiliate programs as interest you (see Figure 5.1). When you add links on your own Web site to the service's merchant partners, you can earn up to a 40 percent commission on all sales made through your site.

**Table 5.1** Comparing Affiliate Programs

| Service | Number of merchant partners | Single sign-up? | Notes |
|---|---|---|---|
| Commission Central | About 10 | Yes | Commission Central uses BeFree's reporting.net technology, but you'll need to log in to Commission Central to look up these merchant partners. |
| LinkShare | 500 | Yes | The multiple affiliate site report lets you see how your merchant partner links compare to each other. |
| BeFree | Hundreds | Yes | Superior tracking and reporting tools. |
| Refer-it | Over 3,000 | No | Exhaustive, detailed listings of individual companies and their affiliate programs. |

**Figure 5.1**
From a central administration page on Commission Central, you can read information about each of the affiliate programs you've joined.

If you don't yet have your own Web page, Commission Central promotes prominent links to go create your own for free at Tripod or Angelfire (see Chapter 4)—which, like Commission Central itself, are Lycos properties.

### Getting started:

As part of the registration process, you'll be asked to choose which merchant affiliate programs you'd like to join. Upon return visits, you can access the Your Merchant Partners page. To add additional merchants at a later time, just click on the words "Apply to Other Merchants" in the navigation bar anywhere within Commission Central. Required information includes

- your site's name and URL
- your mailing address
- country
- telephone number

- primary contact name and title
- pay-to address (if different from above)

You'll also be asked how many unique visitors your Web site logs each month and how many page views your site receives per month.

**Big spender:**

No premium services.

URL: http://commission-central.lycos.com/

**Contact:**   commission-central-help@lycos.com

   _X_  SOHO                          _X_  Small business

# LinkShare

This comprehensive affiliate program includes over 500 merchant partners. Given the range of partners, you're more than likely to find a number of programs and merchants you'll be interested in linking to. Just click on the merchant's name to create links for the merchant programs you want to join. Copy and paste this HTML code into your Web pages. You can return to the LinkShare site at any time to run reports to see how effective your links are and how many click-throughs you've received.

**Getting started:**

Log in to your account with your username and password, then click on the Create Links tab of your control panel. When you register, you're asked for the following information:

- your site's name and URL
- your tax identification number
- one or more categories to describe your site
- information about your site's statistics and visitor demographics
- your full name and e-mail address
- your mailing address
- country
- telephone number
- billing name

You're also prompted to complete a W-9 form so that payments for any commissions that you earn will not be delayed.

**Big spender:**

No premium services.

URL: http://www.linkshare.com/

**Contact:**   contact@linkshare.com

  X  SOHO           X  Small business

# BeFree

BeFree, a technology provider for affiliates, provides a one-stop means for signing up with hundreds of affiliate partners on its site. You can then find additional affiliates, using BeFree's Web-based tools, and quickly distribute promotions via those tools.

The company's Webmaster management tools and affiliate reports are their strong suit, and are licensed by other affiliate clearinghouses like Commission Central.

**Getting started:**

Merchant names are listed in both a categories and an alphabetical list. Check the checkbox next to each merchant's name and click the Add Selected Merchants button. When you're done selecting merchants, you'll be asked for the following registration information:

- your site's name and URL
- your mailing address
- country
- telephone number
- primary contact name and title
- pay-to address (if different from above)

**Big spender:**

No premium services.

URL: http://www.befree.com/

**Contact:**   http://www.befree.com/docs/contact/

  X  SOHO           X  Small business

## Refer-it

Launched in December 1997, Refer-it.com is an extremely extensive directory of Web-based affiliate and referral programs, with more than 3,300 programs listed in its database to date. Each of its affiliate programs are rated across a common set of criteria, including amount of revenue share, ease of implementation, responsiveness, reporting capabilities, clarity of the terms and conditions, and availability of free content.

In addition, each listing on Refer-it.com includes a description of the program, links to join the program, fee information, launch date of the program, the program category, and even a list of Web sites that currently belong to that program.

One big difference between Refer-it and the other affiliate program clearinghouses described here is that Refer-it does not offer a one-stop registration process to simplify your signing on to multiple merchant programs. You must select the programs that you are interested in and then apply to each program individually.

**Getting started:**

To add merchant partners to your site, you can search the categories from the Refer-it home page to find individual merchants and sign up directly with these individual programs. You can also register separately at the Refer-it site as a Webmaster or Merchant to access additional tools and resources. Webmasters are asked for the following information:

- your site's name, URL, and a descriptive category
- your e-mail address
- an estimate of your site traffic in terms of page views and unique users per month
- your company name
- your full name
- mailing address
- telephone and fax number
- pay-to address (if different from above)

**Big spender:**

Refer-it's Premium Webmaster account costs $49.95. It includes a one-year subscription to *Business 2.0* magazine and capabilities for creating your own online store with all the revenue-sharing programs you've joined.

URL: http://www.refer-it.com/

**Contact:** carko@internet.com

   X   SOHO                 X   Small business

# AUCTIONS . . . . . . . . . . . . . . . . .  - - - - .

In general, online auctions aren't really free—small fees for listing your items for sale are common, and these services usually take a small percentage of the final sale price as a transaction fee. Many, though, offer free listings. For aggregating interested purchasers and enabling the bidding process, these sites can extend your commerce capabilities far beyond what you could provide without outside assistance. Table 5.2 lists the fees charged and escrow services used by the auction sites described in this section.

**Table 5.2**  Comparing Auction Sites

| Service | Fees | Escrow services used | Notes |
|---------|------|----------------------|-------|
| eBay | Sellers are charged an insertion fee just for opening an auction, which is usually between $0.25 and $2.00, depending on your opening bid. Sellers are also charged at the end of the auction, generally ranging from 1.25% to 5% of your final sale price. | i-Escrow, Inc., a subsidiary of Tradenable | Difficult to customize the look and feel of the auction pages, so they're not easy to integrate into your own site. |
| Amazon.com Auctions | You're charged 5% for items whose final sale price is less than $25. For items that sell for between $25 and $1,000, you're charged $1.25 plus 2.5% of the final sale price. For items that sell for more than $1,000, you're charged $25.63 and 1.25% of the final sales price. | i-Escrow, TradeSafe | Take-It feature makes it easy to end auctions earlier than planned. Simpler than eBay for posting items for sale. |

# eBay

eBay is by far the largest auction site. While it is mostly focused on consumer-to-consumer, many traditional retailers put their wares up for auction on eBay rather than create their own e-commerce Web site. If you're looking for an easy introduction to e-tailing, online auctions are a fun approach. The cost is minimal and the bidding nature of each sale can drive the selling price way up.

If you're a seller, you'll be charged an insertion fee just for opening an auction (see Figure 5.2). This fee is usually between $0.25 and $2.00, depending on your opening bid. You're also charged a final sale price fee at the end of your auction, which generally ranges from 1.25 percent to 5 percent of your final sale price. Sellers are judged on the basis of feedback—comments that buyers leave about a transaction. Smooth transactions that are carried out expediently, without any disagreement about the quality of the goods provided, will add to your feedback rating, which is affiliated

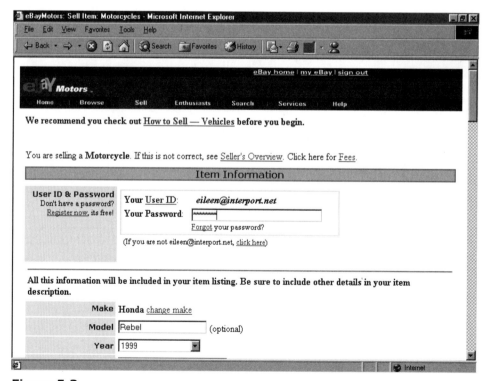

**Figure 5.2**
When you open an auction to sell goods, you may be prompted to enter details based on the sales category you choose.

with different colored stars. A yellow star is granted after 10 feedback points, while those with over 10,000 feedback points get a "shooting star." This can, of course, take years to achieve.

eBay has partnered with TradeOut, an online business surplus marketplace, for businesses that wish to sell or buy bulk surplus goods. The site also offers additional listing options and features, including Gift Icon, 10-day Auctions, Shipping and Payment Terms, and Gallery and Featured Gallery options.

On the down side, it's difficult to customize the look and feel of your pages on eBay, which can have a jarring effect if you're driving customers visiting at your home page onward to bid on your wares. Many retailers do list their home page URLs on every auction they run on eBay, though, and eBay provides an About Me feature, where you can include information about yourself for your fellow sellers and bidders to see.

### Getting started:

To use the Mister Lister Composer application, you must be a registered eBay user who meets the following requirements:

- maintain a credit card on file with eBay
- feedback rating of 10 or more
- registered on eBay for 60 days or more

Mister Lister includes a Composer part, an easy-to-use software tool that helps you list a collection of items on your computer before sending to eBay, and Online Mister Lister Reviewer pages where you can preview, edit, and approve your item collections. Note that there are several commercial alternatives to Mister Lister, not created by eBay, with more features for frequent sellers.

When you register for eBay, you'll need to provide a valid credit card number before you can list your goods and services—even if you only plan to sell goods and not buy them. You'll also need to provide

- your name
- billing address
- credit card expiration date

### Big spender:

eBay can connect you with third-party appraisal services to verify or provide an extra opinion on an item's worth. When you list an item for sale, you can also pay for additional listings to further market your listings.

eBay's escrow service, i-Escrow, Inc., a subsidiary of Tradenable, gives sellers the opportunity to inspect and approve a returned item before the buyer gets refunded. i-Escrow's fees are based on the amount of the transaction and the method of payment.

URL: http://www.ebay.com/

**Contact:**   http://pages.ebay.com/help/

_X_  SOHO                  _X_  Small business

## Amazon Auctions

Amazon.com is one of the numerous online retailers that have copied eBay's lead by adding auctions to their sites. Amazon's offering, though, is a combination of auctions and traditional sales. In addition to straight auctions and Dutch auctions (for multiple, identical items), merchants and independent sellers can use Amazon's zShops program to offer wares for a fixed price through Amazon. Prospective buyers, in turn, can search through those items on Amazon's main site.

In an Amazon auction, buyers may end an auction immediately by agreeing to pay a price preset by the seller. Amazon calls this its "Take-It" feature.

Sellers are charged listing and completion fees—steeper than eBay and some other competitors—as well as fees for any optional display features they select to enhance their listings. You're charged 5 percent for items whose final sale price is less than $25. For items that sell for between $25 and $1,000, you're charged $1.25 plus 2.5 percent of the final sale price.

**Getting started:**

Once you register, setting a price and selling your item is as simple as clicking on the Sell Items button that appears at the upper right corner of every Amazon.com page.

All that's needed to sell an item on zShops is a title, a description, a price, a category, and a location. You can provide much more information in the Sell Your Item Now form—from shipping terms to your location to a photo (see Figure 5.3)—to ensure your 14-day listing is as successful as possible.

If you have already registered on Amazon.com to buy books, you just need to sign in with your username and password to access the site's auctions.

If you're signing up for the first time, you register when you create your first auction listing. Required information includes:

- full name
- e-mail address

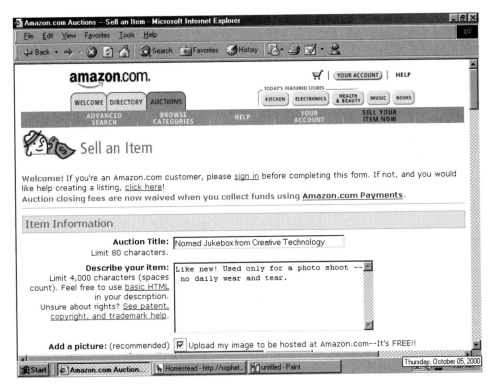

**Figure 5.3**
Detailed instructions on Amazon.com's site make it easy to put up goods for sale.

**Big spender:**

A $0.10 listing fee is charged for every item you list. If you create a zShop listing, you'll be charged $39.95 a month for listing up to 5,000 items, and $0.10 more monthly for each additional item.

There's also a completion fee for all sales. For both Amazon auctions and zShop transactions, the completion fee is based on the final sale price.

| Range of Final Price | Closing Fee |
| --- | --- |
| $0.01–$25.00 | 5 percent |
| $25.01–$1,000.00 | $1.25 plus 2.5 percent of any amount over $25.00 |
| $1,000.01 and up | $25.63 plus 1.25 percent of any amount over $1,000.00 |

In the case of a Dutch auction, the fee is based on the amount of the minimum winning bid multiplied by the quantity of items sold. If you plan to list frequently, you can save on fees through the Amazon.com Pro Merchant subscription. For an extra fee, you can highlight your listing's display in several ways.

| Bold listings: | $2.00 per listing |
| Category features: | $14.95 per listing |
| Home page featured listings: | $99.95 per listing on the zShops or Auctions home page |

For escrow service partners, Amazon.com offers a link to Tradenable's i-Escrow, Inc.

URL: http://auctions.amazon.com/

**Contact:**    http://s1.amazon.com/exec/varzea/subst/help/send-us-auction-email.html/
    _X_ SOHO                         _X_ Small business

# ESCROW SERVICES . . . . . . . . . . . . . . . . . . . . .

Escrow services exist to secure the transaction between buyers, sellers, and the auction company. An escrow company acts as a neutral middleman in the auction process, holding the buyer's money in trust until the seller sends the product to the buyer and the buyer indicates that he or she is happy with the purchase. Like all middlemen, escrow companies take a cut—usually between 2 and 5 percent of the item's price. Some escrow services also charge a minimum fee to cover transaction costs. Table 5.3 compares fees and services offered by the leading players described in this section.

For sellers, escrow services can provide protection against credit card fraud, insufficient funds, and credit card chargebacks. An escrow service can also enable you to easily accept payment by credit card.

## Tradenable's i-Escrow

If you make or offer major online auction purchases and you fear a rip-off, Tradenable's i-Escrow service will hold a payment in trust until the goods are examined and the buyer can check things out. The money is held in trust until the buyer is satisfied with the delivered goods, and then is transferred to the seller. Everybody's happy, especially Tradenable, which takes up to a 4 percent cut of the final sale price.

**Getting started:**

You may buy or sell goods using i-Escrow either directly from the Tradenable site or from an auction site that offers its services (see "Free Auctions" in the previous section). When you log in by entering your e-mail address and password, you will be taken to the QuikTrack interface, which lets you view a summary of all your i-Escrow transactions, including the transaction status.

**Table 5.3**  Comparing Escrow Services

| Company | Services offered | Fees | Partners/alliances |
|---------|------------------|------|--------------------|
| i-Escrow, Inc., a subsidiary of Tradenable | A feature called QuikTrack lets customers track their transaction history and access transaction updates. Includes international sales. | Transactions under $100 are charged a $2.50 fee. Credit card transactions between $500 and $2,500 have a 4% fee; for cash transactions in the same amount, the fee is only 2%. | Has marketing alliances with a number of leading auction sites, Yahoo! Auctions, LookSmart, and Amazon.com. |
| TradeSafe | Includes a built-in fee calculator, transaction history reports, and an alliance program in which vendors can post the TradeSafe seal on their sites. | Charges 3.5% of the dollar amount of the sales plus $0.50 for credit card transactions. For cash payment, charges 2.5% for transactions up to $2,500. | Alliance partners include Lycos. |

At registration, you're asked for the following information:

- full name
- mailing address and country
- telephone number
- your preferred method of payment
- birth date

**Big spender:**

i-Escrow's service fee is based on the transaction amount and the method of payment used by the buyer (see Table 5.4). The transaction amount is defined as the merchandise purchase price plus the shipping fee, if any.

The i-Escrow service fee may be paid for by the buyer or seller, or split equally between the two—during the negotiation process at the beginning of the transaction,

**Table 5.4**   Service Fees

| Transaction amount | i-Escrow fee (using a credit card) | i-Escrow fee (cash) |
|---|---|---|
| Up to $100.00 | $2.50 | $2.50 |
| $100.01–$25,000.00 | 4% | 2% |
| $25000.01–$50,000 | 4% | 1% |
| Over $50,000 | Currently not accepted | 1% |

both parties must mutually agree upon who pays the fee. The buyer is responsible for paying the i-Escrow service fee for all returns, no matter who had initially agreed to pay the fee at the beginning of the transaction.

URL: http://www.tradenable.com/

**Contact:**   http://www.tradenable.com/contact_index.html

_X_ SOHO                          _X_ Small business

# TradeSafe

TradeSafe handles online payment orders for both auctions and online stores. Once visitors fill out the TradeSafe entry form, they're shown a selection of payment types.

Express payments expedite the payment process, but TradeSafe offers buyers a money-back guarantee. The exchange payments offer is a more typical escrow service: Buyers get to inspect their purchases before accepting them, and sellers are then paid only after buyer acceptance.

TradeSafe includes a list of the items it will not represent, such as cash advances, firearms, and illegal items.

You can also use TradeSafe to sell merchandise on your own Web site by creating one or more custom SiteSeller buttons that display the TradeSafe logo. When visitors click on the button, they will see the purchase details and can pay by credit card through TradeSafe—which eliminates any difficulties you'd have with accepting that form of payment.

**Getting started:**

Once you're registered, you can use your e-mail address and password to log in. At registration, you're asked for the following information:

- full name
- mailing address and country
- e-mail address

**Big spender:**

For credit card transactions, the fee is $0.50 per transaction plus 3.5 percent of the final sale amount, including the shipping costs. The cost for cash transactions is 2.5 percent of the final sale amount up to $2,500. For transactions over $2,500, the fee is $62.50 plus 1 percent of the amount over $2,500. Fees on all orders may be paid by either the seller or the buyer.

URL: http://www.tradesafe.com/

**Contact:**   http://www.tradesafe.com/contacts.cfm

  _X_  SOHO                  _X_  Small business

# FREE ONLINE PAYMENTS . . . . . . . . . . . . . . . .

Online auctions and the burgeoning numbers of small businesses going online have created a demand for services that can supply a secure, convenient, and inexpensive way to make person-to-person payments to, for instance, settle online auction deals. The following services are making it easier to accept credit card payments or otherwise transfer funds over the Web. Neither buyers nor sellers need to exchange personal information, credit card information, or bank account numbers. Table 5.5 displays the main features of each service's offerings at a glance.

## PayPal

X.com's PayPal payment system lets you send money electronically to others via e-mail or beamed through Net devices like Web-enabled cell phones. Best of all, PayPal is a completely free service. You won't be charged a percentage of the cost of the item or pay any transaction fee to use PayPal's Auction Payment services. The customer's funds are first backed by a credit card, debit card, or personal check, then depsoited in a PayPal account. The company's revenue comes from the float between the time the funds are sent and when they are actually cashed in.

PayPal transmits money from an existing PayPal account, credit card, or bank account to the recipient's e-mail account. After registering for the free service, consumers enter the recipient's name, e-mail address, and a dollar amount (see

**Table 5.5**  Comparing Online Payment Services

| Company | Means of payment | Fees | Security |
|---|---|---|---|
| PayPal | Payments can be made from an existing PayPal account, credit card, or bank account. | None | All information is transmitted via the SSL protocol. |
| ecount | Payments are made from your ecount account, which works just like a debit account. You can only deposit funds with a credit or debit card, not a check. | $6.95 one-time fee to obtain an ecount card, which can be used in stores and at ATMs. To add funds (via credit card) or withdraw funds (via check or ATM) from your ecount account, you're charged a $1 transaction. | All information is transmitted via the SSL protocol. |
| ProPay | The buyer's credit card (MasterCard or Visa) is charged directly. | As the seller, you pay all fees, which include 3.5% of all sales transactions, plus $0.35 per transaction. You are also charged for failed deposits to checking accounts ($5) or charges refused by credit cards ($30). | All information is transmitted via the SSL protocol. ProPay is designated a Verisign Secure Site. |

Figure 5.4). The money is debited from the payer's credit card or bank account and credited to the recipient. Buyer and seller alike must be registered with PayPal.

PayPal uses the Secure Sockets Layer protocol (SSL) with the highest level of encryption (128-bit) commercially available to encode confidential information during transmission for payment processing, to prevent third-party data interceptions. Before you register or log in to PayPal's site, its server checks that you're using an approved browser—namely, one that uses SSL 3.0 or higher.

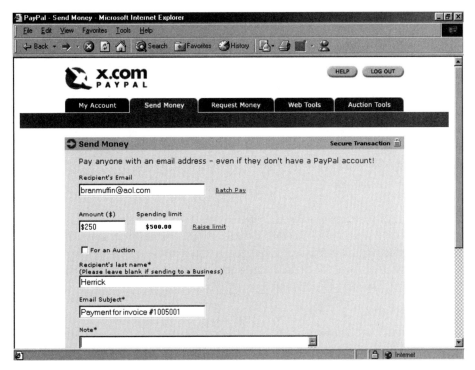

**Figure 5.4**
PayPal facilitates quick online payments, suitable for auction transactions or for any personal payment.

Sellers can accept MasterCard or Visa credit cards for free, and receive instant payment. You can use it on any auction site; PayPal boasts that it has become the top payment service on eBay. A current program (in the U.S. only) gives new members $5 just for signing up and $5 for each referral.

Since PayPal is not an escrow service, be warned that it cannot provide any assurance for goods you have purchased.

**Getting started:**

After you register, log in to PayPal.com, click the Auction Tools navigational tab, and click on Basic Logos. This section details how to place the PayPal logo and a brief statement explaining PayPal's service in the Description area of your auction listing. If you are selling on eBay, the PayPal AutoLink feature lets you automatically place a PayPal.com logo in all of your auction listings.

To request payment, you can send the buyer an Auction Payment Request. This is a customized bill found in the Auction Tools section. You create it by adding the buyer's e-mail address, the winning bid, and other optional details about the auction, such as the item, URL, and title. PayPal will automatically send this Payment Request to the buyer's e-mail address. The buyer can click on your unique referral link in the e-mail, sign up for PayPal, and send you the payment.

Required information includes

- your name
- mailing address
- evening phone number
- e-mail address

As part of the sign-up process, PayPal will send you a unique Street Address Confirmation Number via U.S. mail. To raise your charge limit to $5,000 and activate all the withdrawal features, you must enter this number after logging in to your PayPal account. This process is an added security measure that makes sure no one else can claim money in your account.

**Big spender:**

A Premier account, with a fee of 1.9 percent plus $0.25 on incoming payments, includes the following features:

- The ability to accept direct payments on your Web site or for your auctions
- A daily sweep of funds into your primary bank account
- The ability to accept unlimited credit card payments or batch payments
- A downloadable transaction history
- Round-the-clock call-center customer service

URL: http://www.x.com/

**Contact:**   http://www.paypal.x.com/cgi-bin/webscr?cmd=_contact-general

  X  SOHO                          ___  Small business

## ecount

With an ecount account, you can make free person-to-person payments via e-mail and readily shop online with money stored in your ecount account.

Using established financial services and Web infrastructures, ecount lets you conduct secure online transactions through prepaid personal accounts—just like a debit card. You can even obtain a physical ecount card, which you can use to spend the cash in your ecount anywhere offline and make withdrawals at ATMs.

You can create an ecount account at the company's Web site, where you can add funds, send money to anyone via e-mail, request and receive payments from others, shop at any online merchant, or transfer funds to a credit card account. You can add funds instantly to an ecount from a credit card account. You should be able to instantly spend your ecount funds at any online merchant that accepts credit cards.

The company has licensed its e-mail-based payment platform to popular portal sites such as cNet and also has licensing arrangements with AT&T, Charles Schwab & Co., and Ford Motor. In addition to its standalone online payment service, ecount powers Webcertificate.com, an online and offline gift certificate service, and Private-Buy.com, an anonymous shopping service.

**Getting started:**

Visit ecount.com and click the Sign Up button on the home page. Required information for setting up an account includes:

- your name
- e-mail address
- billing address
- phone number

A confirmation message is sent to your e-mail address and to your billing address. You'll then need to verify your e-mail address to activate your account.

**Big spender:**

If you want to obtain the ecount card, you'll be charged a one-time fee of $6.95. Anytime you withdraw money from your ecount account via check or an ATM withdrawal, you'll be charged a $1 transaction fee. There is also a $1 transaction fee to place funds in your ecount account when you do so using a credit card.

URL: http://www.ecount.com/

**Contact:**   customerservice@ecount.com

   _X_  SOHO           ____  Small business

# ProPay

ProPay lets you accept credit cards as payment for products and services without applying for a merchant account first. The company delivers the service by holding a master merchant account and allowing customers to transact under its umbrella. In this way, customers can preserve the full fraud protections afforded them when they pay for goods with a MasterCard or Visa credit card.

To charge your customer's credit card through ProPay, you need to first establish a ProPay account. Then, visit ProPay.com and click on the Web Pay button. You enter your customer's e-mail address and the amount you are requesting, along with the reason for the charge (see Figure 5.5). Your customer will then immediately receive an e-mail from ProPay containing your request. After your customer clicks on the URL embedded in the e-mail and provides his or her credit card information, ProPay will then put the fund into your account.

**Getting started:**

Visit ProPay.com and follow the link on the home page to sign up for a new account. Required information for setting up an account includes:

- your name
- e-mail address

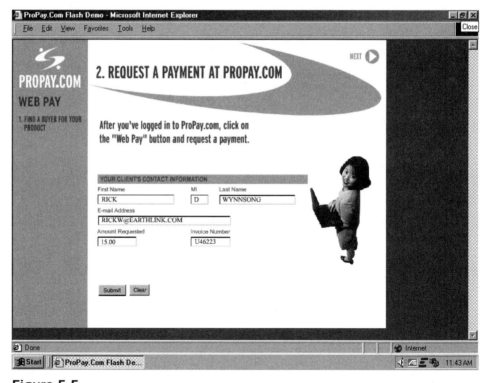

**Figure 5.5**
ProPay offers an online demo that details what happens at each step of a transaction using its services.

- billing address
- daytime and evening phone numbers
- Social Security number
- birth date

You will then receive an e-mail on the status of your account within three to five business days, after the company verifies the information you submitted. Currently, only applications from U.S. residents with valid Social Security numbers are accepted.

**Big spender:**

While setting up your account, adding, and exchanging funds are free, you start to incur transaction fees for all sales transactions and for moving funds to your account. With ProPay, the seller pays all transaction fees. You're charged 3.5 percent of the total sale, plus $0.35 to move funds to your bank account.

URL: http://www.propay.com/

**Contact:**   customerservice@propay.com

   X  SOHO                    X  Small business

# FREE SELLING . . . . . . . . . . . . . . . . . . . . . .

Simple sites are great for promoting a service or explaining your products, and auction sites can start you on your way to selling. But ultimately, you may want to truly customize your online store. The following Web sites focused on Internet selling can help you launch your small business onto the Net. Table 5.6 weighs their offerings in a single at-a-glance view.

## Bigstep

Bigstep.com gives you free online services to build and maintain a Web site. One of the niftier do-it-yourself Web-building tools here lets you create your own customized catalog or portfolio without needing to know any HTML. To add items to your catalog, you fill out a form for each item, although you may find this time consuming if you already have your data stored electronically. You can add any number of items to your site and ease navigation by creating any number of sections, which you can publish separately as you finish them. You'll have an unlimited number of Web pages and can store 12 MB worth of files for free.

**Table 5.6** *Comparing Services for Selling Online*

| Feature | Bigstep | eCongo | FreeMerchant |
|---|---|---|---|
| Custom catalog support | Yes, but you'll need to fill out a form for each item to add to the catalog. You cannot upload a database or spreadsheet. | Yes, you can choose from predesigned templates and upload your own images. | Yes. If your products are in a database/spreadsheet, you can upload them with the Catalog Importer after setting up your category structure. |
| Credit card payment processing | Yes, as a premium service with real-time verification. | Yes, as a premium service with real-time verification. | Yes, but you'll need to purchase a merchant account and a processing interface from a merchant service provider, not FreeMerchant. |
| Shipping and delivery support | No shipping outside the U.S. | Support for tax and shipping tables is built in seamlessly. International shipping is available. | An intuitive interface lets you set up shipping parameters, tax options, and shipping and return policies. |
| Shopping cart support | Yes | Yes | Yes |
| Inventory verification | No | Yes | Yes |
| Free disk space | 12 MB | Unlimited | Unlimited. For best performance, FreeMerchant recommends that its sites have no more than 1,000 items, nor more than 100 items in a category (or 50 with images). |

As you progress through the creation of your site, all of the tasks you have yet to complete are automatically added to a to-do list. You'll see icons that show you the status of tasks, indicating whether they are started, completed, or published. The site also features an extensive set of marketing ideas and tools for sending online newsletters.

Although Bigstep.com touts its free commerce capabilities (Figure 5.6), the site's credit card transaction processing is conducted through site partner Cardservice

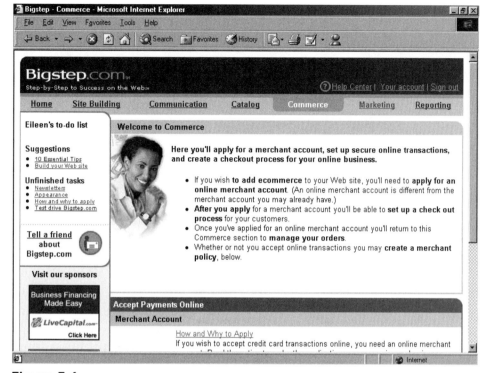

**Figure 5.6**
Bigstep.com provides instructions about how to accept credit cards, promote events, and move through its hosting services.

International, which charges both a monthly fee and a per-transaction fee. Note that non-U.S. credit card transactions are not supported; neither is shipping outside of the U.S. You can register your own domain name and have it hosted on Bigstep.com, if you wish, so that customers see your own URL and not a subpage off of Bigstep.com.

**Getting started:**

To use the Bigstep.com service, you'll need to meet the following technical requirements:

- A PC running Windows 95/98/NT or Macintosh operating system 7.0 (or newer)
- Netscape Navigator version 4.0 and up or Microsoft Internet Explorer version 4.*x* and up
- A modem capable of 28.8 kbps or greater

After you register, you'll be prompted to pick a unique, free Bigstep.com Web address, even if you plan to set up your personalized domain name with your Bigstep.com Web site.

Required information includes

- your e-mail address
- your full name
- business name
- zip code
- country
- a category that describes your business
- your role at your company and how many employees work in your business

**Big spender:**

To accept credit cards, you'll pay a $24.95 monthly fee plus an additional fee, which depends on the credit card, for each transaction. Other fees include a per transaction cost, and a $0.15 batch fee charged for each day you process transactions for that month.

URL: http://www.bigstep.com/

**Contact:**   support@bigstep.net

   X   SOHO                    _____  Small business

# eCongo

eCongo.com's e-commerce services include a Web store builder and administrator (no HTML knowledge necessary), multiple integrated payment methods, Web customer service, shipping and delivery management, and advertising and promotion services.

The service offers integrated real-time credit card processing as a premium paid service—starting with at least $34 in monthly processing fees—which is important to remember, since eCongo bills its services as enabling free commerce. Visitors to your site can pay by check, COD, phone ordering, and credit card capture. eCongo.com has also partnered with Cybergold to offer a flexible micropayments system for eCongo.com merchants.

As you create your basic online store, you can modify the overall appearance of the store by choosing from among 18 predefined design templates or by uploading your own custom images. The eCongo catalog lets you create departments, categories, and items; as a result, you'll want to plan, from the user's point-of-view, where visitors might go to look for certain items for sale. The service supports shopping carts so your customers can store items online before checkout.

As well as a product catalog, each eCongo store has four information pages automatically added in to it: a contacts page, an FAQ, a help section, and a returns policy page. You can specify the content of each of these four sections by completing a simple form. However, the tools make it difficult to preview your changes in progress. You must select a Manager/Publisher function to request a preview update—which can be time consuming to run—instead of seeing your changes on the fly.

### Getting started:

When you begin to create an eCongo storefront, you can choose a URL for the store as a subdomain of eCongo—for example, http://www.mystore.econgo.com/—or you can use a custom domain name. Next, you specify basic data for the store: its name and description, what categories of products are to be sold in it, and which payment methods and tax assessment will be used (see Figure 5.7), as well as which shipping options are to be available. The final step is to enter the storeowner's contact information.

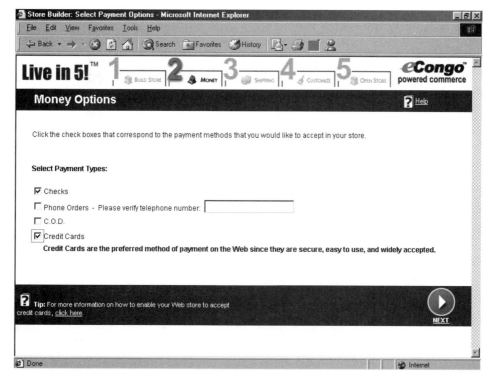

### Figure 5.7
You can indicate which payment methods you're prepared to accept when you set up your eCongo storefront.

When the store is ready to go live, eCongo.com will automatically submit your Web store's info to five search engines, with the option to define both the store description and keywords. You'll also find an advertising generator that is used to produce text advertisements, which can then be exchanged with other eCongo storeowners. Required information includes

- full name
- e-mail address
- phone number
- mailing address
- country

You will then be guided through a setup process that will ask for information about your business. If you apply for an online merchant account, you'll be asked for the following information:

- contact information for your business
- information about your business (including location, type of ownership, tax ID number, number of employees)
- sales data (annual sales, annual credit card sales, average sale, sales tax, return policy)
- business methods (sources of sales, delivery times, advertising, current fulfillment, and credit card processors)
- information (including Social Security number) of principals in business
- bank reference information (including average balance, total loans, total other business)
- bank account information

**Big spender:**

eCongo offers credit card processing as a premium service. It enables its online credit card transactions through Cardservice International, just like Bigstep.com, but here the fees are much higher; there is a monthly cost of $34 in addition to a discount rate of 2.8 percent plus $0.30 per transaction. These costs include the provision of a merchant account and real-time transaction fees.

URL: http://www.econgo.com/

**Contact:**   info@econgo.com

   X   SOHO                              ____   Small business

# FreeMerchant

FreeMerchant.com provides all the basic site-building features of a Web storefront service: a secure e-commerce transaction system, including a shopping cart system, browsable product database system, and an easily customizable Web interface—all completely free. The service does not offer credit card processing, though; if you choose FreeMerchant for your storefront, you may want to consider one of the free credit card processing services mentioned a little earlier in this chapter.

There are some 50 different templates to choose from in designing your site's look and feel. Like Bigstep.com, FreeMerchant.com can import a street map to show your physical store's location. The builder's tools are especially helpful for setting categories, subcategories, and items for sale.

The Payment Gateway lets you establish precisely how you want shipping, taxation, and transactions to work. The catalog maintenance includes an automatic inventory checker that alerts you when you're low on a product and will either let customers place their orders (which will be labeled "on back order") or will stop taking orders for that item. You can also import catalog data from Microsoft Excel and Lotus 1-2-3 spreadsheets or dBase, FoxPro, and Paradox databases. To keep track of invoices, freemerchant.com can export invoice data to Intuit's QuickBooks. FreeMerchant.com's site-traffic logging system is unfortunately limited to reporting only the numbers of hits per specific period, not the most popular paths by which visitors traverse your site. The service also offers an online coupon generator application for you to create coupons you can issue to your customers (see Figure 5.8).

When you fill out a form with your site's title, description, and keywords, the Site Promotion system will list your site with AltaVista, Excite, HotBot, and others. FreeMerchant.com's eBay promotion feature requires that you first establish an account with eBay and then fill out a form within FreeMerchant.com so that eBay can point to the product you intend to auction.

### Getting started:

When you first register with FreeMerchant.com, you're prompted to acknowledge that you will not use the service to host an adult site. You're prompted to create a unique username that will form part of your URL. Your URL is of the form http://www.yournamehere.safeshopper.com/, where *yournamehere* is replaced by your unique username.

Required information includes

- your e-mail address
- full name
- company name and address

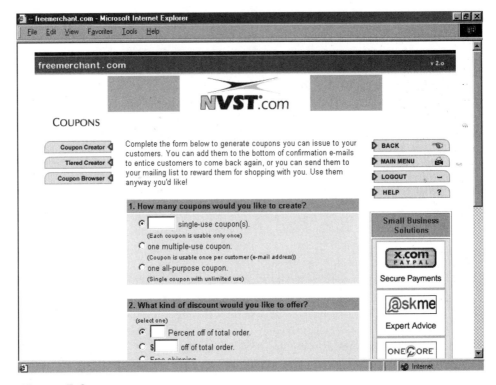

**Figure 5.8**
As a promotion tool, you can generate online coupons through
FreeMerchant's service.

- telephone number
- information about number of employees, annual revenue, and industry
- country

**Big spender:**

No premium services. If you don't have a merchant account, you'll need to purchase one. Two FreeMerchant partners, OneCore and U.S. Merchant Systems, sell merchant accounts.

URL: http://www.freemerchant.com/

**Contact:**   freemerchantsupport@freemerchant.com

   _X_  SOHO                          ____  Small business

# Mal's Free E-commerce Service

Mal's E-commerce is a little different from the other services described in this section. It simply lets you set up a virtual shopping cart system for your site that it hosts on its server, totally for free. You'll need to have your own Web page set up—see the free services listed in Chapter 4 if you're just getting started. You can customize the cart with your own look and graphics, so some knowledge of HTML would be most helpful on that front. This shopping cart will handle an unlimited inventory, too.

Mal's online help files and extensive FAQs will walk you through enabling the shopping cart system from start to finish. The shopping cart system encrypts the information sent, using SSL. When you receive an order, you'll be notified by e-mail, which will contain details of the order plus a unique shopper ID but minus the credit card number. You will have to collect the card number using an SSL-secure browser and the shopper ID number from Mal's site.

This system doesn't offer payment processing, but you'll find a complete online tutorial with detailed advice on securing a merchant account or finding other ways to accept and process payments (see Figure 5.9).

The site has a message forum where you can ask questions if you're looking to extend your site's system. The service includes calculators for shipping, taxes, and discounts, and is available in 13 languages, with support for the Euro. A demo storefront is available for you to peruse for brainstorming before you take the plunge.

**Getting started:**

Click the Join Up button on the home page to join.

Required information includes

- your name
- company or organization
- telephone number
- fax number
- country
- e-mail address
- type of organization
- your site's name, URL, and a description of what you sell

**Big spender:**

A $5-a-month premium account lets you directly integrate the cart into the credit card payment gateways of Cybercash, Authorizenet, Linkpoint, or Secpay.

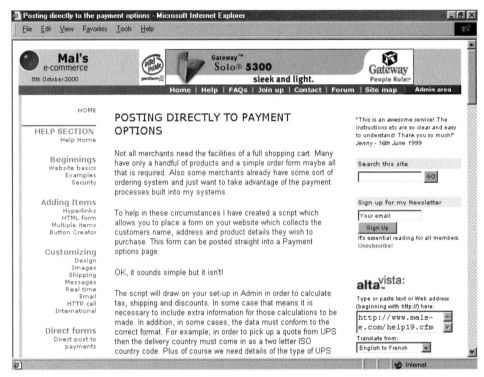

**Figure 5.9**
Mal's Free E-commerce site offers extremely useful information for small business owners who are looking to get started with e-commerce.

URL: http://www.mals-e.com/

**Contact:**   http://www.mals-e.com/contact.cfm

  X   SOHO                    ____ Small business

# FREE ADDRESSES AND REDIRECTION . . . . . . . .

You've finally got something worthwhile to show your customers. Now how will they find it? Just like in the real world, your address is key to having people find you. Unfortunately, you may find it difficult to find an easy-to-remember address, because many good ones have been taken. However, several sites can provide memorable Web site addresses to help.

···································································································

## BIG SPENDER: REGISTERING YOUR DOMAIN

If you haven't yet gotten around to registering your own domain name, here are a few good reasons to not put it off any longer:

If you decide to switch to a new Web host, you can take your domain name—and your site's identity—with you. Your regular visitors or customers who knew your site name would not have to be educated about finding your site's new home; they would be automatically directed there through their Web browsers.

If you are conducting business online, a domain name will lend credibility to your operation.

When your domain name picks up on or extends your company's business or name, users will be more likely to remember the name easily and can return to your site without help.

Purchasing a domain name involves registering your name with InterNIC through a registrar such as Network Solutions (http://www.networksolutions.com/). To register a name like mynamehere.com, you can apply online for that name and pay a $70 registration fee (see Figure 5.10). You will then have the right to that name for two years, at which point you can renew it for $35 a year.

Some commercial Web hosts will register your site's name for you and pay for the name for free (such as NameZero); others will do it for you but you'll have to bear the domain registration costs.

If you still do not have a Web host, you can use Network Solutions' services that allow you to register for a domain name and maintain it at a page that's specially designed for you. Although this service comes at an additional cost, it's useful for reserving a good name when you're not quite ready to launch your Web site yet.

## Come.to

It's come.to this: V3, the Internet Identity Company, powers a redirection service that lets you append your name—or company name or any words you choose—to one of several possible URLs. (".to", by the way, is the top level domain for the country of Tonga.) In this way, your URL will become http://come.to/yourname/—or http://run.to/yourname/, http://listen.to/yourname/, http://start.at/yourname/, or any of a dozen or so other snappy URLs. You'll also receive a matching e-mail address to go with your new short URL—for example, yourname@come.to.

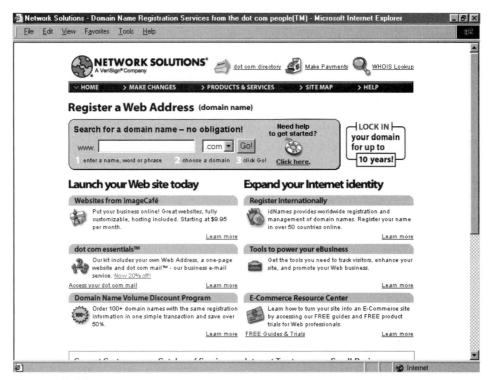

**Figure 5.10**
Network Solutions is now one of a number of resources at your disposal for registering a domain name.

The site promotes its Cloaking Device function, which hides your target URL at all times so that users see only your redirect URL.

Unless you pay a premium, the service requires you to either post an ad banner, pop-up window, or a delay page on your site's pages. A delay page—either a pop-up window or top or bottom frame—appears for several seconds before your site loads and will contain a message by V3 or their clients. You can choose options for how this delay page will appear.

**Getting started:**

After you choose a V3 URL (e.g., http://go.to/yourdomainname), you provide your e-mail address and your site's current URL. You can search the list of domains to see if any of the domain names you would consider are available (see Figure 5.11). The service then e-mails you a password and a URL to visit to activate your account.

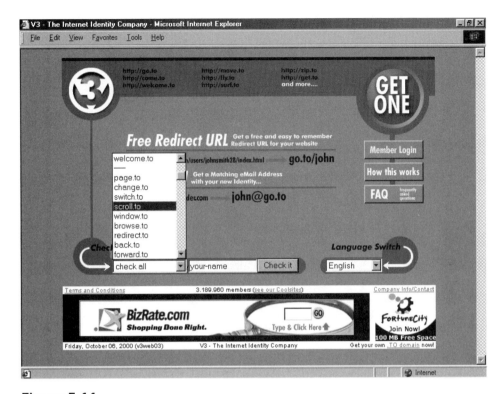

**Figure 5.11**
Browse the list of .to addresses available at V3.com.

You're required to provide the following information:

- full name
- birth date
- gender
- country
- zip code
- occupation
- your site's title, as well as a description, relevant keywords, category, and language

**Big spender:**
An advertising-free option is available for $18 per year.

URL: http://www.v3.com/

**Contact:**   support@v3.com

   X   SOHO                      \_\_\_\_ Small business

## NameZero

NameZero will absorb the cost of registering your desired domain name, as well as provide the portal and e-mail services related to the domain in exchange for hosting it on their site with their advertising. After one year, you can take over the domain name or continue to let NameZero host it. The standard fee for registering a domain for two years is $70; in addition, if you had to pay for a hosting service it might typically run $10 to $25 a month, or $120 to $300 a year.

Your new domain's portal will have a substantially sized application toolbar at the bottom of the screen, with buttons for software applications, online shopping, e-mail, and instant messaging, as well as an ad banner. As visitors browse within your portal, the toolbar will remain ever-present. Once they exit to go to a different site, the toolbar will disappear.

**Getting started:**

After you fill out the online registration form, an e-mail containing follow-up instructions is sent to the e-mail address you specified. The online application asks for your top three preferences for custom domain names, but it's a good idea to query the domain search at Network Solutions or InterNIC's site first so that you'll know for certain if your selections are available. Required information includes

- full name
- e-mail address
- the domain name you'd like to preregister
- street address
- country
- zip code
- how you heard about NameZero
- your gender
- age
- education level

**Big spender:**

For $24.95 annually, NameZero's Personal and Business Plus package includes

- Ownership of a domain name
- No NameZero-affiliated advertising (The domain name holder can of course place his or her own advertising or storefront marketing there.)
- Domain name POP- and Web-based e-mail, accessible from anywhere
- Unlimited URL forwarding and one domain transfer

An equivalent set of services would typically cost over $100 from competitors such as Register.com.

URL: http://www.namezero.com/

**Contact:**  customerservice@namezero.com

    X  SOHO               ___  Small business

# FREE PROMOTION . . . . . . . . . . . . . . . . . . .

Two of the easiest—and cheapest, since they don't have to cost anything—ways you can promote your Web site are by submitting it to search engines and linking to exchanges.

Most search engines will index the other pages from your Web site by following links from a page you submit to them. But sometimes they miss, so it's good to submit the top two or three pages that best summarize your Web site if you have more than one significant destination page on your site.

Free link exchanges are essentially mutual advertising arrangements that are made through a third party; you display another site's banner in exchange for their displaying yours. Most banner exchanges give you a 2:1 ratio for your ad banners; in other words, for every two times you display another site's banner, yours will be displayed on another site once. The free online graphic services mentioned in Chapter 4 can be helpful for you to use to create your own banners.

## Net Services

Submitting your site's information to a large number of search engines at once is this page's sole purpose (see Figure 5.12). You can also pick and choose among the search engines you want to submit to. Options include HotBot, InfoSeek, Lycos, AltaVista, Excite, WebCrawler, Northern Light, radarUOL, Anzwers, PlanetSearch, and whatUSeek.

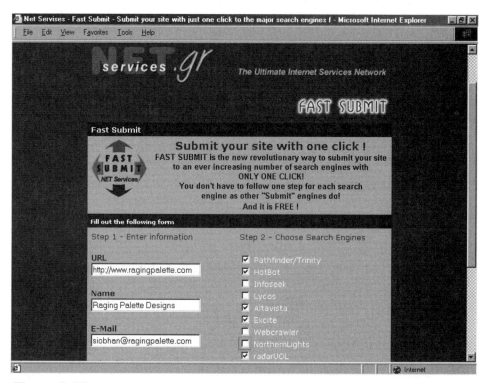

**Figure 5.12**
With the Net Services form, you click on the checkboxes next to the names
of the search engines you want to apply to.

**Getting started:**

Just enter your URL, name, and e-mail address and click the Submit button to send
your site to 12 search engines.

**Big spender:**

No premium services.

URL: http://www.netservices.gr/fsubmit

**Contact:**    webmaster@netservices.gr

   X   SOHO                    ____  Small business

## Promotion 101

Brought to you by NetPromote, this all-in-one guide to online promotion and traffic generation is a tremendous resource for Web marketing. It covers everything from search engine placement tutorials to free promotion tools, articles on branding, public relations, Usenet newsgroups, e-mail marketing, and more, plus links to other important Web promotion resources. The service includes a free newsletter to stay updated on Web promotion developments and search engine news.

You can follow links from this site to download a trial version of some of NetPromote's commercial services. For example, NetPromote Free is a free trial service for registering your Web site with about 20 search engines and online directories.

You can also obtain a 45-day trial version of WebPosition, which shows you how well your site ranks under your most important keywords and keyphrases in the top search engines such as AltaVista, Excite, HotBot, LinkStar, Yahoo!, WebCrawler, InfoSeek, Lycos, Magellan, PlanetSearch, whatUSeek, MSN, and AOL Netfind. The service then shows you how to improve your search engine placement.

**Getting started:**

No registration is necessary. Follow the links from the home page to read articles about how search engines work, discover more information about the services that interest you, or download trial software.

**Big spender:**

Premium services include NetPromote Gold (registration with over 400 online search engines and directories) and NetPromote Gold Plus (registration with over 850 online search engines and directories).

URL: http://www.promotion101.com/

   _X_  SOHO                          ____  Small business

## bCentral

Formerly known as Link Exchange, the banner exchange program now owned by Microsoft gives you a 2:1 ratio for displaying a standard 468×60-pixel banner.

The site offers a tutorial on creating your own ad banners, marketing tips (see Figure 5.13), and incredibly enough has enlisted several banner makers among the bCentral volunteers—one might even create a banner for you!

You have some control over who will see your banner and what ads will appear on your site. The service offers free statistics to show who is visiting your site (see Figure 5.14).

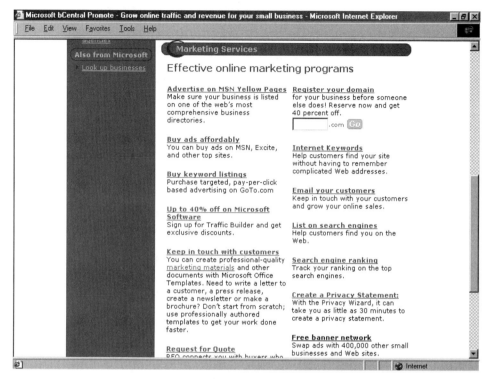

**Figure 5.13**
You can find a repository of tips for promoting your site at bCentral.

**Getting started:**

When you register, you're first asked to agree to the site's terms of service, which in-clude averring that your site does not contain adult material. You must also have cookies enabled on your site in order to sign up.

Required information includes

- full name
- e-mail address
- street address
- country
- phone number

**Big spender:**

For $19.95 per month, you can receive a combined package of banner advertising, search engine submission, a listing in the MSN Yellow Pages, and e-mail list creation service.

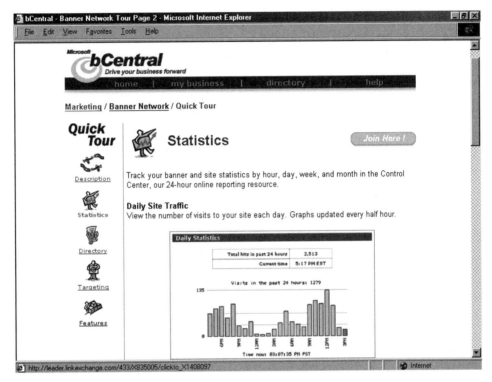

**Figure 5.14**
You can see graphical reports or numerical sum names of your banner traffic statistics at bCentral.

URL: http://www.bcentral.com/

**Contact:**   http://www.bcentral.com/help/bn/contact.html

  X   SOHO                          ____   Small business

## LinkBuddies

The LinkBuddies Free Banner Exchange program offers a high exchange ratio that is determined by your click-through rate, so it goes up as banners get better traffic on your site. The service also provides detailed statistics about your visitors. You can tell the number of visitors to your Web page, the number of times your banner was displayed, and how often it was clicked on, all tracked on an hourly basis. You can specify the maximum number of impressions you would like to receive on an hour-by-hour basis in the Hourly Targets setting (see Figure 5.15). You can set your

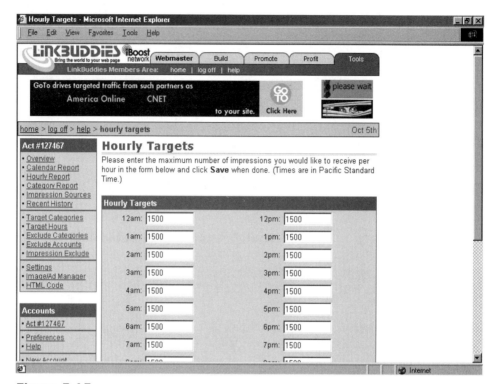

**Figure 5.15**
You can specify to the hour when you'd like your ad banners shown on other LinkBuddies sites.

account to auto-target categories for displaying your ads, which targets the best categories based on where you've received the most click-throughs in the past.

LinkBuddies also has a strong viral-marketing referral program. Whenever you refer a new member to LinkBuddies, you will receive a percentage of the new member's activity.

When you join, you receive a sign-up credit in which your banner ad will be displayed 500 times. Best of all, you can specify which categories of banners should not be displayed on your site, to ensure that ads from your competitors are not inadvertently shown.

**Getting started:**

LinkBuddies banners must be 468 pixels wide and 60 pixels tall. When you sign up, you'll be prompted to agree to the site's terms and conditions. You will then be given a link and e-mailed a password, which will allow you to log in and fill out the registration form. When you complete the form, you're given a LinkBuddies account number, and an e-mail message explaining some of the service's features is sent to you. A Web-based form walks you step-by-step through uploading your new banner images and helps you specify the settings you want for their display. At registration, you're asked for the following information:

- full name
- e-mail address
- your site's URL
- category for your Web site
- your site's title
- a description and keywords for your site

**Big spender:**

Additional advertising is available as a premium service.

URL: http://www.linkbuddies.com/

**Contact:**   support@linkbuddies.com

   <u>X</u>  SOHO               <u>   </u>  Small business

# FREE MAILING LISTS . . . . . . . . . . . . . . . . . . .

Getting visitors to your site is one thing. Keeping them is another. While there are all kinds of tricks you can employ to make your site "sticky," a great way to bring visitors back is by staying in touch through e-mail. Traditionally, creating e-mail discussion groups has been difficult, but several sites have made it easy—and free—to create e-mail lists. One service even lets you automatically inform customers whenever anything has changed on the site.

## Topica

Topica is a free, advertising-supported service that lets you create moderated and unmoderated mailing lists.

Topica offers several features that are absent from most basic Web-based mailing-list services. If you go on vacation, your mail can be held for you while you're gone. Subscribers can also set up signatures that are automatically appended to mail messages sent online. You can read and post list mail entirely from the Web, so that large mail messages from your lists won't fill your e-mailbox to overflowing.

As a list maintainer, you can control how often digests are sent—for example, every 10 messages or once a day—or automatically approve or reject new subscribers based on e-mail address. You may also indicate preferences for message archives, whether or not new subscriptions require your approval, and who may access the sub-scriber list. You can upload a number of e-mail addresses at once to prevent rekeying in your mailing list in a new forum (see Figure 5.16), but to prevent spamming, Top-ica may review the batches you upload. Subscription requests must be confirmed by end users to protect against list bombing.

Unlike eGroups, there's no way to post file libraries or calendars, or to schedule chats via Topica. It is possible, though, to schedule events on Topica via Evite.com.

**Getting started:**

After you register, you will be sent an e-mail to which you'll need to respond in order to verify your e-mail address. You will not be able to subscribe, create lists, or

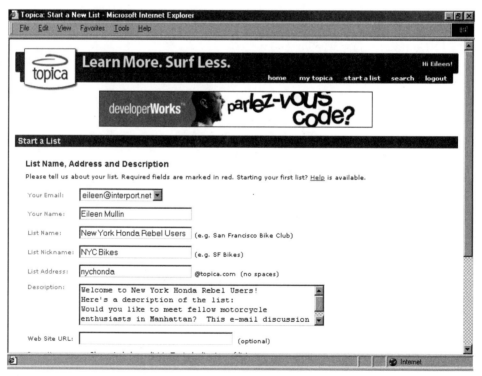

**Figure 5.16**
When you start a new list on Topica, you need to create an initial welcome message.

participate in lists until you have at least one verified e-mail address. You're asked to supply the following information:

- full name
- e-mail address
- gender
- birth date
- zip code
- country
- who referred you

**Big spender:**

No premium services.

URL: http://www.topica.com/

**Contact:**   support@get.topica.com

  _X_ SOHO                          ____ Small business

# Yahoo! Groups

With feature-rich mailing lists for moderated or unmoderated broadcast use, the free Yahoo! Groups (formerly eGroups) service outperforms many of its commercial mailing-list competitors. The service displays advertising on your mailing list pages, but these can be removed for a $4.95 monthly premium.

More than just mailing lists, Yahoo! Groups lists also sport chat rooms, individual and group event calendars, online voting, and more. The polling facility allows you to publish a multiple-choice or checklist-style questionnaire and tally the results.

When you create a new group, you indicate whether the postings are moderated or unmoderated, and whether or not the general public can access and join the list (see Figure 5.17).

**Getting started:**

When you sign up, you first provide your e-mail address. A message with a validation number and the rest of the sign-up instructions is then sent to you.

Required information includes

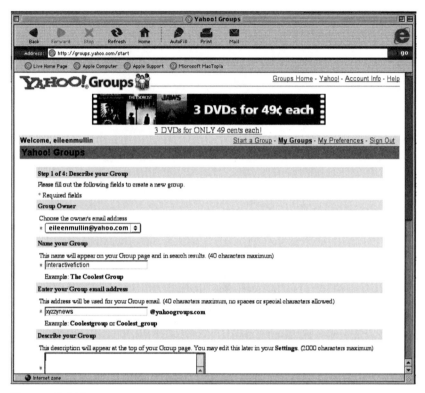

**Figure 5.17**
With Yahoo! Groups, you can create both moderated and
unmoderated mailing lists.

- your name
- e-mail address and password
- zip code
- date of birth
- gender
- country

**Big spender:**

For $4.95 a month, your online mailing list can display with no advertising.

URL: http://groups.yahoo.com/

    _X_  SOHO                    ____  Small business

## MessageBot

Formerly known as eList.com, this free service lets you maintain any number of your own exclusive lists of e-mail addresses easily and automatically.

If you have your own Web site, you can insert the code provided by Message-Bot on your site so users can leave their e-mail addresses when they visit. You can use the MessageBot service for any number of end uses, such as collecting subscribers for an e-newsletter or registering users who wish to be notified of upcoming changes or announcements about your site.

If you don't run your own Web site, you can start your list at the MessageBot site and return there to update the page.

**Getting started:**

Click Register for a new list on the MessageBot home page to start your own mailing list. After you fill out the short registration form, you'll see a page generated dynamically that tells you your new list is created, and the HTML code for you to copy and paste into your pages is displayed. You'll be asked for the following information:

- your name
- e-mail address
- your URL (if applicable)
- your list's name
- a title for your mailing list

**Big spender:**

No premium services are offered.

URL: http://www.messagebot.com/

**Contact:**   cameron@bloke.com

   X   SOHO                           ____   Small business

## NetMind

Ever worry that visitors to your site may not realize that you've posted new content? NetMind's free Mind-it service notifies visitors of relevant changes to your Web site via e-mail and spurs them back to view these changes. The service provides copy-and-paste HTML code and graphical buttons you can utilize in your pages for this purpose (see Figure 5.18).

NetMind has partnered with YesMail to provide free e-mail offers to Mind-it users. When visitors to your site sign up with Mind-it, they will see this optional offer in the new user registration.

Another new service from the company is NetMind Search-it, a free remotely-hosted search engine that lets Webmasters add search tracking capabilities to sites up to 500 pages. NetMind Search-it and the Mind-it application will be integrated in a search engine that tracks searches and notifies end users when the results of their search change.

Like Mind-it, Search-it is available for free to Webmasters and is easy to install on your site via copying-and-pasting HTML code into your pages.

**Getting started:**

When you register, NetMind will provide you all the customized HTML code you need for your site—just copy, paste, and publish.

**Figure 5.18**
If you want to ensure your site's visitors know when you've updated your site, offer the NetMind Mind-it service.

Note that the URL you provide to Search-it should be a directory or subdirectory URL, not an individual HTML page. If you specify an HTML page, such as index.html, Search-it will not index your site.

Required information includes

- your name
- e-mail address
- your URL

**Big spender:**

No premium services.

URL: http://www.netmind.com/

**Contact:**   http://www.netmind.com/html/contact_us.html

  X   SOHO               \_\_\_\_ Small business

# SELLING YOUR SERVICES . . . . . . . . . . . . . . .

Most of this chapter has focused on selling goods online, but what about services? There are many specialized sites that allow freelancers to look for jobs, and there are also, of course, big recruiting sites. But several sites tailor to individuals who own their own businesses and are blazing their own trails.

## Guru.com

Guru.com, a free service focused on serving the needs of independent professionals, provides community, advice-oriented content, job-matching, and deals on products and services to solo professionals (see Figure 5.19).

In addition to posting your resume, you can use the site to network with other professionals who can advise you and with prospective clients who can hire you.

You'll find a Q&A column full of marketing tips, and guides on important issues such as who owns the copyright for your work. A "gig matching engine" is designed to pair freelancers with clients.

### Getting started:

Once you sign up and return to log in, the first thing you should do is fill out your profile. Your fellow gurus and clients can then check out your skills and experience, and contact you for potential gigs. Required information includes

**Figure 5.19**
If you have freelance or small business services to offer, you can make your presence known to project managers by creating a profile at Guru.com.

- your name
- e-mail address
- city, state, and zip code
- country
- your area of expertise

You'll also be asked how you heard about Guru.com and whether you'd like to opt in to receive Guru.com's weekly e-newsletter.

**Big spender:**

No premium services.

URL: http://www.guru.com/

**Contact:**   http://www.guru.com/cgi-bin/feedback

  X   SOHO                                    ____ Small business

## FreeAgent.com

FreeAgent.com acts as a giant virtual contractor or temp agency. After registering, freelancers can create and store detailed resumes—called e.portfolios here—that employers can browse at will (see Figure 5.20). The e.office feature at FreeAgent.com is a premium service but definitely one that is important to freelancers—e.office enables members to buy and manage benefits, and it also handles invoicing and collections.

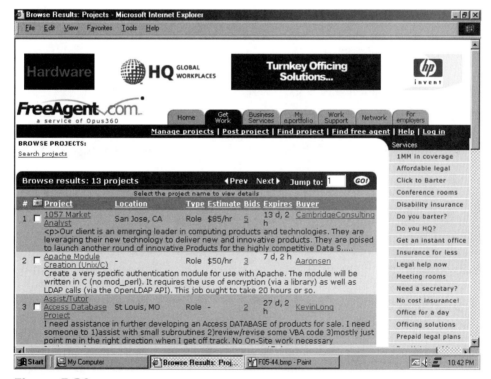

**Figure 5.20**
You can search available opportunities on FreeAgent.com based on location or fee.

You'll also find free services like Xchange project searches (which aim to match freelancers with employers who have specific project needs), online discussions and networking with others in your industry, your own free e-mail account, and more.

You can upload file attachments to your e.portfolio so that prospective employers can download and review more samples of your work.

There are industry-specific networking forums with accompanying discussion topics, profiles of freelancers working in that field, and online polls.

**Getting started:**

You can search jobs by keyword or use the advanced search feature to expand the list of search criteria. The Browse function displays all project postings by category. If you have created an e.portfolio with skills information, you can use Quick Search to immediately generate a list of all open matching projects. You can also decide to store search criteria for return visits.

Required information includes

- your name
- e-mail address
- your primary field of work

You will be asked how you heard about FreeAgent.com and can choose to store a cookie so that you won't need to log in again upon return visits. You can also opt in to receive bi-weekly newsletters.

**Big spender:**

For $274 a month, you can sign up for FreeAgent's e.office service, which provides payroll and other services. Technically, this makes you an employee of FreeAgent.com, but with the freedom to accept other assignments and employment. When you line up a client and negotiate the billing rate for the contract, FreeAgent.com will then help review the contract and discuss its terms with you. You submit regular timesheets of your work, either by fax or online, along with your monthly expenses, to FreeAgent.com. They will invoice your client and await payment according to the terms negotiated with them. When FreeAgent.com receives payment, it performs the payroll service and sends you your net pay. The service reimburses your expenses and handles all the deductions and payments that you've authorized, including insurance, payroll taxes, membership fee, 401(k), and local, state, and federal income tax withholding. FAQs about your 401(k) plan, taxes, insurance, and more are on the site.

URL: *http://www.freeagent.com/*

**Contact:** http://www.freeagent.com/help/contact.asp

  X   SOHO        ____    Small business

# SUMMARY . . . . . . . . . . . . . . . . . . . . . . . .

You've covered a lot of ground in this chapter and learned about the free tools and services at your disposal for realizing the unique thrill of receiving your first sale or order from an online customer. The promotional services covered at the end of the chapter for promoting your site through link exchanges and search engine promotion are just the tip of the iceberg for starting the buzz about your brand.

Next up in Chapter 6, you'll learn about free online resources for taking your small business to the next level of success, from the day-to-day concerns of managing your office to long-term strategic issues.

# 6
# Growing Your Business

..........................

Business is booming for you ... or maybe it's not. Either way, you've moved beyond selling online to the next frontier: developing your business. But there are so many things to worry about—finding goods and services, checking out the buzz of your customers, doing market research, and of course keeping pace with the ever-changing Internet. This chapter explains how your business can find the best information and deals online, including Net resources just for small businesses.

## SMALL BUSINESS PORTALS . . . . . . . . . . . . . . . .

Small businesses stand a middle ground between the average consumer and big business. In purchasing practices, small businesses are more like the consumer—they buy in smaller quantities, usually without purchase orders, and without the volume discounts available to large businesses. On the other hand, in order to offer their customers reliable service, small businesses rely on their vendors to provide the high level of service given to larger businesses. Small businesses will find mega-portal sites like Yahoo! and AltaVista helpful for some things, but for others, small business demands a community all its own. The portals discussed in this section aggregate a wide variety of content and services with a special focus on the needs of small businesses.

### Bizzed.com

Brought to you by e-Citi, the e-commerce unit of Citigroup, Bizzed.com is a portal to help entrepreneurs readily gain access to big-business resources. It provides access to free support services from Citigroup, such as e-commerce capabilities, payroll and electronic banking, credit-card processing, insurance and retirement planning, marketing and advertising support, and obtaining business services at discounted prices (see Figure 6.1).

With the site's resources and tools, you can learn how to take advantage of online banking (through Citigroup services, of course). You'll also gain insights into building a free business Web site, generating traffic, and conducting e-commerce. There are online articles and workshops on topics for entrepreneurs, such as how to write a business plan or market more effectively to your customers.

**Getting started:**

Provide your name and e-mail address to register at the site. You can then browse the site's categories, which include financial services, business services, marketplace, human resources, sales and marketing, and news and information.

**Figure 6.1**
Search for help on Bizzed.com based on functional need, or the problem you're trying to solve.

**Big spender:**

No premium services available.

URL: http://www.bizzed.com/

**Contact:**   info@mail.bizzed.com

  _X_  SOHO                  _X_  Small business

# OnVia.com

OnVia.com helps you manage your day-to-day operations as a resource for business services, products, customer leads, tools, breaking news, and expert advice. All OnVia services that can be purchased are accessible directly through OnVia.com. There are no outside links to complete your transaction.

The products OnVia offers range from paper clips to printers. The services are introduced in an online exchange that connects small business buyers and sellers across 75 business services such as marketing, human resources, and technical support. OnVia can tell you where to find Internet access, payroll services, long-distance plans, and a slew of other services.

Site categories include My Business, Request for Quote, Purchase Now, and News and Tools (see Figure 6.2). It also contains sections spotlighting breaking news, daily tips, how-to advice, and a community forum.

My Business presents the options to request a quote or check out buyer and seller activities. In the Tool Center, you can visit the discussion forum, ask for expert advice, download and print helpful forms, or visit a database of links. You can also track your account information in the My Business section.

Request for Quote brings together buyers and sellers. As a buyer, you can compare online sellers and local sellers to determine which partner best meets your needs. As a seller, you can cost-effectively reach new customers.

Purchase Now lets you shop for more than 25,000 business products, including computer hardware, software, office supplies, business machines, and telephone systems. News and Tools focuses on information, statistics, and data updated hourly; business building blocks to help you work more efficiently; business advice and strategies for success; and a community where you can network with other small business owners.

You can also sign up to receive e-newsletters on topics such as marketing, technology, and finance.

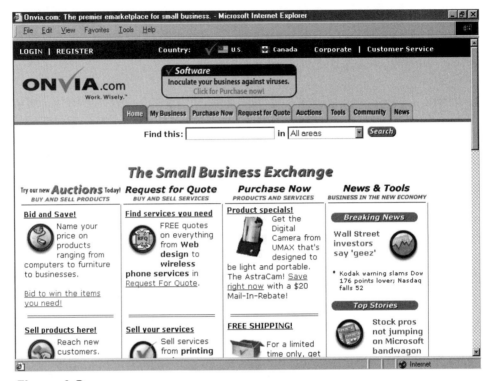

**Figure 6.2**
From the OnVia home page, you can find resources for all aspects of running a small business.

**Getting started:**

When you register, you're asked for the following information:

- full name
- company name
- e-mail address

**Big spender:**

No premium services available.

URL: http://www.onvia.com/

**Contact:**   customerserviceUSA@onvia.com

<u> X </u>  SOHO                          <u> X </u>  Small business

## Office.com

Office.com combines content, commerce, and community in a portal that offers your small business the advantage of industry trends, news, and gossip in 17 industries, 124 sub-industries, and 8 business management-focused areas.

Office.com also offers an Online Business Resource Center powered by SmarterWork, which lets you post projects on which others can bid (see Figure 6.3).

Office.com is divided into departments to meet specific business needs.

- Industries presents focused news stories on different economic sectors. It includes headlines, trends, and feature stories.

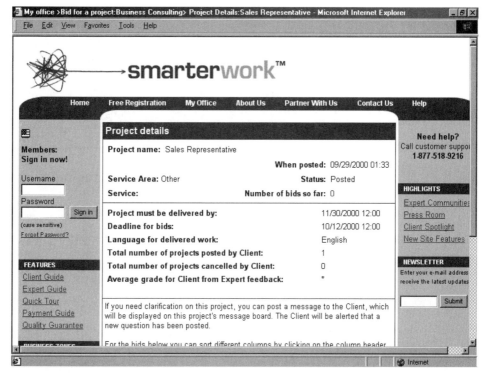

**Figure 6.3**
Office.com offers a forum for collecting bids on project work you wish to outsource. ("Office.com" and "Office.com A Service from Winstar" are registered service marks, and the Office.com logo is a service mark, of Winstar Communications Inc.)

- Run Your Business provides expert advice on everything from financing and franchising to product launches and promotions.
- E-Business explains how you can better use the Internet and technology to run your business.
- News & Research offers financial news, breaking business news, business research resources, and a series of wizards that guide you through business processes.
- Community lets you connect with other small businesspeople. You can find out what business leaders are talking about and voice your opinion.
- On the Air provides video spotlights of business stories and insights.
- Marketplace allows you to purchase a wide range of business supplies, from pens to plane tickets.

Across the top of every Office.com page is a Fast Find feature to search for information about a company, ticker, or person. An advanced search option lets you search by specific industry.

**Getting started:**

To register and personalize your home page, you'll need to complete a form that asks for the following information:

- full name
- e-mail address
- your organization's primary business activity

You can also sign up to receive the Office.com weekly business newsletter by e-mail.

**Big spender:**

Establishing a purchasing account lets you make purchases through the site, including premium content. Corporate accounts for multiple users are also available.

URL: http://www.office.com/

**Contact:**   http://www.office.com/global/help/ws_feedback/

  X   SOHO                        X   Small business

## AllBusiness.com

A portal that spotlights the daily concerns of your business and its long-term strategic issues, AllBusiness.com is comprised of an expert staff and links to online communities. The combination gives you a mixture of information and the ability to buy office supplies or services, as well as to access tools to complete tasks such as calculating startup costs.

In all, AllBusiness.com offers more than 40 Smart Business areas (see Figure 6.4), 250 downloadable business forms, practical solutions such as payroll processing, background checks on prospective employees, bad debt collections, and help in finding help in new sales leads. The wide array of business services available through the site's main center range from free Web-based computer backup utilities to Internet faxing services.

The major site categories—home, services, products, and community—cover procedures and strategies for posting jobs, building staff, organizing departments, managing decisions, documenting information, outsourcing projects, sending materials, and selling products and services to grow your start-up or small business.

**Getting started:**

You'll need to become a registered user to take advantage of some of the site's free tools. At registration, you're asked to provide the following information:

**Figure 6.4**
*AllBusiness.com covers a wide variety of small business advice and services.*

- full name
- name of business
- type of business
- number of employees
- e-mail address
- zip code
- country

**Big spender:**

No premium services available.

URL: http://www.allbusiness.com/

**Contact:**   http://www.allbusiness.com/general/customer_feedback.asp

 X  SOHO                     X   Small business

# SmartOnline.com

With SmartOnline you can start, manage, and grow your business with Web-hosted applications and information resources that cover business plans, financial statements, incorporation, job descriptions, legal forms, and sales and marketing.

These interactive software applications are combined with business guidance, business-to-business collaboration and commerce, and e-communication services to deliver productivity solutions to help improve your small business. Some of the online applications are limited unless you sign up as a paying subscriber. For example, one online application lets you create your own human resources manual with over 100 employee policies. However, this full application is only available to paid subscribers; non-subscribed users can only view and edit the policies in the first two chapters.

The site's major categories include applications, reference, and community. SmartOnline.com includes a number of useful online forms and insightful questionnaires as well (see Figure 6.5).

You'll find a list of how-to features with topics covering how to start your business, finance for growth, market and incorporate your business, protect yourself legally, build your team, and expand globally. Each topic page has a brief description of the topic's applicability to your business plan and a menu bar for access to specific advice and information. These topic pages all sport links to Get It Done, Learn About It, and Ask an Expert.

**Getting started:**

Supply your e-mail address and you'll receive a password to access members-only areas.

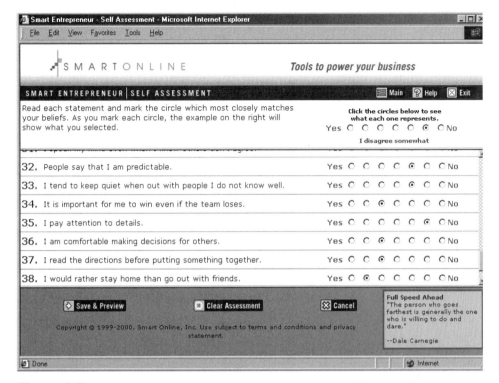

**Figure 6.5**
You can take online questionnaires at SmartOnline.com to assess your potential on many fronts.

**Big spender:**

For $14.95 per month, you'll gain full access to the site's business-planning tools, Web-based applications, and expert services.

URL: http://www.smartonline.com/

**Contact:**   http://smartonline.custhelp.com/cgi-bin/smartonline?People/

  _X_  SOHO                          _X_  Small business

# DigitalWork

DigitalWork.com offers online workshops in a wide range of topics, including marketing, sales, and public relations. Some are free, and most cost less than $100. Its partners include companies like IBM, Dun & Bradstreet, and Business Wire.

Through a variety of online classes and a simple question-and-answer forum, you can obtain hands-on help on a variety of topics, from writing an effective press

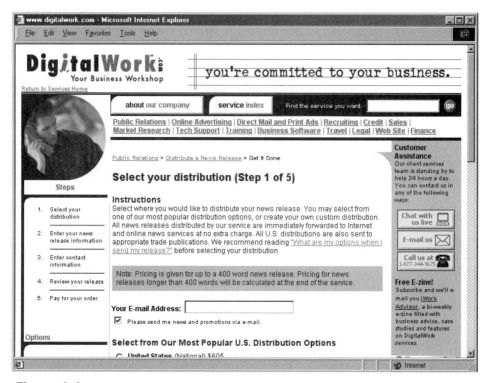

**Figure 6.6**
The hands-on tutorials at DigitalWork walk you step-by-step through activities designed to grow your business.

release (see Figure 6.6) to choosing the right media outlet. For example, you'll find tips from online banner advertising company Flycast on how to advertise effectively on the Internet.

Workshops are available in the following subjects: public relations, online advertising, direct mail and print ads, recruiting, credit, sales, market research, tech support, training, business software, travel, legal, Web site, and finance. You'll see a short summary of each workshop when you drag your mouse over the subject title on the home page; each page also offers the option of learning more about the subject area.

**Getting started:**

By supplying your e-mail address, you can register and receive workspace.

**Big spender:**

Some workshops are fee-based, starting under $100 each.

URL: http://www.digitalwork.com/

**Contact:**   customerservice@digitalwork.com

 X  SOHO                          X  Small business

## workz.com

Designed with the Vulcan-like intention of "helping small businesses grow and pros-
per online," workz.com offers a one-stop resource for running a Web site and maxi-
mizing your e-commerce opportunities. The workz.com network of sites provides
objective articles and how-to checklists with step-by-step instructions on Internet utilities, resources, references, and tools that can help you build, manage, promote, and
maintain your business online.

Workz.com has three main sections: InternationalWorkz, MerchantWorkz, and
BannerWorkz.

- InternationalWorkz has free tools for promoting and marketing your Web
  site globally. You'll learn critical information about shipping and trans-
  port, taxes, and Web site maintenance.
- MerchantWorkz can serve as your rating system to identifying successful
  merchant account providers (see Figure 6.7) who can help you take credit
  cards on your Web site. These articles and resources will help you to better
  understand how credit card merchant accounts work and what to look out for.
- BannerWorkz is a small-business service source for online banner ad creation, affiliate program collateral, and other graphic design services.

A site monitoring service lets you see your site performance, notifies you when
your site is down or serving pages slowly, and serves as a benchmark for comparing
your site's success.

Workz.com provides link options in a printer-friendly format. If you find something you think a colleague would find interesting, you can quickly direct those pages
to your colleague. If you have a specific question, you can just "Ask the Experts" for
answers through asktheexperts@workz.com. Workz.com also facilitates site building
using the following features:

- Build Your Site contains checklists to help you build a Web site that
  meets your budget and your business plan.
- Attract Customers guides you through nine cost-effective promotional
  strategies and techniques that can increase traffic to your site.
- Make Money contains checklists to identify key site strategies to achieve
  profit.

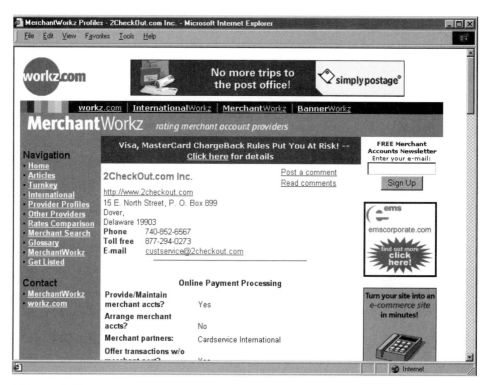

**Figure 6.7**
The MerchantWorkz overview provides a continually updated comparison of online merchant services. (Copyright 1995–2000. Pinnacle WebWorkz Inc.dba.workz.com. All rights reserved. Do not duplicate or redistribute in any form.)

- Manage Operations covers day-to-day guidelines for making sure that your online business is effective.
- Resources sends you to link libraries that will help you accomplish given goals, such as learning new terminology, submitting a site to a search engine or directory, or choosing banner software.
- Bookstore updates you on new and recommended titles at discounted prices.

**Getting started:**

You don't need to register to start using workz.com. To sign up for workz.com newsletters, discussion lists, and informational e-mails, you just need to submit your e-mail address where prompted on the home page.

**Big spender:**

No premium services available.

URL: www.workz.com

**Contact:**   info@workz.com

    X   SOHO                   X   Small business

# FREE PRODUCT RESEARCH . . . . . . . . . . . . . . .

When purchasing business products, you want to be sure that you are investing wisely in quality products that meet all of your requirements. This often involves digging through product reviews, asking others about their experiences with particular products or brands, or taking time from your busy schedule to comparison shop. Fortunately, a group of free sites allows you to easily judge vendors and products according to verdicts from consumers and experts. You'll find questionnaires that help determine the best feature set for your needs. Read on, and you'll even find out about an online store where just about everything is free.

## Active Buyer's Guide

Active Decision's Active Buyer's Guide provides free product research on thousands of products. Active Buyer's Guide doesn't make any broad product recommendations, but rather steers you toward your purchase through an interactive quiz designed to elicit what product features really matter to you. This highly personalized process reduces your research time to a matter of minutes and answers the question, What's right for you?

Active Buyer's Guide supplies product specifications, pictures and reviews, and side-by-side comparisons based on product features that you specify, then completes your search with links to the best sites from which to purchase the product you've selected (see Figure 6.8). The site's Adaptive Recommendation technology automates the selection process for you.

From the home page, you must choose a category that contains the product you want to buy or investigate. You can then choose to learn the basics about your choice or move straight to the Guide. The basics option provides a quick overview of facts. A glossary defines unfamiliar words and subjects.

Active Buyer's Guide then hones in on a couple of product options specifically tailored to fit your needs. The Guide recommends the products by compiling your

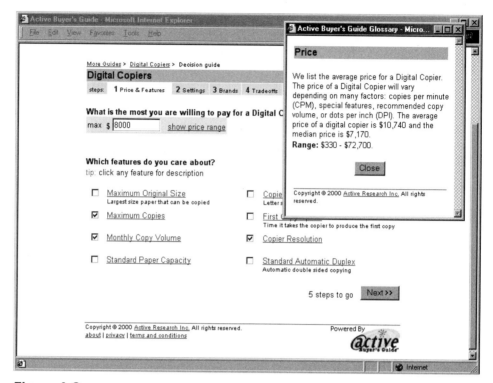

**Figure 6.8**
To derive your personal recommendations on the Active Buyer's Guide, you need to specify which product features matter most to you.

selections and presenting your results, with the option of comparing your final products list in greater detail.

You can go to several links that go directly to a product page to purchase, compare prices, and even seek consumer reviews on your product.

**Getting started:**

The Guide takes 5 or 10 minutes and poses a few simple questions about your personal needs, preferences, and tastes. The Guide determines its results through a series of selections you provide based on how you value features, requirements, brand, and trade-offs (see Figure 6.9).

Once you finish your search and create an account, you can save your work by clicking on the Save Info icon. Once your results are saved, you can retrieve the product recommendations by entering your e-mail address and a password.

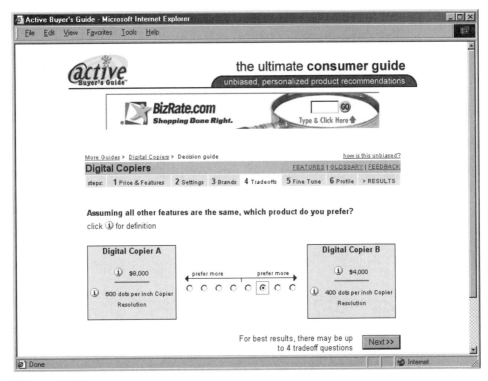

**Figure 6.9**
Your personal preferences will be the deciding factors in determining which of the leading candidates is the best product for you.

**Big spender:**

No premium services available.

URL: http://www.activebuyersguide.com/

**Contact:**   info@activebuyersguide.com

    X   SOHO                          ___   Small business

# BizRate

BizRate.com claims to be the "first people's portal" to e-commerce, saving you up to 25 percent every time you shop. By continuously collecting direct customer feedback on which Web sites provide the best service, BizRate.com lets you decide for yourself which site offers the best shopping features. BizRate.com uses a five-star rating system to distinguish the vendors on its site.

BizRate.com pays for its consumer research through a Customer Certification Program, distributing to its users commission checks that can be redeemed for purchase rebates at participating sites. The company earns money by selling aggregated marketing research based on the survey feedback it receives from customers at the point of sale.

You can start your shopping by utilizing the Super Find feature located on the home page, then choosing a category to guide you to a list of stores that provide the service you're looking for (see Figure 6.10). Links cover a wide variety of shopping categories, including apparel and accessories, auctions, books, computer hardware, computer software, consumer electronics, electronics, food and drink, gifts and flowers, health and beauty, home and garden, music, office supplies, online investing, sports and outdoors, toys and games, and travel and leisure.

**Figure 6.10**
Customer feedback forms the basis of the reviews of online stores on BizRate's site.

A Merchant Report Card contains one of two rating classifications (Gold Customer Certified Stars or Silver Staff Reviewed Stars). In each shopping site performance review, BizRate details the store description, store features, its return policy, and contact information. The Merchant Report Card is broken down into a number of categories to cover all your basic e-commerce concerns. These include ease of ordering, product selection, product information, price, on-time delivery, product representation, customer support, privacy policies, and shipping and handling.

**Getting started:**

Follow directions on the home page to register online, where you'll choose a username and password, and supply your e-mail address. You can download the BizRate Shopping Toolbar, which lets you automatically fill forms and track your transactions by storing copies of your receipt pages on your secure account page. You'll then also gain the site's Member Exclusives shopping offers.

**Big spender:**

No premium services.

URL: http://www.bizrate.com/

**Contact:**   http://www.bizrate.com/content/contact.xpml

   X   SOHO                          ____   Small business

# Epinions

Boasting over one million product reviews, Epinions provides consumer-generated testimonials (see Figure 6.11) to help you shop. In particular, the depth of discussion by the writers and judges at Epinions.com is quite extensive in terms of what contributors love, hate, buy, and use, which fosters a very strong sense of community. Epinions also offers a superior motivator for reader participation: cash rewards are offered for successful reviews.

Epinions.com doesn't take money from merchants to include or recommend specific products or edit its reviews, but will reward its customer base with cash for opinions that are beneficial to other members. Aside from earning thanks from members who benefit from your advice, you can also profit from your review if people rate it highly. The more recognition you get, the more Eroyalties you can earn.

You will be awarded a designated number of Eroyalties for every unique user who views a Web page on which the full review you authored is displayed. The more reviews you write, and the more other users like them, the more Eroyalties you will be eligible to earn. Eroyalties are redeemable for $10 cash. If your friends are members, you'll earn more Eroyalties. And if they're not, you can sponsor them and earn

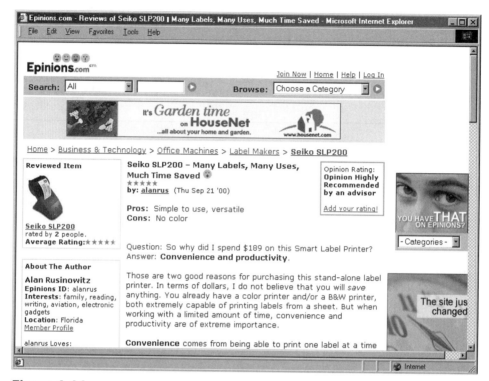

**Figure 6.11**
You can discover in great detail what other customers think about the products you're considering purchasing.

an additional 10 percent of whatever money they make on the site. You can track your earnings on your account.

Member profiles can include how many opinions you have written; how many times your opinions have been read by other members; and a Web of Trust, which chooses relevant opinions and product recommendations based on the members you trust and rate highly, and who your trusted members recommend.

You can also get alerts when specific members, whose opinions you respect, submit feedback.

**Getting started:**

To find a desired product, click through the categories or launch a search. When you reach your desired category page, you'll have the opportunity to compare and investigate a number of reviews of the same product. In digital cameras, for example, you can read both in-depth and not-so-detailed explanations of why some people like certain cameras and why others don't. If you reach a purchasing decision, you can utilize the Where To Buy function to find the product at leading retailers.

To create your Epinions.com ID, you'll need to register with your e-mail address, country, and zip code.

**Big spender:**

No premium services.

URL: http://www.epinions.com/

**Contact:**  http://www.epinions.com/feedback_general.html

  X  SOHO                    ____ Small business

# FREE PRODUCTS  . . . . . . . . . . . . . . . . . . . . .

Who doesn't like receiving free samples or free software? These direct marketing sites connect you with merchants that will ship you the goods you decide you want in exchange for some market research feedback.

## FreeShop

Online marketing engine FreeShop offers a site where you'll discover a broad selection of free and trial products. You choose from the categories you're interested in and give FreeShop permission for marketers to contact you in exchange for receiving free goodies. FreeShop also offers coupons on items that are not-quite-free (see Figure 6.12).

Club FreeShop has over 3.3 million members and stakes its claim as one of the most successful opt-in e-mail programs on the Internet. As a member you can receive newsletters featuring the latest free and trial offers on the site, alerts on special contests, exclusive benefits, and links to sponsors.

FreeShop highlights each week's special interest topics across the top of its home page. The other categories are classified by subject matter, with recently added offers topping the list. Other topics include auto, business and careers, newsletters, computers and more, entertainment, family and kids, health and sports, hobbies, home and living, personal finance, magazines, software, men's style, women's style, travel, and more.

Each product's order page includes a brief description of the product or service, what you get, and how you receive it. Rush order options for express delivery are available for some goods. Other items, such as free software products, may be readily downloaded. A tell-a-friend feature lets you forward an offer page directly to a friend or colleague.

**Figure 6.12**
From the FreeShop home page, you can see how many offers are available in the product categories that interest you most.

**Getting started:**

To register for Club FreeShop, type your e-mail address in the registration box on the home page.

**Big spender:**

The company's premium services are targeted to merchants who wish to buy e-mail lists or receive targeted market research.

URL: http://www.freeshop.com/

**Contact:**    custserv@freeshop.com

      X   SOHO                    ____  Small business

## YesMail

When you sign up with online direct marketing firm YesMail, you'll receive via e-mail offers, promotions, and other information from its merchants on the subjects you choose.

You have a wide choice of interests about which to receive information. To avoid e-mail overload, though, it's a good idea to specify your interest in individual topics within a broad-level category.

After you register, you can set up a user profile to select or deselect your chosen interest categories. A MyEvents feature can be used to track your personal calendar and show upcoming events linked to your interests. The Tools section includes links to spam filters and other e-mail privacy software—which you'll need because your opt-in e-mail address is sold and resold on lists—and links to privacy organizations where you can report e-mail abuse.

### Getting started:

To register, you just need to submit your e-mail address at the site. You're then prompted to choose the categories you're interested in receiving offers about.

### Big spender:

The company's premium services are targeted to merchants who wish to buy e-mail lists or receive targeted market research.

URL: http://www.yesmail.com/

**Contact:**   webmaster@yesmail.com

   X  SOHO               \_\_\_\_ Small business

# FREE SHOPPING SERVICES . . . . . . . . . . . . . .

Losing the overhead associated with traditional retail and even printed catalogs in order to offer inexpensive goods online was just the first stage of online commerce. Now, retailers have advanced, innovative business models that could either only happen online or are greatly facilitated by the Internet. This new wave of dynamic Internet pricing has at its crux the empowerment of consumers to name their own price through a variety of means.

- Auctions. We've described how you can sell your own goods in this way, but it's also a great way to stock up yourself.

- Group buys. By combining orders from multiple buyers into a higher-volume transaction, these services pass the savings of volume-based buying on to smaller buyers.
- Reverse auctions. Here, sellers can respond to buyers' bids.
- Automated price cuts on liquidations. These services help find closeout sales on the products that interest you.

Browse the following sites to find some of the best deals on the Net.

## Mobshop

Mobshop.com supports a "more the merrier" ideology by aggregating buyers to drive a discount. Big businesses have been buying in bulk for years, and now it's your turn to do it over the Internet. Mobshop and its partners pool interested buyers from across the Web through Web-based tools the company calls transaction formats. A period of time (known as a buy-cycle) is set for buyers to come together to aggregate their purchasing power to buy a product at a large discount. As more people join your buy-cycle, the price of the item drops (see Figure 6.13). When the buy-cycle closes, Mobshop will do the legwork and place a substantial volume order with the supplier. Because of the increased volume, the price of the product is driven down to a cost much lower than if you purchased a single item.

The categories include computer hardware, computer software, electronics, entertainment, PDAs, small business, and sports and fitness.

To be part of a purchasing group, you'll need to link to Browse Categories, Hot Deals, or Closing Soon from your home page, and then click on any of the products that suit your fancy. You can use a search function to find a specific product. After you choose the item you want, you will be taken to that product's details page, where you'll get more information. You'll see the date the buy-cycle closes, a graph depicting how many people are already in on this product, and how much money you're saving on it. You'll also get a detailed description of the featured item. If you want to lock in the price the item is being sold for, click Buy Now. The price may still drop if more people join the group before the buy-cycle ends.

A Click & Tell feature permits you to easily pass along e-mails to encourage your friends and family to get in on your buy-cycle so they may join and increase the critical mass for maximum savings. You will receive an e-mail when the buy-cycle closes, telling you the final price of the product and the final number of people who accompanied you to great savings.

The Save a Spot feature lets you delay purchases until they reach a specific price. You can also choose Buyer Flash, and an e-mail alert will notify you that a product in a buy-cycle has dropped to your desired price tier.

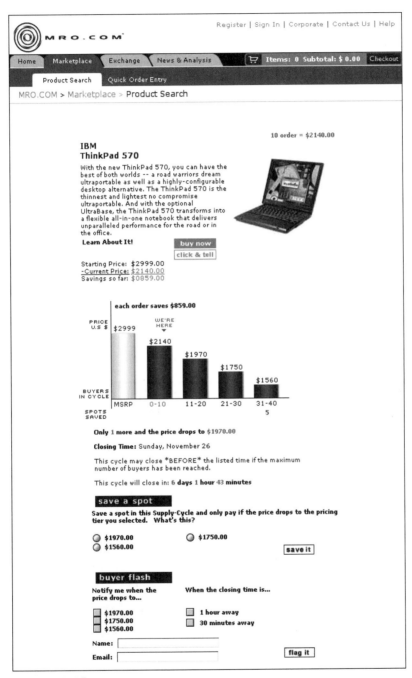

**Figure 6.13**
Mobshop's unique transaction formats enables buyer- and seller-initiated trading.

**Getting started:**

When you set up your account, the My Account link allows you to check the status of your most recent orders, review your past purchasing history, or update your credit card and shipping information. To become a member, you must provide the following information:

- full name
- e-mail address
- street address
- telephone number

**Big Spender:**

No premium services available.

URL: http://www.mobshop.com/
**Contact:**   service@mobshop.com

   X   SOHO               X   Small business

# Buy.com

Buy.com presents you with a vast selection of brand names at their guaranteed lowest prices. Offering a mall-structured online shopping experience, Buy.com is able to provide a wholesale shopping advantage by supplementing its service costs with advertising dollars and sometimes with shipping and handling charges, although several special incentives do have limited offers for free shipping and handling.

If you do find a better deal at another Internet store within 24 hours of your purchase, you can request a price match. Buy.com sticks to its Low Price Guarantee and will refund the difference, though there are some restrictions (see Figure 6.14).

Product categories include computers, software, electronics, golf, books, videos, games, music, travel, sports, and a clearance section offering you closeout specials for more savings. Your purchases are combined into one virtual shopping basket that's accessible from all the specialty stores.

Once you decide to wander through the virtual superstore, you can choose a product tab according to your shopping interest. When you're searching through the product area, you'll have the option to shop by brand, scan through the top 25 products in that category group, or hunt for specials. Closeout bargains can always be found by visiting the clearance area. While you're shopping, all your purchases will be placed in your shopping cart, which will tell you what you've got and how much it costs.

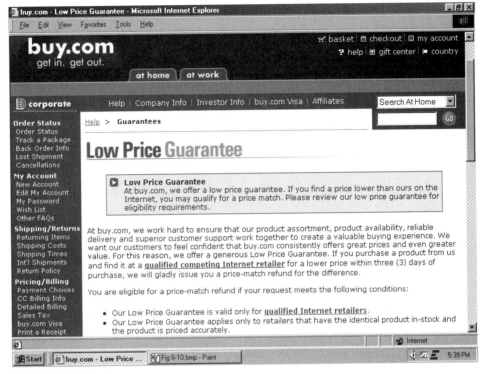

**Figure 6.14**
Buy.com details on its Web site how its lowest price guarantee works.

If you can't find what you're looking for, an eSearch feature offers advanced searching power, with product-specific categories and search hints. You can also find the information you want by contacting a 24-hour customer care agent through an instant message or a toll-free phone call.

When you are finished shopping, go to the checkout area and your account will reflect all your purchases, including shipping and handling. Your account lets you quickly access your order history, past and present. You can track your order with an auto-tracking feature that follows the UPS delivery status.

**Getting started:**

To register for your account, you have to supply

- billing information
- shipping address
- payment and shipping information
- e-mail address

**Big spender:**

No premium services available.

URL: http://www.buy.com/

**Contact:**  Customer care agents are available round-the-clock at 1 (888) 880-1030.

     X   SOHO                         X   Small business

## Priceline

As you may have heard William Shatner tell you, Priceline is based on the proposition that you should be able to name your own price when you buy its offered products and services. Priceline uses a reverse auction theory with a "demand collection system" that lets you place a bid in an effort to save on services and products you need. Sellers participate because they have surplus inventory and Priceline suppliers are guaranteed buyers.

The product and service categories include airline tickets, hotel rooms, and long distance, as well as consumer services such as home financing.

Before you "name your price," there are some things you still need to know. Once Priceline accepts your bid, you are going to have to guarantee your purchases by locking in your bid with a credit card. If your bid is rejected, you pay nothing. Priceline usually requires approximately an hour to directly communicate to participating sellers of to their private databases the price you are willing to pay. If they agree to match your bid, your service will be booked or your product will be purchased, and it generally cannot be changed, transferred, or cancelled. You will have to be flexible with respect to brands, sellers, and product features, in most cases.

Airline tickets (see Figure 6.15) can only be purchased for round-trip travel, domestically or internationally, and you pick the day (whether it is a few months or a few days away). All flights are on major airlines and their affiliates, and most flights are booked non-stop; however, there is a chance you may have to make up to at least one stop or connection each way.

You can make one request (for up to eight people traveling together) for each trip by filling out the full first and last names of the people traveling. If your offer is not accepted, you can resubmit another request right away, but you will have to change your travel dates and/or add airport choices. Although you choose the dates you want to travel, the airlines will choose departure times (always between 6 a.m. and 10 p.m.) on flights that have seats available.

To purchase hotel rooms, you tell Priceline what city you want to go to, the part of that city you prefer to stay in, how many rooms you need, your check-in and check-out dates, and the quality level (1–5 stars) of hotel you'd like to stay in.

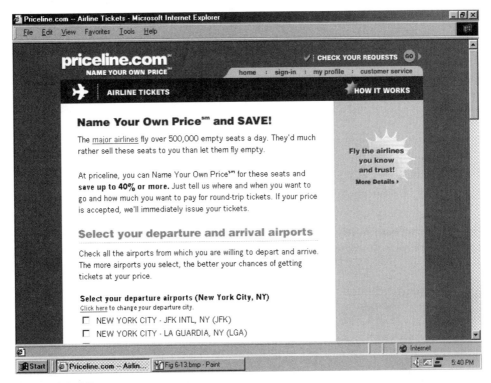

**Figure 6.15**
When bidding on airline tickets, you select the dates and provide identifying information about all travelers.

Priceline checks with participating hotels. If the hotel accepts your bid, Priceline immediately purchases the room and charges your credit card.

**Getting started:**

The registration process involves filling out details for each service, but all services require your

- full name
- street address
- credit card billing information

When registering for a service, you will be asked if you'd like free sponsor dollars with which you can save additional money by trying a national sponsors' services.

**Big spender:**

No premium services available.

URL: http://www.priceline.com/

**Contact:**   http://www.priceline.com/PricelineASPCustomerService/email/email_main.asp

  X  SOHO                  X  Small business

## DealTime

DealTime is an online comparison shopping service for searching online merchant sites, auctions, classifieds, and buying groups to locate the items you're looking for at the lowest prices (see Figure 6.16). The service creates automatic search agents known as "crawlers" that continually check for the newest information, price updates, and availability of the products you want to buy.

Before launching a product search, DealTime takes a variety of factors into consideration, including third-party merchant ratings; the popularity of the site with consumers; its customer service track record; the amount, quality, and price of the merchandise it offers; and feedback from consumers.

DealTime chooses which products to search for based on consumer demand for the product and the number of merchants offering the product.

When you begin a product search, you're prompted to define your search parameters such as brand, model, and price. Category listings include apparel, appliances, babies and kids, books, computers, electronics, financial services, flowers and gifts, food and wine, health and beauty, home and garden, jewelry and watches, movies, music, office, pet supplies, software, sports and fitness, tools and hardware, toys and games, and video games.

When you click through the results of your search, you're sent to the online merchant's own site for more details and purchase information. DealTime is not a merchant and does not sell the product to you directly.

If you prefer to wait for a better deal, click on Track It, and have your search continue over a selected period of time. To pick the methods by which you'd like to be notified, go to the Your Alert Methods page.

You can opt to view the status of your searches at any time by going to the Your Deals page. To delete a search, go to the Your Deals page and click on Delete in the product tracking summary banner.

**Getting started:**

You won't need to register to use DealTime's search services—just follow the links on DealTime's home page. If you wish to sign up for an e-mail newsletter or receive alerts about an upcoming bargain, you'll need to provide your e-mail address.

**Figure 6.16**
Access the current deals or search a broad product category from the Deal-Time home page.

**Big spender:**

No premium services.

URL: http://www.dealtime.com/

**Contact:** customerservice@dealtime.com

  X   SOHO               ___ Small business

# FREE LEARNING . . . . . . . . . . . . . . . . . . . .

Contrary to the saying that advocates the importance of who you know, what you know *does* matter. Knowing where to do research online is an important skill in keeping up with your customers and community. These sites will let you drill down to specific domains of expertise so you can stay ahead of the crowd and quickly bone up on the subjects you need to expand your business into new areas. Table 6.1 provides a brief comparison chart of these services' main features.

## About.com

A self-contained network of over 650 highly targeted subject matter sites (see Figure 6.17), About.com has a designated expert guide moderating each of its satellite sites. The topic-specific nature of each site also creates a community atmosphere where you can share your experiences and opinions with other members.

You can conduct a directory search by clicking the site index. The categories include arts and literature, autos, computing and technology, education, games, health and fitness, hobbies, home and garden, Internet and online, kids, news and issues, shopping, sports, teens, and travel.

After you choose a topic, the site presents a page that provides comprehensive information and a link to your topic guide. This definitely adds a human touch that personalizes the About.com experience. You'll also find Internet links to other directories, original content from a seasoned professional's perspective, community features, and online shopping opportunities. Shopping links take you to a comparison buying site and a group buying service that's powered by Mobshop.com (see profile earlier in this chapter). If you'd like to chat, the home page gives way to Hot Forum Topics in a Talk About section.

**Getting started:**

You don't need to register to use the site, but you can sign up to receive any number of e-mail newsletters by supplying your e-mail address.

**Table 6.1**  Comparison of Free Online Learning Sites

| Service | Number of guided subject matter areas | Provides e-mail service? | Discussion groups? | Provides online calendar? | Online chat? |
|---|---|---|---|---|---|
| About.com | Approximately 650 | No | Yes | No | Yes |
| 4anything.com | Approximately 1,300 | Yes | Yes | Yes | Yes |
| Northern Light | N/A | No | No | No | No |
| ScheduleEarth | N/A | Yes | Yes | Yes | Yes |

**Figure 6.17**
Small Business is one of the hundreds of useful subject categories to delve into at About.com.

**Big spender:**

No premium services are available.

URL: http://www.about.com/

**Contact:**   reachus@about-inc.com

　X　SOHO                                _____ Small business

# 4anything.com

If you're looking for just about anything, just put a "4" in front of it and a ".com" behind it. That's the easy-to-remember format behind the 4anything.com concept, a set of sites that eliminates unnecessary pages. 4anything.com structures itself around a main site that contains a number of general interest sites, such as 4entertainment.com,

4shopping.com, and 4news.com. There are also some 875 vertical interest sites, such as 4wine.com and 4bizops.com (see Figure 6.18), which are destination sites as well as entry points to the network and quick links to 425 city guides, such as 4newyork.com and 4losangeles.com. Your link options on each topic page are selected by site editors based on their findings and opinions of the most useful and relevant Web sites that pertain to your interest.

Your personal interests drive 4anything.com's online community. You can create a forum— recent news, online discussion, yellow pages, chat boards, shops, and an e-mail service—around every topic that may appeal to you.

You can link directly to a site with a 4 URL or access a subtopic under one of the 14 category indexes on the home page that contain all 1,000-plus sites. If you can't locate a page, just use the search bar located next to the logo at the top of the page. If 4anything has an exact match to your search term, you'll be sent to that site. If there are other topics that come close to what you want, you'll see a list of a few options. If there's nothing that comes close to what you want, then 4anything.com expands its search to cover the entire Web. Each page in the network contains around

**Figure 6.18**
Try 4bizops.com to learn about sites targeting entrepreneurs.

70 to 80 of the best links about a topic and puts them on one site. For example, you'll find its best choice links for chocolates on 4chocolates.com.

Each page in the "4" site network contains tabs that can bring you to a discussion, a chat room, and an e-mail station for that particular section. The network can connect you to people of common interests through an online community.

You can even use a "4" site as your e-mail domain address and have your passion or interest branded right on your e-mail—for example, sweettooth@4 chocolate.com.

**Getting started:**

You don't need to register to use the site. To obtain a free e-mail account at your favorite "4" domain, you'll need to supply the following information:

- birth date
- gender
- zip or postal code
- country

**Big spender:**

You can read your e-mail using a POP client for $11.95 per year.

URL: http://www.4anything.com/

**Contact:**   contactus@4anything.com

   X   SOHO               _____  Small business

## Northern Light

Northern Light is a research engine that enables you to scan the Web and seek out information from 6,900 premium sources in an original, in-depth, and organized manner. In an effort to pull high quality information from all relevant materials and place them into one search, Northern Light accesses books, magazines, databases, and news wires that you probably wouldn't find in any other search engine (see Figure 6.19).

Northern Light formats your search results prioritized by best match and organized into blue folders that help target your best search option and other search avenues. Organized Custom Search Folders are created specifically to your individual request, integrating Web results with a Special Collection access that contains over 8 million full-text articles from data sources such as investment reports, *Wall Street Journal* abstracts, *Business Week*, *Fortune*, news wires, city and regional papers, college papers, and broadcast news transcripts. Special Collection is accompanied by

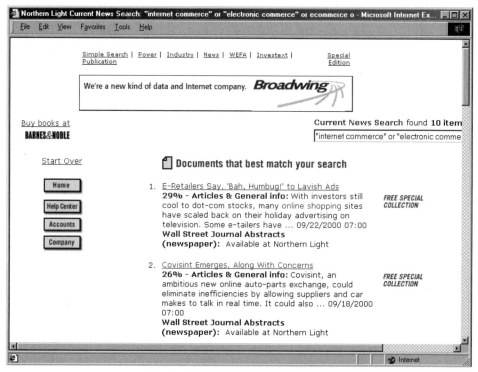

**Figure 6.19**
The Northern Light research engine uses classification intelligence and precision relevancy ranking to improve Web searching.

free summaries with every document, free medical abstracts compliments of Medical Data Exchange, and free Magill book reviews.

You can conduct a variety of searches. For example, the Power Search acts as a complete toolkit for advanced searching by subject, source, document type, and date. The Business Search is a specialized search of industry-focused Web pages, market research, economic analysis, and company reports for business professionals. The Investext Search browses thousands of investment research reports written by expert analysts. The Stock Quotes link brings you to a detailed market research station. And the Search News spotlights current stories from a two-week archive of real-time news from 56 continuously updated news wires.

Channel buttons provide a help center, your account information, search alerts, and a portfolio button that contains your personal stock tracker. A Special Editions link, compiled by a team of librarians, is located on the home page and contains updated accounts of today's pertinent issues, combining relevant links from authoritative Web sites, with free documents from Northern Light's own online publication and a live queries forum. You can customize Northern Light Special Editions or live queries for your office or business.

**Getting started:**

Type your keywords in the search box on the home page to conduct a search. You'll be directed to a research page heavily saturated with links to information. You're asked for your full name and e-mail address when you register.

**Big spender:**

When you sign up for a member account, you will receive a $5 bonus to use towards your first Special Collection purchases. If you choose to purchase Special Collection documents, you will be charged on a pay-per-document basis. Most articles are priced between $1 and $4.

Your credit card will be charged for purchases on the twenty-eighth of each month, or when your document purchases have reached $20, whichever comes first.

URL: http://www.northernlight.com/

**Contact:**   cs@northernlight.com or call 1 (617) 621-5100

   X   SOHO                          X   Small business

# ScheduleEarth.com

ScheduleEarth is a marketing and brand-building portal that can provide you with information for personal and professional development. The site serves as a source to promote your small business products and services (see Figure 6.20), and also a source for continuing education classes, seminars, and career enhancement courses for your employees or yourself.

An appointment calendar, discussion groups, newsletters, e-mail service, and a marketplace where you can display and sell your products are some of the features ScheduleEarth offers. To promote events such as association meetings, awards dinners, college reunions, conferences, conventions, fundraisers, holiday galas, seminars, speaker events, or training classes, all you need to do is post it.

**Getting started:**

The home page includes links to the many functions and services the site hosts. Quick Jump sends you to a list of links such as home page, membership, power search, information center, free e-mail, discussion groups, calendar options, and travel section.

To promote your business through an event, you can just click Add an Event and submit information about the event, its sponsors, and its target audience. An information center lets you manage your membership, update your contact information, promote your business, sign up for an event, or find additional information.

**Figure 6.20**
ScheduleEarth targets marketing professionals in providing information about upcoming seminars, continuing education, and training events throughout the world.

To register, you'll need to provide the following information:

- full name
- e-mail address
- zip code

**Big spender:**

You can pay to run a message in the Target Banner section and spotlight your event on the home page.

URL: http://www.scheduleearth.com/

**Contact:**   support@scheduleearth.com

  X   SOHO                          X   Small business

# FREE RESEARCH . . . . . . . . . . . . . . . . . . . . .

Machiavelli, the famous princely power broker, admonished that you should keep your friends close and your enemies closer. What was true for the sixteenth century politician is also true for the twenty-first century business person. Keeping an eye on your competitors or partners (which can sometimes be the same in the Internet economy) is a daunting task. But the Web can help. Free research sites can let you loop up public information about other companies and stay up to date on the latest consumer and Internet research.

## Company Sleuth

If you're interested in a behind-the-scenes look at publicly traded companies, log on to companysleuth.com, an Internet covert specialist that provides free, legal, inside information.

Acting as your personal investigator, Company Sleuth tracks your business investments, partners, and clients' activities. It also provides revealing scoops on your competition's financial moves, Internet dealings, patents (see Figure 6.21) and legal actions. Company Sleuth will track only U.S.-based, publicly traded companies that are listed on the AMEX, NASDAQ, and NYSE boards.

Company Sleuth also maintains an e-mail alert service that aggregates hard-to-find information. You can track up to 10 publicly traded companies and have reports sent to you in the form of a daily e-mail that can even be delivered to your handheld computer device.

If you're just looking for quick insight on news, intellectual property, an inside view, an outside perspective, or stock trends, enter the company's ticker symbol at the top left of the welcome page and hit Go. New information is tagged with a "new" burst. If you're unsure of the symbol for a particular company look it up through a link provided right below the ticker box.

You can view any of the top 10 companies being watched on the home page. This list allows you to see who the public majority is interested in tracking. You can also view the companies from links listing the Top 10 Stakeouts Requested This Week. By clicking on any of these links, you will get the insider information that Company Sleuth gathers each night.

When you register to stake out a company, you'll receive detailed updates every day. You can sign up on the home page or on a launched company search page. What you get is information alerts covering topics on SEC filings, earnings estimates, discussion group postings, stock quotes, analyst ratings, charts, technical trading information, new trademarks, insider trades, job postings through Job Sleuth, press

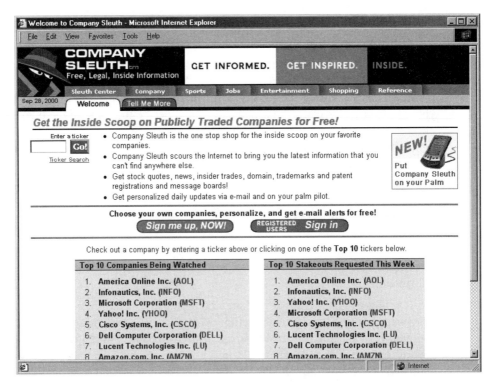

**Figure 6.21**
In addition to tracking the companies that interest you most, Company Sleuth provides great entertainment value in listing the companies most watched by its entire user base.

releases, business news, short interest, stock rumors, federal litigation matters, and audio and video reports.

**Getting started:**

You'll need to register at the site to begin tracking companies. You're asked to provide the following information:

- full name
- e-mail address
- zip code
- country

When you register, Company Sleuth offers special promotions options, such as free issues of *Investor's Business Daily*, a business newspaper.

**Big spender:**

No premium services available.

URL: http://www.companysleuth.com/

**Contact:**   company@companysleuth.com

　X　SOHO                    　X　Small business

# CyberAtlas

CyberAtlas presents you with Internet statistics and market research that enable you to develop a better business model and make more informed business decisions. A Web guide to online facts, CyberAtlas gathers research from a myriad of data resources and presents summaries of and links to the latest analyses and data available (see Figure 6.22).

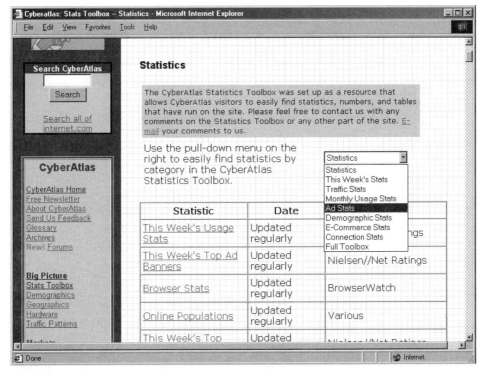

**Figure 6.22**
If you're looking for statistics about Internet usage, CyberAtlas is a good place to start.

CyberAtlas includes a Big Picture link, which groups research content and headlines the information service links. A Stats Toolbox allows you to find statistics, numbers, and tables that have previously run on the site. If you want to find statistics by category in the CyberAtlas Statistics Toolbox, you can use the pull-down menu off to the right. You can also explore data categorized by demographics, geographics, hardware, and trends.

You can check out Web markets by clicking directly on their respective categories. Under those links—advertising, B-to-B, broadband, education, finance, healthcare, professional, small biz, retailing, travel, and wireless—are two sections dedicated to incorporating more Web-specific information through an affiliate program with internet.commerce and CyberAtlas's parent company, internet.com.

**Getting started:**

You won't need to register in order to use this site. If you want to sign up to receive the free e-mail newsletter, you'll need to supply your e-mail address.

**Big spender:**

The site's All Net Research Center is a superstore offering discounted prices on research reports from different research firms.

URL: http://www.cyberatlas.com/

**Contact:**   mapstore@internet.com

   X   SOHO                      ____  Small business

## Iconocast

Iconocast is an influential channel for Net publishers and marketers, reporting on trends and statistics in e-commerce, Net advertising, and online usage (see Figure 6.23). Its Tell Jaco feature is a rumor mill—one that never reveals its sources—where you can leave behind-the-scenes buzz in return for incentives.

You can also express your beliefs on what you read in Iconocast by joining a discussion forum appropriately entitled Iconoclash. Iconocast contains newsletters, live chats, current topics of interest, opinions, and advice sections.

You can search the Iconocast Archives section by issues listed in chronological order or enter keywords in the search area found on the Archives page.

**Getting started:**

To subscribe to Iconocast, enter your e-mail address in the subscription box on the home page.

**Big spender:**

No premium services available.

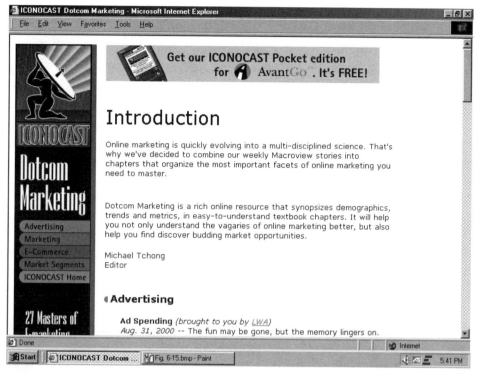

**Figure 6.23**
The Dotcom Marketing section of the Iconocast site provides capsule
summaries and useful links to numerous articles on online marketing topics.

URL: http://www.iconocast.com/

**Contact:**    http://www.iconocast.com/about.html

   _X_  SOHO                     ____  Small business

# eMarketer

Covering all aspects of Internet business, eMarketer consolidates market research
from a variety of different sources. eMarketer products and services consist of eReports, offering a comprehensive and accurate picture of the Internet marketplace; eS-
tats, the lead stories structure around the numbers; an eNews section that gives you
news and analysis on industry issues and topics that have a direct, global impact on
e-business; and the eNewsletter, which highlights the most important news, information, and statistics featured on the eMarketer site.

You'll also find a weekly eList of the site's top 10 eBusiness models, based on
content, image, ease of navigation and usability, and an eCommunity to post your

messages on a billboard list. In addition, an eDirections feature contains instructions, advice, an eGlossary, and an eHistory lesson on the Internet.

**Getting started:**

Navigate through the eMarketer site by clicking on the product, service, or operation page you want to enter. The center column displays the information (see Figure 6.24) or supplies summaries with links to the whole story.

eReports are broken down by eCategory and summarized. Each in-depth overview is available for purchase in the StatStore.

**Big spender:**

For a price, in-depth research reports on Internet-specific topics are available.

URL: http://www.emarketer.com/

**Contact:**   http://www.emarketer.com/aboutus/contactus.html

    X   SOHO                      X   Small business

**Figure 6.24**
The eBusiness section of eMarketer provides links to headline news and thoughtful analysis on Internet commerce topics.

## FreeEDGAR.com

EDGAR (Electronic Data Gathering Analysis and Retrieval) is an information resource that provides up-to-the-minute SEC corporate filings and related business intelligence tools (see Figure 6.25).

The service is the provider of financial news to dozens of leading Web sites, including Yahoo!, Company Link, The Street, *USA Today,* Quote.com, and Planet Direct. You can access third-party research through EDGAR company partnerships with PC Quote, Big Charts, Hoover's Inc., News Alert, Zacks Investment Research, *Wall Street* Research Net, and Company Link.

The site's IPO Express section offers information on new stock offerings. You can register on a personalized watch list for e-mail with news about stocks.

**Getting started:**

To set up a watch list of stocks, you'll need to register by providing the following information:

**Figure 6.25**
At FreeEDGAR.com, you can look up the most recent SEC filings for any corporation. (Copyright EDGAR Online, Inc., www.freeedgar.com.)

- full name
- e-mail address
- birth date
- gender
- zip code
- profession
- description of your firm

**Big spender:**

EDGAR Online Premium offers access to a variety of advanced tools to access data from SEC filings, including tracking of your own portfolio of companies and industries, with real-time e-mail alerts; the ability to search all SEC filings by individual name; automatic notification about new IPO filings, plus daily and weekly IPO summaries; and the ability to get complete printed bound copies of any SEC filing, delivered overnight to your office or home. The price varies from $9.95 to $99.95 a month, depending on how many filings and Insider Trading Form 144s you request each month. There is a special $14.25 per quarter rate for journalists and students.

URL: http://freeedgar.com/

**Contact:**   support@edgar-online.com

     X  SOHO                    X  Small business

# SUMMARY . . . . . . . . . . . . . . . . . . . . . . . . . .

By now, you've seen that there's a wealth of information portals and market research sources that your business can take advantage of to grow more efficiently. In the final chapter, straight ahead, you'll discover additional online resources for expert help in specialty areas, from banking and shipping to legal and travel services.

# 7

# Other Business Resources

..........................

All of us at some point in our lives will likely require professional help from bankers, lawyers, and other advisors. In this final chapter, we come full circle to discussing the Internet's service proposition. While not all the services that a business must use have jumped online yet, the progress these companies are making in convenience are paving the way.

## FREE ONLINE BANKING . . . . . . . . . . . . . . . . . .

There's no shortage of financial services, from low-cost stock trading to bill aggregation, available on the Internet. If your bank hasn't yet opened a Web site yet, you can bet it is planning to. In fact, many of the largest banks and credit card companies have created special small business areas to reflect the commitment they've made to those customers in the offline world.

What kinds of banking transactions are customers going online to conduct most often? Think simple transactions: checking your balance, conducting account maintenance, transferring funds, making payments online—all for free and at your convenience.

### Citibank

At this virtual version of the nation's largest retail bank, you'll gain access to a myriad of the services you need to manage your finances and make routine banking transactions conveniently over the Internet. Citibank Online offers a complete financial management center, free bill payment and account aggregation, and fairly basic financial planning services covering home ownership, insurance, credit, borrowing, and education planning.

The Citibusiness Resource Network offers you discounted products and services and expert advice to help you set up, maintain, and grow your home office or small business. The Citibusiness page opens to reveal three subject categories, headlined: Accounts and Services, Business Access, and the Citibusiness Resource Network.

The Accounts and Services section includes Checking, Savings & Investments, CitiEscrow, Credit Programs, and Global Banking. A Newsstand feature contains tips for financing your office space and guidelines for marketing your practice, as well as information about the Citibusiness Platinum Select Card.

Business Access offers you an online computer banking service designed to help you manage your finances and make routine banking transactions. However, many of these products are not available yet in all parts of the U.S., and some transactions require a paper signature.

The Citibusiness Resource Network offers everything from discounted products and services (see Figure 7.1) to getting expert answers within 48 hours on virtually any financial topic, from setting up to maintaining your small business.

**Getting started:**

To register for Citibusiness products and services, you'll be required to fill out a form that asks for your

- full name
- street address
- day and evening telephone numbers

After submitting this information, you will be contacted by phone by a Citibank representative.

**Big spender:**

To discuss additional services, expand your business relationship, or partner with Citibank, you can contact citicommerce.helpdesk@citicorp.com

URL: http://www.citibank.com/

**Contact:**   www.citibank.com/us/cbna/contactus/

  X  SOHO                          X   Small business

**Figure 7.1**
Citibusiness card members can take advantage of a comprehensive Ask the Expert service. This service provides access to a panel of experts who can address practical business questions.

## Bank of America

The Bank of America site provides links for your online banking, business, and investing needs. Its Business Services section offers tools, resources, and merchant services to assist you with payment processing, Internet commerce, and specialized banking, such as community development banking. In addition, it offers market research and industry-focused commentary from notable analysts, covering the equity and debt markets, foreign exchange, derivatives, and possible global and country risks. You might also be interested in other topics, such as corporate and commercial banking finance services.

The site organizes its information architecture into four categories: Personal Finance, Business Services, Inside the Bank of America, and Financial Tools. Each includes a menu bar that transfers you to specific service overviews.

The Small Business page includes the bulk of products and services for growing companies, including worksheets, advice, and technology that can help your business thrive financially. The Internet Commerce Center helps you sell online by linking your products to a comprehensive online shopping, payment, and settlement process.

If your business isn't already online, the Internet Order Center can create an e-commerce site that makes it easy for your customers to browse and buy. If you already have a working store, the service can handle all your credit card transactions, help you minimize fraud, and save you time and money.

Other products and services listed in the Small Business section include online banking, business checking, business savings, CDs, credit services, merchant services, treasury management, and retirement planning. You're also offered the option of opening a Bank of America account if you don't have one. You can apply online for checking, savings, certificates of deposit, credit, and online financial services.

**Getting started:**

To enroll in the business center and receive tailored information and personalized access, you're required to fill out a profile form with the following fields:

- business name
- business owner name
- street address
- business ID
- administrator name

**Big spender:**

A variety of premium services are available for business customers.

URL: http://www.bankofamerica.com/business/.

**Contact:**   http://www.bankofamerica.com/contact/

  X  SOHO                              X  Small business

## American Express

A recent addition to American Express's portfolio of lending products and financial services is a one-time-only card number that customers can download for online shopping. Called Private Payments, the free service is targeted at consumers and small businesses concerned about online security. Cardholders download software to access Private Payments and, when ready to shop, click on an icon on their desktop or go to the company's Web site to indicate which American Express card they want to link to the temporary number. Merchants won't ever see the cardholder's permanent number.

From the home page, you can select from four basic topic areas to help you as an individual or business. The menu-navigated service areas are broken down into Personal, Small Business, Merchants, and Corporations. A My American Express service on the site's home page lets you easily access the American Express information and services you are interested in from one convenient location.

Click Small Business and you'll find everything you need—from applying for a card to starting your company, to exploring funds to make it grow, to managing your accounts online and consolidating your expenses, to accessing an assortment of human resource, financial planning, and business information.

In the Small Business section you'll find information about applying for cards, financial services, how to save when shopping online, and more. The site offers quizzes that help you tighten your business practices (see Figure 7.2).

The Small Business Exchange's Community for Entrepreneurs is the home base for the bulk of your online banking and news-gathering needs. Most of the products

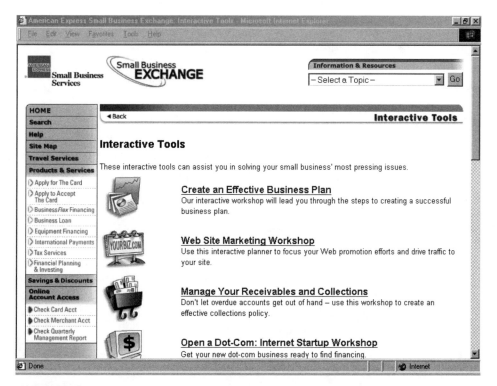

**Figure 7.2**
The interactive tools offered on American Express's small business site helps you focus on your goals and the actions you need to take.

and services sections run through this center and they are presented in a clean and colorful format.

Last year American Express Small Business Services launched a multimillion-dollar communications program it calls Voices from Main Street to engage small-business owners in a dialogue about their issues; more information can be found at http://www.americanexpress.com/voices/.

**Getting started:**

To apply to accept the American Express card, you are required to provide the following:

- name and social security number of an authorized signer
- your bank's name, address, and routing code
- the account type and number of your business bank account

To create your My American Express account, you'll need to provide the following:

- full name
- zip code
- e-mail address

**Big spender:**

A variety of premium services are available for business customers.

URL: http://www.americanexpress.com/

**Contact:**   http://www10.americanexpress.com/sif/cda/page/0,1641,414,00.asp

  X  SOHO               X  Small business

# FREE SHIPPING INFORMATION . . . . . . . . . . . . . .

One of the major challenges faced by product-oriented businesses on a daily basis is shipping. The sites listed here maintain up-to-date tables to help you determine the cost of shipping, along with handling and insurance costs, when you provide information about the size and weight of the package.

## Stamps.com

The free iShip shipping services at Stamps.com makes it easy for you to calculate shipping costs for sending your packages through a variety of carriers. You can avoid the long lines of a shipping center, choosing between confusing service options, and running around to compare prices. Stamps.com delivers comprehensive information on shipping rates, services, and package delivery status from several major shipping carriers, so you can easily choose the right service for each package without spending lots of time shopping. The service currently allows you to compare rates and services among several carriers, including UPS, FedEx, Airborne Express, and the U.S. Postal Service.

There are three major actions you can take when you access Stamps.com's shipping services. Price It allows you to compare rates and delivery times of major carriers in a colorful grid (see Figure 7.3). You'll need to enter the package dimensions and weight, the destination zip code, and any insurance or handling charges you wish to add. You'll see how much it will cost and how fast it will be delivered, and will also have the opportunity to add insurance or request a delivery receipt.

Track It allows you to monitor your package through tracking numbers until it reaches its destination. Stamps.com can track all the carriers for which it provides pricing information with through Price It.

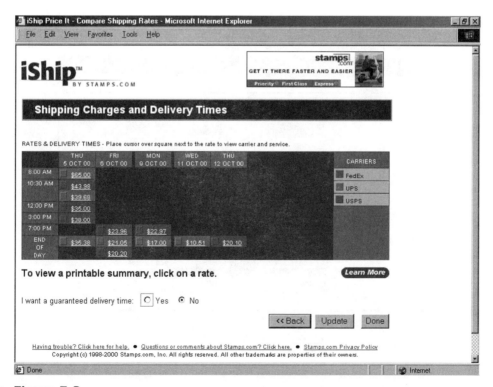

**Figure 7.3**
Use Stamps.com's Price It feature to see what several different carriers would charge to deliver the same package.

Sell It is geared toward auction sites' shipping and handling charges (see Figure 7.4). It is similar to the Price It option but produces a hyperlink that allows perspective purchasers to estimate their own shipping charges.

**Getting started:**

No registration is required to use Stamps.com's shipping services.

**Big spender:**

Beyond handling packages, Stamps.com offers, for a fee, a complete postage meter service that lets you print postage directly onto envelopes or labels.

URL: http://home.iship.com/

**Contact:**   support@iship.com

       X   SOHO                         X   Small business

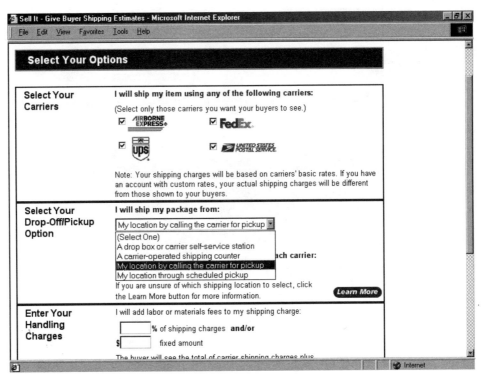

**Figure 7.4**
The Sell It feature is especially useful if you're selling goods at online auction and need to estimate shipping charges.

## UPS

UPS.com offers many of the services of UPS, on a global scale, through the convenience of a clean and easily accessible corporate site. At the UPS site, you can track packages (see Figure 7.5), ship packages, check a price inquiry, find out delivery dates, access an air pickup service, locate a drop-off facility, and, for My UPS.com members, order supplies.

The site features a service guide, the download center (where you can download solutions, tracking software, and zone and rate information), and a customer service station.

With the tracking tool, you can track up to 25 shipments at once, using the tracking number, or reference number. You can also send an e-mail message with your UPS tracking numbers to totaltrack@ups.com; you'll receive your tracking summary in a reply message. Register for a ship tool and you're entitled to complete shipping history, various preferences, full support, and help. A quick cost calculator will

**Figure 7.5**
Enter the UPS tracking number assigned to your package, and the company's online service can report who signed for it and when.

tell you the shipping prices when you provide the shipments' origin, destination, and package information. You can find out worldwide delivery times and see U.S. ground maps under the transit time tool. You can also have your package picked up by providing destination information.

When you register for My UPS, you can access a supplies tool so you can quickly reorder supplies, start an address book, and track your packages.

**Getting started:**

To become a member of My UPS, you'll need to provide the following information:

- full name
- street address
- country
- telephone number
- e-mail address

**Big spender:**

There is an additional charge for UPS On Call Air Pickup service, depending on your delivery. That charge can be determined through the quick cost calculator.

URL: http://www.ups.com/

**Contact:**   customer.service@ups.com

   X   SOHO                           X   Small business

# FedEx.com

FedEx has a comprehensive site that provides shipping services, from basic time-saving tools that can track your package to building blocks for creating your own on-line storefront.

Tools designed for various shipping needs can give you centralized control of your company's shipping process through options that help you better manage shipping, billing, and reporting, and reduce the time you spend shipping. A real-time link to your business's infrastructure allows access to in-depth product information, shipment tracking, and other services, such as printing labels (see Figure 7.6).

**Getting started:**

On the FedEx home page, you're asked to identify your country. On the country home page, the tabs on top access tools that provide shipping, tracking, drop-off, and rate-finding services. On the right of the home page, you can track up to 25 air bill numbers. News, information, updates, and a spotlight round out the home page.

**Figure 7.6**
Print shipping labels online with this FedEx.com feature.

The FedEx interNetShip tool lets you store your FedEx Express account number online to speed up the logon process. You can complete inkjet or laser-printed shipping labels, store a 300-name address book, arrange for a scanner, and see a 45-day shipping history—all from your browser window.

To open on online account, you are required to provide the following information about your company:

- contact name
- street address
- telephone number

**Big spender:**

E-commerce solutions are based on your shipping needs. Call 1 (800) Go-FedEx for more information.

URL: http://www.fedex.com/

**Contact:**  webmaster@fedex.com

   <u>X</u>  SOHO                  <u>X</u>  Small business

# LEGAL . . . . . . . . . . . . . . . . . . . . . . . .

Have you heard the one about the lawyers who went online? They became extremely helpful! While the legal industry hasn't yet seen the online explosion that the health industry has, several sites offer a wealth of legal information on the Web. In fact, some even let you speak with a live lawyer online. As with some of the online health sites, the legal sites can be aimed at professionals, so watch out for legalspeak.

## FindLaw.com

Looking for general legal information or a specific link? You'll probably find it here. FindLaw.com contains comprehensive legal information for all, covering everything from cases and codes to technology deals and Internet contracts. FindLaw contains a list of services that include a legal dictionary (see Figure 7.7), message boards, SEC EDGAR information, a bookstore, newsletters, and a LawCrawler search feature. Other categories include a legal subject index, law firms and lawyers, consultants and experts, a FindLaw library with over 15,000 publications, and more.

To make your hunt for small business-related legal information more efficient, FindLaw has grouped its findings in an easily accessible small business page, which encompasses all your legal needs in one well-designed resource.

**Getting started:**

The site sports a section aimed at small business owners where you'll discover several law-oriented features that can benefit your small business, especially in its early stages.

At the Small Business Online Bookshelf, you can read an online version of *Legal Guide for Starting & Running a Small Business,* a book containing 24 structured chapters of small business legal knowledge. There's also a section containing a SOHO Guide, with countless pages of startup, finance, managing, and marketing solutions. A Business Tools section is where you can download a step-by-step checklist, model business plans, forms (see Figure 7.8), and other documents.

To receive news and updates, click Newsletters on the home page, choose your interests, and enter your e-mail address.

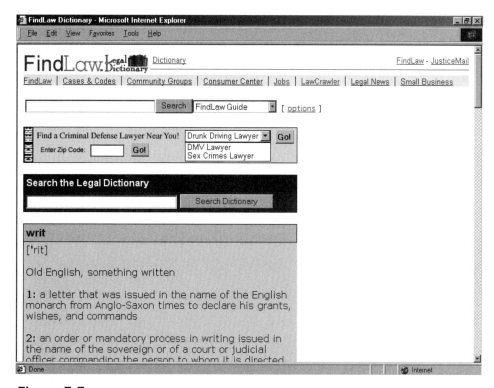

**Figure 7.7**
FindLaw's online dictionary is useful for referencing legal terms on demand.

**Big spender:**

No premium services available.

URL: http://www.findlaw.com/

**Contact:**   write@findlaw.com

  X  SOHO                    X   Small business

## USLaw.com

Offering a variety of solutions for your small businesses, USLaw.com is a real-time Internet link to legal information services and resources. Topics include immigration, family, employment, real estate, finance, health and injury, crime and the courts, and commercial and small business.

**Figure 7.8**
If you're just setting out to establish your business, the online forms and business plans at FindLaw.com can help streamline your efforts.

The site allows you to conduct an interactive one-to-one chat with a trained lawyer for a small fee (see Figure 7.9), research information from a library on virtually every legal topic, or visit a directory of qualified lawyers in various practice areas and geographic regions.

If you'd like to speak with a lawyer about general legal concepts (available online for five hours a day on weekdays, with additional Saturday hours), you must first read and agree to the terms of service. This will explain that the site does not form an attorney-client relationship. The attorney will not provide advice, but will explain legal concepts and principles, as well as empower you with useful information so you can address your legal concerns. The lawyer may also guide you to other sources of information that may help you. To find the nearest lawyer, you'll need to provide the legal topic you need advice on and a zip code.

Equally useful are the online tools to crafting legally binding documents in such areas as bills of sale or hiring employees. In the Small Business Resource Center, you'll find articles on sole proprietorships, corporations, hiring and firing, partnerships,

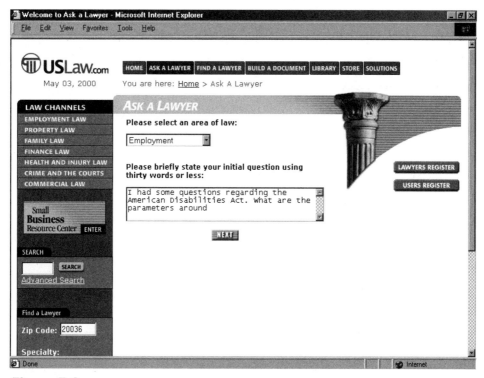

**Figure 7.9**
You can gain some direction—though not binding legal advice—from chatting interactively with an attorney on USLaw.com.

home-based businesses, licenses and permits, and more. After you register, you're entitled to receive e-mails specifically geared to your interests, as well as important date reminders.

### Getting started:

To become a member of USLaw.com or register to Ask a Lawyer, you'll need to leave your e-mail address and fill out a registration form. Required fields include

- full name
- birth date
- zip code

### Big spender:

A single, 30-minute real-time chat with an attorney costs $9.95, or you can sign up for an annual chat subscription for $24.95. You can also purchase a legal report, which allows you to submit a question on a legal issue, and an attorney will respond with useful legal information in an easy-to-understand format, all within two business days. Legal reports cost $14.95 each.

URL: http://www.uslaw.com/

**Contact:**   questions@uslaw.com

  X   SOHO                                X   Small business

# TAXES . . . . . . . . . . . . . . . . . . . . . . . . . . . .

If you need information on tax codes, help with your taxes, or a Schedule C form, you can visit your local Internal Revenue Service (IRS) office and wait in line—or you can go online to try to find the information yourself. Read on for some online resources that can help make the ritual of paying taxes slightly less, um, taxing.

## IRS

You'll find just about every document that the IRS publishes at the IRS Web site, as well as numerous links to help you with your taxes. Some of the site's most useful resources include forms, pointers to your local IRS office, and tax publications.

You can download tax tables and forms from the Forms and Publications link. Tax forms are available in several file formats, including PDF (Portable Document Format), PCL (Printer Control Language), and PostScript.

You can also use the site to find the toll-free number and the address of your local IRS office, where you can get walk-in assistance. The site also offers Tax Topics, a section with links to tax tips and software that can assist you with preparing your taxes, audits, and negotiation services.

The site's image-boosting attempt at lightheartedness though often frivolous home page stories can make it difficult to immediately find information on refunds, tax schedules, or extensions—but all of that good information can be retrieved through the Site Tree or search features (see Figure 7.10).

**Getting started:**

Follow links from the home page to reach current tax forms and those from previous years, as well as frequently asked questions and information about IRS e-file, a paperless electronic tax return service.

**Big spender:**

No premium services available.

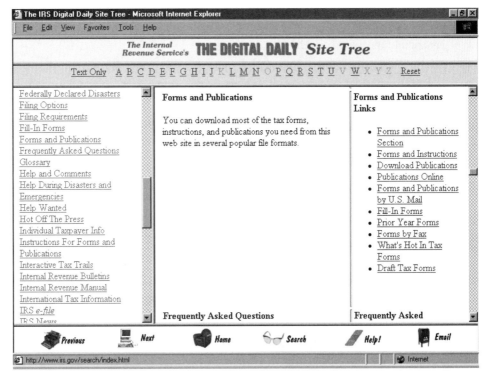

**Figure 7.10**
The Site Tree listing at irs.gov can help you find whatever arcane tax form or regulation you're looking for.

URL: http://www.irs.gov/

**Contact:**   http://www.irs.gov/where_file/

  X   SOHO             _____ Small business

## Quicken.com

Quicken.com brings helpful advice and interactivity to other online personal finance tasks. You can find out how to get the best rates on a mortgage or insurance and how to apply for them; conduct your online banking and bill paying; prepare for and file taxes, and plan for major life events. The site's My Finances section lets you consolidate all of your online financial information in one place. Service sections, including breaking news, market quotes and alerts, solutions, and a personalized portfolio, grace the home page.

The Financial Health Checkup feature can give you a good snapshot of your overall financial situation if you fill out its lengthy questionnaire. You can use the financial report card to set long-term goals.

You can visit a small business message board that posts frequently asked questions in an organized folder. There are forms and tools, such as a look into loans (see Figure 7.11) to help your start-up.

Quicken.com also brings you constantly updated money-related news and data, an industry library on a list of small business subjects, and a book of the week suggestion.

**Getting started:**

A small business link on the home page takes you to the small business home page. To receive a monthly newsletter and stay abreast of topics like tax breaks for small businesses, you can subscribe by entering your e-mail address.

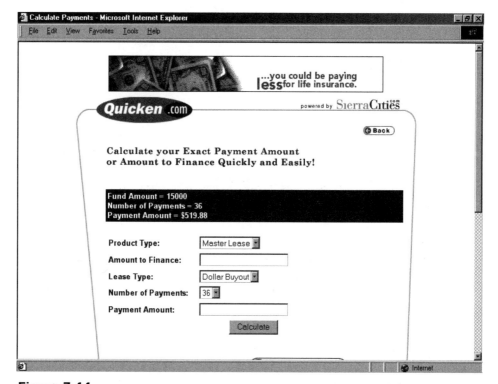

**Figure 7.11**
The online calculators at Quicken.com can help you easily crunch numbers for a housing or car loan.

**Big spender:**

Turn to the site's products section for commercial software purchases. You can obtain a free 30-day trial of Turbo Tax software. Should you choose to keep it, the software costs $29.95, or $49.95 for the deluxe version, which includes a state edition.

URL: http://www.quicken.com/

**Contact:**   http://www.quicken.com/support/help_center

  X  SOHO                    X   Small business

# TRAVEL SERVICES . . . . . . . . . . . . . . . . . . .

Big businesses may have the budget to fly employees in first or business class, with wide seats, wine lists, and individual TV screens. Small businesses, on the other hand, pinch pennies at every turn—and the pinching goes a lot further when economizing on travel compared to many other business costs. Here are some quick tips to bear in mind for making your travel dollars go further:

- If have a preferred airline, check its Web site before turning to the travel portal sites listed below. Some may have cheaper fare or special offers not advertised elsewhere.
- If you're planning a trip with plenty of lead time—say, months into the future—activate a fare watcher service to send you e-mail alerts of great fares that meet your criteria for departure and arrival dates and locations.
- Sign up for online access privileges to your frequent flier account. This lets you monitor your miles so that you won't lose any through expiration and also allows you to redeem them more conveniently.

The travel sites listed here can help you locate fares lower than those quoted by travel agents, with the added convenience of booking fares around the clock, not just during office hours.

## Travelocity

This major travel portal lets users book flights, hotels, and rental cars and provides localized travel planning news. You can plan, price, and book your trips online from package and vacation deals.

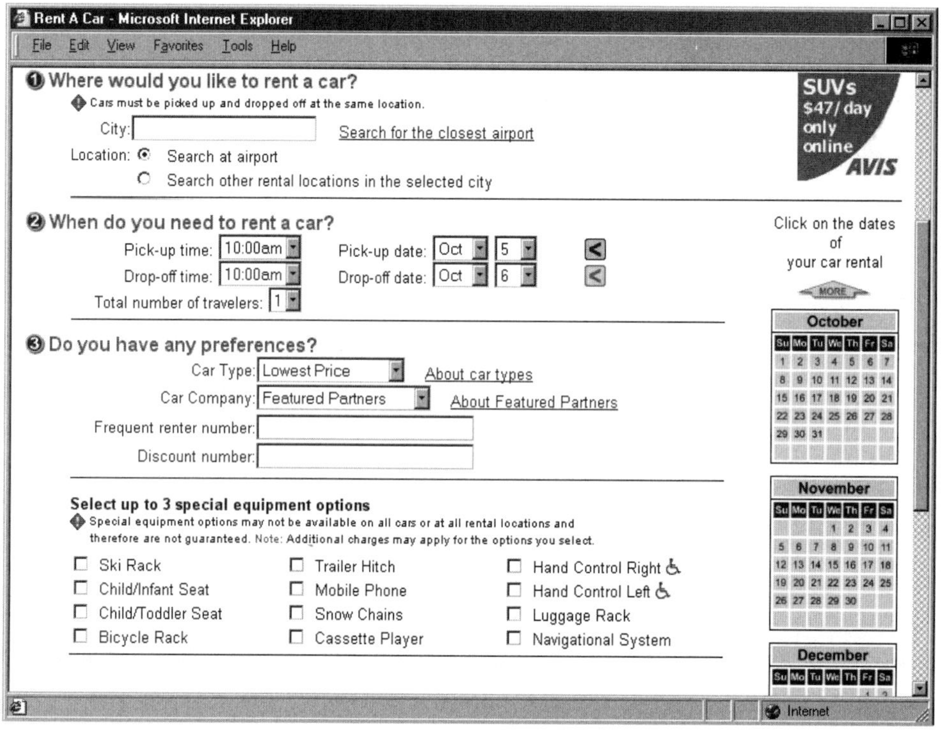

**Figure 7.12**
Instead of waiting on hold to speak with a customer service representative, you can book a car rental online with Travelocity.

One of the most useful features is a fare watcher service that you can use to search for the lowest available airline fares. Results are displayed using an interactive calendar that highlights the days the fares are offered.

The site's Destination Guide provides information on global destinations by leveraging content from third-party sources like Frommer's, Lonely Planet, and the World Travel Guide. You can also use the site to check weather forecasts, read reviews, consult exchange rates, and create your own custom mini-guides.

With the car rental service, you choose your pickup location at either your destination airport or another rental location (see Figure 7.12). When renting, you can select up to three special equipment options, such as a luggage or bicycle rack, cassette player, or a built-in navigational system, just as if you were making a reservation in person or over the telephone.

You can also check the current status of a flight with real-time departure and arrival information, or choose to receive updates on important flight information directly to an alphanumeric pager.

**Getting started:**

With Travelocity, you can submit several kinds of search queries right from the home page. Enter your destination's name or airport code in the Search Travelocity.com box to find in-depth planning information for your trip. With the fare checker feature, you enter your travel dates, starting and ending destinations, and number of adult travelers; the service immediately displays the results in incremental price order (see Figure 7.13). If you have flexibility in the time of day you can travel, though not the travel dates themselves, the 9 Best Itineraries service searches for the best-priced itineraries for the available dates, then displays the total price.

After you register, you can make and track reservations on the site or personalize the Fare Watcher on Travelocity's home page for your frequent destinations. You're asked for the following information:

- full name
- e-mail address

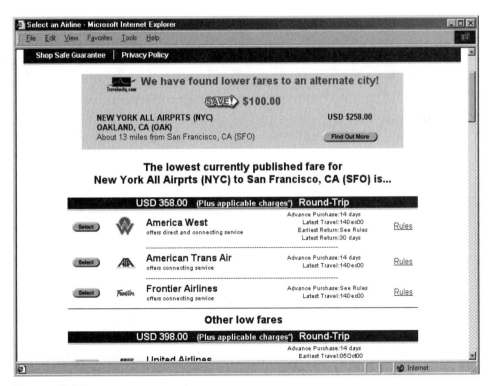

**Figure 7.13**
The price comparison for airfares at Travelocity can eliminate much of the effort that manual research would require.

292

- company name
- street address and country
- home and business telephone number

**Big spender:**

No premium services available.

URL: http://www.travelocity.com/

**Contact:**  Click the link to customer service at the bottom of the Travelocity home page.

  X  SOHO    X  Small business

# Expedia

A member of the Microsoft Network, Expedia is another one-stop resource for online travel planning. It offers flight booking (see Figure 7.14), car rentals, hotel room reservations, package vacations, cruise offers, destination information, and point-to-point mapping.

When searching for flights, modifiable search fields persist in the left-hand margin, so you can easily edit flight dates and times as you fine-tune your searches. Many packages boast an Expedia Special Rate icon, which presents low-cost combination rates made possible by Expedia's acquisition of Travelscape. As you search, you can view hotels on a map or access a local destination guide. Hotel details include the nightly rate for each day of your stay. Expedia distinguishes itself among travel portals through its mapping resources, thanks to integration of Microsoft's own mapping capability. You can store information in My Maps & Routes for future reference.

A My Trips function keeps track of your itineraries, lets you customize your account, and offers links to all of Expedia's services. The site also offers a fare calendar, which helps to determine the cheapest dates to travel. A Mileage Miner (see Figure 7.15) keeps track of all your frequent flyer accounts. A Quick Round Trip Flight search is also available.

**Getting started:**

Expedia delivers a unique way of presenting air, car, and hotel query fields on the home page. Instead of unduly taking up space, reservation fields appear after you click on the appropriate icon. You need to create a user profile to begin personalizing the My Trips page. After you register for an account by leaving your e-mail address, you add traveler information for each person traveling. This profile information includes the following:

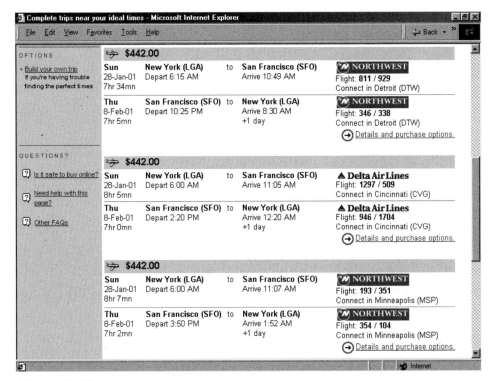

**Figure 7.14**
The extensive search results you see when you compare fares at Expedia help you make a better informed decision when it comes to booking your flights.

- full name
- type of traveler (e.g., senior, adult, child)
- telephone number
- country in which passport is issued
- emergency contact information

Once you create a traveler profile, you can add travel preferences for flying, hotels, and car reservations. For Express Booking, you provide your credit card information. Your e-mail address will be used to confirm your travel purchases, notify you of a reservation change, and advise you of special travel promotions.

**Big spender:**

The Mileage Miner service is free for the first 12 months. After that, you pay an annual fee of $9.99, unless you book three air tickets through Expedia during the year.

**Figure 7.15**
Expedia's Mileage Miner simplifies tracking your frequent flyer miles.

URL: http://www.expedia.com/

**Contact:**   http://www.expedia.com/daily/service

 X  SOHO                         X   Small business

## biztravel

Travel portal biztravel.com presents flight search results in two different ways—one is an express search complete with air, car, and hotel included in your itinerary, and the other is a build-your-own search, which can be more time-consuming and less intuitive. But what has really put biztravel in the headlines is its Customer Service Guarantee, which includes money back when its customers suffer airline delays.

The site's sophisticated handling of frequent flyer miles includes helping customers to maximize awards by suggesting accommodations.

Once you enter your profile information, you can automatically have flights upgraded where available. Note that biztravel.com can offer ticket purchases only on United States or Canadian issued credit cards and will deliver paper tickets only to United States or Canadian addresses.

You can also access biztravel's services through a mobile phone, PDA, or other wireless devices (see Figure 7.16).

**Getting started:**

The actions you can take on biztravel's site are intuitively arrayed on the site's home page and within the Travel Planner tab; Plan a New Trip, Open a Saved Trip, Repeat a Trip, Book a Vacation, and Charter a Flight are a few.

At your request, you can have biztravel contact you via pager an hour before your scheduled departure with your flight status, gate number, and weather in your destination city. You sign up for this service through the Traveler Toolkit tab, which also helps you locate additional services in the city you're traveling to—for example, in case you need to rent a computer or cellular phone (see Figure 7.17).

**Figure 7.16**
Sign up for bizAlerts to check your flight's status in real time.

**Figure 7.17**
With biztravel.com, you can search by city to find useful resources for business travelers at your destination.

When you fill out your bizReservations Member Profile, you're asked to provide the following information:

- full name
- e-mail address
- postal code and country

**Big spender:**

Biztravel@MyCompany is a premium online travel management service for companies and frequent business travelers. For more information, contact sales@biztravel.com.

URL: http://www.biztravel.com/

**Contact:**   You can reach customer service 24 hours a day, seven days a week at 1 (800) BIZTRAV or 1 (701) 227–7036.

# CITY GUIDES . . . . . . . . . . . . . . . . . . . . . .

You've put the travel sites in the previous section to work in getting you where you need to go—now take advantage of the guides in this section to help you get around town like a native, choose restaurants, and fit in sightseeing.

## CitySearch

City guide portal CitySearch offers an abundance of links to news, business, and recreational sites for dozens of U.S. cities and a growing number of non-U.S. locales as well. The content sources that support CitySearch include ticketmaster.com, cityauction.com, match.com, sidewalk.com, and livedaily.com, and the site also features online horoscopes and job search functions.

**Getting started:**

Choosing your desired city is the first step. Once you click to the local guide, you can use the site-wide search function to find a specific establishment. You can also drill down through the vast directory for help in locating local services, such as restaurants or clubs for entertaining clients.

No registration is necessary.

**Big spender:**

No premium services available.

URL: http://www.citysearch.com/

**Contact:**   http://www.abouttmcs.com/contact.html

  X  SOHO                             X   Small business

## Yahoo! Get Local

List-happy Yahoo's Internet guides include get-around-town info for major metropolitan areas in all U.S. states.

For locales ranging from Bangor, Maine, to Honolulu, Hawaii, you'll find subcategories such as entertainment, employment, travel, and real estate. You can check out classified ads, local news, or look up a friend in the white pages. You can easily access information about local lodging, dining, car rentals, driving directions and maps throughout the area. For local color, browse the listings to find out about hot bands, the club scene, or how the area's sports teams are doing.

Yahoo! GetLocal focuses in on information for up to 30,000 U.S. zip codes.

**Getting started:**

Enter a zip code or browse through listings of states and their respective cities. International users can select from a wide range of countries and languages also listed on this page.

**Big spender:**

No premium services.

URL: http://local.yahoo.com/

**Contact:**   http://www.mail.com/cgi-bin/mailcom/noframes/support

  X  SOHO                              ____  Small business

# BUSINESS DEVELOPMENT . . . . . . . . . . . . . . . .

The bad news: Starting a new business is tough. The good news: Plenty of help is available for the asking. Best of all, much of this advice is free for the asking and on-line to boot. For our final site summary, let us point you to a site that can provide help with planning, setting up, operating, and maintaining your business—and that offers a human touch through networking as well.

## SCORE

The Service Corps of Retired Executives is a nonprofit organization dedicated to helping small businesses develop themselves strategically. The SCORE Association consists primarily of working and retired executives and business owners who volunteer their time and expertise as business counselors.

Partnering with the U.S. Small Business Administration, SCORE can counsel you on a broad range of business topics through in-person meetings or confidentially through an e-mail counseling program.

You can search for an e-mail counselor from a list of experienced advisors. Use the counseling-by-e-mail service to briefly describe and submit your business question via an online form (see Figure 7.18). Your SCORE counselor will reply with his or her answer. The About Workshops section features monthly how-to tips, covering previously addressed topics and providing insight for small business owners and aspiring entrepreneurs.

The Business Resource page provides a spotlight on links to vital resources for entrepreneurs, such as the Business Resource Index, Business Hotlinks, a special Guest feature, and highlighted sites.

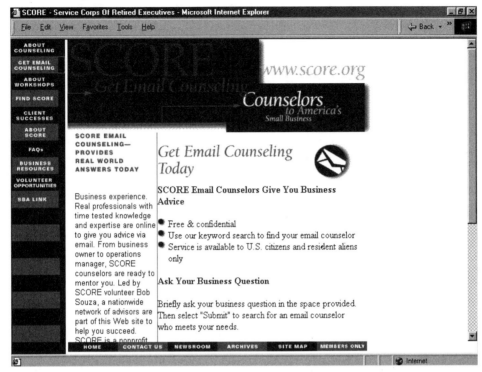

**Figure 7.18**
At the SCORE Web site, you can search by keyword to locate a counselor you can submit business questions to.

### Getting started:

The site's navigation is fairly intuitive, with persistent left-hand navigation throughout the site for accessing the counseling services, workshop information, FAQs, business resources and links, and volunteer opportunities.

If you'd like to visit a SCORE center in your local community and meet with a SCORE counselor face-to-face, you can locate one through a Find SCORE function or call the SCORE Association toll-free at 1(800) 634-0245.

No registration is necessary. There is a Members Only section available for SCORE members.

### Big spender:

No premium services available.

URL: http://www.score.org/

**Contact:**   score@sba.gov

_X_  SOHO                    _X_  Small business

# SUMMARY . . . . . . . . . . . . . . . . . . . . . . . .

Congratulations. You've encountered some of the top online sources for free start-up
help and advice on running a small business and home office. You'll continue to uncover others as you continue to surf the Net and interact with the people you meet
through your networking adventures. Our best advice is to keep your eyes peeled and
always be prepared to do your research online—it's a sure bet you'll uncover more
information than you need and for a price that can't be beat.

# Index

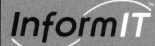
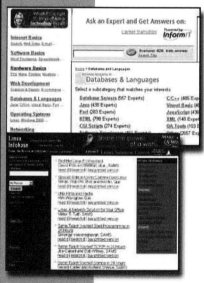